The Church

H. H. WALSH

The Church in the French Era
From Colonization to the British Conquest

Volume One of *A History of the Christian Church
In Canada.* General Editor: John Webster Grant

THE RYERSON PRESS TORONTO

To Becky, Nikki, Erika and Lisa

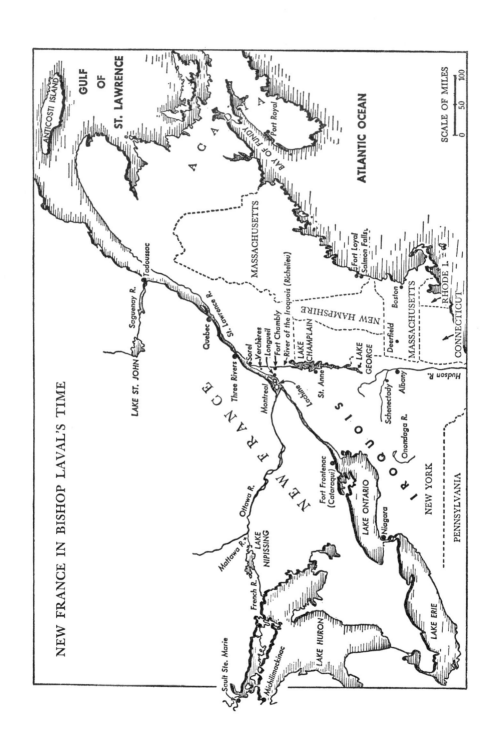

NEW FRANCE IN BISHOP LAVAL'S TIME

Foreword by the General Editor

The publication of these volumes is a direct result of the initiative and persistent prodding of the late Dr. Lorne Pierce. Dr. Pierce had determined many years in advance that The Ryerson Press, of which he was Editor-in-Chief, could most fittingly contribute to Canada's centenary celebrations by sponsoring a definitive study of the place of the Christian Church in her history. His hope, now brought to fruition, was that a team of church historians should collaborate on a three-volume work. Dr. Pierce foresaw not only the need but the difficulty of such an undertaking. There were a number of specialized studies, and a few denominational histories, but source material was scattered and the necessary community of scholars was lacking. Instead of admitting defeat he set out, typically, to create the conditions under which an inclusive history could be written. He stimulated the collection and organization of archival material, especially within his own communion, The United Church of Canada. He played a leading part in the formation in 1959 of the interdenominational Canadian Society of Church History, within whose membership he hoped to find his authors. He published a number of studies upon which a larger work could be based, notably Dr. Walsh's *The Christian Church in Canada* (Ryerson, 1956).

The team of writers took shape during early meetings of the Canadian Society of Church History, and the story most naturally lent itself to division into periods of French, British and Canadian dominance. Assignments were soon made: the French Era to Professor H. H. Walsh, the British Era to Professor John S. Moir and the Canadian Era to myself.

The work now being offered is the most comprehensive account of the history of the church in Canada that has yet been written.

In the main it is based on past studies, but these have been exten-
sively supplemented by original research. We hope that readers will
find it both useful and enjoyable, and that students will find in it
suggestions for areas of future research.

Each author has been left free to interpret the evidence in his own
way, and it is only to be expected that some differences in viewpoint
will be evident. Nevertheless, the project has been a team effort.
There has been constant mutual consultation and criticism, and all
the writers have accepted two general assumptions about the nature
of their task.

One of these assumptions, embodied in the reference of the title
to "the Christian Church" rather than to churches, is that this history
should be ecumenical in both range and sympathy. Such a commitment does not imply an ironing out or even a playing down of the
controversial elements in the story. It does involve a recognition that
the history of each communion is part of the history of all com-
munions. This assumption is not easy to maintain in dealing with
periods when Canadians tended to regard their various denomina-
tions as in effect so many separate religions, but without it the story
loses any vital link with the common source and common destiny
that are integral to the existence of the Christian Church.

The other assumption is that the Canadian locale should be taken
seriously. Once again writers are bound to no particular estimate of
the significance of the existence of Canada as a nation but only to
an awareness of the setting within which the church has lived and
worked. This assumption is no easier than the other, for much of
Canadian church history has seemed to consist of little more than
the importation of European and American forms and folkways.
Inevitably, however, the Canadian environment has affected the
churches and in turn been affected by them, with results that have
sometimes received inadequate recognition from both religious and
secular historians. The writers of these volumes concern themselves
not only with the institutional development and the devotional life of
the church but also with its public witness and especially with its
relation to the development of the Canadian character.

The time at which the present project comes to fruition is in many
ways fortunate. On the one hand, the recent spectacular broadening
of dialogue among members of various branches of the Christian
Church is beginning to make an ecumenical perspective more natural
for all of us. On the other, the growing interest in church history
evident in many university departments is initiating a dialogue with
secular historians that promises to be equally rewarding. This work

will amply justify itself if it leads to a quickening of interest that will result in the filling of some of the many gaps in our knowledge and understanding that still remain.

Each writer will undoubtedly wish to acknowledge some particular debts. I should like to express my appreciation to Dr. Walsh and Dr. Moir for their unflagging efforts and for their constant willingness to give and receive criticism gracefully, and to Mr. Earle Toppings of The Ryerson Press for his helpful and always tactful advice. It is our collective wish that this project when complete may be a worthy memorial to Dr. Lorne Pierce, scholar, churchman and Canadian.

JOHN WEBSTER GRANT

Preface

As a footnote to the foreword by the General Editor, the author of this present volume would like to express his gratitude for the advice he received from specialists in related fields of research; particularly is he indebted to the Reverend Louis Campeau, S.J., a specialist in Acadian church history, for his meticulous examination of Chapter Five, "The Acadian Adventure," which led to many revisions of this chapter; my indebtedness must be extended to the Reverend G. E. Giguère who called my attention to certain errors in my first draft of Chapter Three, "The Religious Background of New France," and also suggested a more modern bibliography on the subject. I am also indebted to Professor Jacob Fried, formerly of the Department of Anthropology at McGill University, for his comments on Chapter Four, "The Challenge of the Aborigine." My greatest indebtedness, however, is to my two teammates in this project, Professors Grant and Moir, who have read my manuscript more than once and have always come up with helpful suggestions for its improvement. Needless to say none of these scholars are responsible for my final conclusions for which I must assume full responsibility. My list of indebtedness could be greatly expanded, if space permitted, to include librarians in Canada and France who helped to smooth the paths of research; nor should I overlook the Canada Council, which made it possible for me to pursue part of my research in France.

And now for a few intimate words of thanks: first to Dean Stanley B. Frost, for an act of intercession which secured for me a grant from the McGill University Research Committee at a time when, because of a serious illness, I was unable to complete the final details of publication. With this grant, for which I am extremely grateful to the committee, I was able to get very efficient help to assist in arranging a bibliography and also to provide an index for the book. My thanks are also due to Mrs. Larissa Bida, who before she took over the task of indexing was always available to help in tracking down an elusive book and publisher, and to Mrs. Florence Mitchell for much of the typing of the manuscript, as well as to my wife who was always willing to use a typewriter. A special word of thanks is due to Mr. Earle Toppings, General Books Editor of The Ryerson Press, whose strong encouragement during my recent illness has been particularly appreciated, and to Mrs. Audrey Coffin whose editing has been a surprise and a delight.

A word of explanation is probably due to the English Protestant reader, who may find here a view of church history of New France not usually stressed in English-speaking circles. I can only plead in extenuation that I have tried to follow Collingwood's advice and to get into the minds of my subjects and try to think their thoughts. If this approach leads to a more kindly judgment upon the policies and actions of such dominant personalities in French-Canadian history as Bishops Laval and Saint-Vallier than is usual with English-speaking scholars in this field, and an appreciative understanding of the cultural background of our French-Canadian compatriots who share with us the responsibility for building a more spiritually united Canada, I will be content.

Weymouth, Nova Scotia   H. H. WALSH
July, 1966

The Church in the French Era

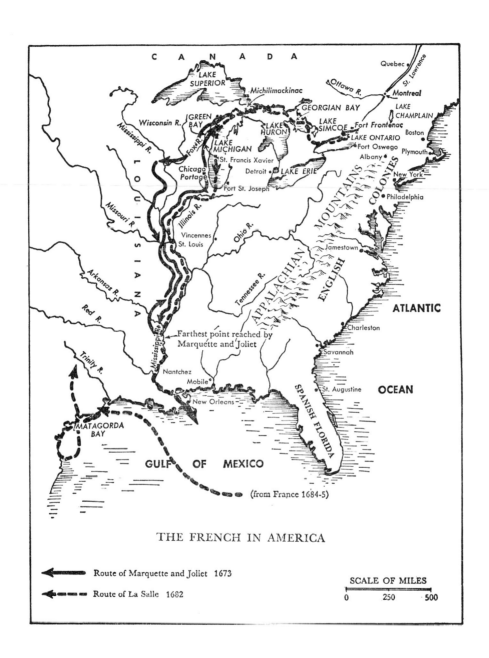

C A N A D A

LAKE SUPERIOR

Michilimackinac

GEORGIAN BAY

Quebec

St. Lawrence R.

Ottawa R.

Montreal

Wisconsin R.

GREEN BAY

Fox R.

LAKE MICHIGAN

LAKE HURON

LAKE SIMCOE

Fort Frontenac

LAKE CHAMPLAIN

Mississippi R.

St. Francis Xavier

LAKE ONTARIO

Fort Oswego

Boston

Chicago Portage

Detroit

LAKE ERIE

Albany

Plymouth

Fort St. Joseph

New York

L O U I S I A N A

Missouri R.

Illinois R.

Philadelphia

Vincennes
St. Louis

Ohio R.

M O U N T A I N S

C O L O N I E S

Jamestown

Arkansas R.

Tennessee R.

A P P A L A C H I A N

E N G L I S H

ATLANTIC

Red R.

Charleston

Farthest point reached by Marquette and Joliet

Savannah

Mississippi R.

Nantchez

Mobile

St. Augustine

OCEAN

Trinity R.

New Orleans

S P A N I S H   F L O R I D A

MATAGORDA BAY

GULF   OF   MEXICO

(from France 1684-5)

THE FRENCH IN AMERICA

← ——— Route of Marquette and Joliet 1673

← – – – Route of La Salle 1682

SCALE OF MILES

0   250   500

ONE

Introduction

Since Canadian Christianity is part of the missionary outreach of the European church, its history in the main has been regarded as a codicil to European church history.[1] Such a status has hardly added to the prestige of Canadian church historiography, nor attracted many students into this field of historical research. It is a status, however, that Canadian church history shares with the history of all the younger churches both on this continent and in Asia and Africa,[2] and it is only very recently that the story of non-European Christianity has begun to be told on its own merits. One reason for the long delay has been the difficulty of adapting the history of the younger churches to the normative canons of European church history—a difficulty that has sometimes led to the conclusion that genuine church history of these younger churches cannot be written.[3] Because of this reproach, several American church historians have made a frontal attack upon the so-called normative canons of church history and are insisting that "changes must come not only in definitions, approaches and methods, but also in the attitude toward the content and subject matter of church history."[4] This is an attack in which Canadian historians may well join to strive for a church history discipline which is comprehensive enough to deal with the whole body of Christ's church throughout the world.

BASIC ASSUMPTIONS

There are, however, certain basic assumptions which distinguish church history as a discipline from other historical disciplines and with which it will be difficult to dispense, even in the interest of comprehensiveness. The first of these is the conception of the

1

church as a people related to God through the redeeming work of Jesus Christ.[5] As a member of the redeemed community the church historian is called upon to record what God has wrought through the witness of the church; he must at all times help the members of the church to "look backward in time—backward on the path along which they have come,"[6] so that they may understand the true cause and hope of their status as a people of God.

A second assumption of no less importance is that church history is universal in its outlook. In point of fact, church historians have always acted on the principle that they were engaged in a universal study; it is extremely doubtful if any historian today, whether writing in Europe or America, would take exception to Eusebius' dictum that "he who would commit to writing the history that contains the Church's narrative must needs begin from the first with the beginning of the dispensation of Christ Himself . . . a dispensation more divine than most men imagine." By this afterthought Eusebius meant that "Christianity is as old as creation" and church history actually should begin with Adam and Eve and include such worthies as Abraham and Moses and all "those friends of God in days of old."[7] Many an earlier church historian has tried to do just that, but in modern days it is customary to follow Eusebius' example and simply salute the distant ages before getting down to more recent events.

These then are the controlling assumptions of the church historian, and they do pose a problem when one is dealing with the variety and exclusiveness of sectarian Christianity on the American continent. It is possible, no doubt, to write about the churches apart from these two assumptions; a great deal of study has been given to the sects in Canada, with particular emphasis upon their cultural influence in Canadian life,[8] but such research belongs to the field of sociology rather than church history. Because of the sectarian nature of both American and Canadian Christianity, even church historians have been tempted to write Christian sociology rather than church history; but if the church historian abandons his controlling assumptions and becomes a sociologist or a mere chronicler of religion he is depriving himself of the unique interpretative insight which distinguishes him from the secular historian. As it has been said of the historian generally: only he "who is excited by his participation in history . . . will be able to understand history,"[9] so it can be said specifically of the church historian: only he who is excited by his participation in the church is able to understand church history.

It may be contended that such participation detracts from the objectivity of the historian, but his involvement in the church need imply no more bias than is common to all historians who must necessarily belong to a human culture and are dependent upon some common orientation towards experience if they are to communicate with their readers. And once it is conceded that all history must necessarily be subjective—Professor Bultmann goes so far as to say that ". . . the most subjective interpretation of history is at the same time the most objective"[10]—then the church historian is on an equality with his secular colleagues who also have their controlling assumptions; and along with these assumptions, which may well include "the central events of the faith,"[11] he can also make use of all the techniques and tools of secular history; he can be just as "critical and discriminating in his judgments" and just as conscientious in his "choice and sorting"[12] as the most scientific historian. Nor will he, since Collingwood, indulge in mere "scissors and paste" history, or depend "altogether upon the testimony of authorities";[13] nor will he forget Collingwood's warning that if the events of the past are to live in the present "they should vibrate in the historian's mind."[14] But in order that the Canadian historian may do this very thing and take cognizance of all the many vital aspects of Canadian Christianity, it is necessary that he free himself from much of the methodology and presuppositions of European church historians.

PATCHING-ON VIEW OF CHURCH HISTORY

At least two of these presuppositions must be summarily dismissed as of no value in the New World. The first is what has been described as the "patching-on" view of the continuity of church history; the second is a concentration on national church history to the depreciation of dissenting or so-called heretical churches. The "patching-on" view no doubt arose out of the concept of the church universal in which the historian would take "a comprehensive backward look to the Garden of Eden,"[15] a view that was further strengthened by the historiography of the post-Renaissance period, when classical interests began to dominate Western thinking. Under this influence all true history was regarded as beginning with Greece and Rome and national histories were conceived as something to be added on to the history of the Greco-Roman world. Church historians, under the same influence, thought of church history in terms of the church fathers who were either Greek or Roman; consequently the history of the various national churches of Europe appeared as sequels to the regular church histories of the fathers.[16]

Although this patched-on type of history does retain the continuity of the church from apostolic days to the present time, it hardly does justice to the autonomous development of European churches, particularly to the history of dissent; and it becomes almost unmanageable when applied to the American continent, where "patching on" becomes twice removed from the original church.

This disservice is even exceeded when Europeans, preoccupied with a national or established church, regard it as the true church and retain, as it were, a catholic covering for the separated churches under the titles of dissent or non-conformity. Such terms with their derogatory implication will not do in the New World where very frequently an Old World dissenting religion may well have become the dominant cultural influence in large areas of the American continent.

NEW TECHNIQUES

While New World church historians continued to adhere to the Old World canons it remained almost impossible to write a comprehensive history of either American or Canadian religious development. The first church historian to challenge the European concept and to pioneer in new methods and techniques was Professor W. W. Sweet; with the appearance of his *The Story of Religion in America* in 1930, a new era in the field of church history began; but even as late as 1950 Professor Sweet complained that "religion has been the most neglected phase of American history," and he underlined his complaint by saying, "The average college student could pass a better examination in Greek mythology than in American church history and is better informed on the medieval popes than he is on the religious leaders of America."[17]

In seeking a new method of making American church history more than a mere "appendage to general church history on the one hand or denominational monographs on the other"[18] Professor Sweet perhaps relied too much on the discipline of secular American history;[19] nevertheless, he did infuse a new spirit into the study of American Christianity and has succeeded, as he intended, in reminding "secular historians of the religious factors that have helped to shape America" as well "as impressing denominational and other historians of religion of the significance of other religious groups, and the secular forces, in shaping their particular groups."[20]

Since Professor Sweet's pioneer effort there has been a growing accumulation of publications on American church history (Professor

Sweet himself was godfather to more than thirty Ph.D. theses on some aspect or other of American church history) and an intense discussion by students of the subject on the best interpretative approach to what is still an almost untilled field of research. In all this discussion an interpretative method is being sought which will avoid the temptation of becoming mere Christian sociology, but will at the same time provide themes sufficiently comprehensive to do justice to the complex history of Christianity on the American continents.[21] A careful study of this literature[22] can help materially to smooth the path of the Canadian church historian as he tries to wend his way through a religious development as complex as that in the United States.

CONCEPT OF THE CATHOLIC CHURCH

One conclusion that has become quite generally accepted by American historians is that the term "Catholic" can no longer be identified, as it often is by European historians, with an institutional expression of Christianity. As Professor L. J. Trinterud has rightly observed, "Seldom do these institutional expressions allow of easy harmonization"; consequently "church history becomes largely the history of the warfare within and between these various ecclesiastical institutions which we know as 'churches.' "[23] Because of this lack of harmony in defining the church and also because all ecclesiastical institutions have had a historical development, it is now pretty well agreed among American church historians that they have no firm standard whereby they can exclude any church or sect from the history of the church universal. Therefore, it follows that the concept of the Catholic church must be broad enough and inclusive enough to embody all those who at any time past or present have claimed or do claim redemption through Jesus Christ. It must be admitted that this larger concept of the Catholic church imposes a particularly onerous burden upon both American and Canadian church historians because of the many types of Christianity they have to deal with; nevertheless, the church historian must consider sympathetically and with understanding all religious groups, however fanatical or bizarre, if he is to do complete justice to church development on this continent.

This does not mean that he abandons his critical faculties or that he does not have his own perception of the Gospel; in point of fact he does permit himself the same freedom of judgment in treating the claims of a sect as he permits himself in judging his own particular branch of the Church Catholic; but he must always remain aware that he himself, unless he claims infallibility, cannot be the final judge in these high matters of spiritual discernment.

NEW THEMES

In providing sectarianism with a more respectable status than has been customary in European church histories it becomes necessary to look more closely at its theological origins and its European development. Such an investigation soon reveals the inadequacy of the older church histories in which the sects are very often portrayed from a negative point of view, as threatening the norms and structures of the national church or as culturally divisive forces. Because of this older approach to a religious phenomenon that has, in America, created the typically free and popular churches of the frontier, it becomes almost a necessity to rewrite the religious background of New World Christianity. This, to some extent, has been done by Professor J. H. Nichols who, in the opening pages of his *History of Christianity 1650-1950*, states quite frankly that he is going to treat the many separated church traditions "as if they were all part of the Christian society, the church, or as if the church were to be found in significant measure with them."[24]

Such a treatment brings into prominence many themes that are only lightly touched upon by older church historians. One is revivalism, which opens up a whole series of allied issues, the most significant being voluntaryism, namely, that religious institutions should depend upon the free-will contributions of the membership. To the European historian the American interest in these themes may seem excessive, since revivalism has perhaps played only a minor role in European cultural development; but the interest is by no means excessive when it is realized that revivalism and many of the principles it fostered, such as voluntaryism, lay-participation in religion and democracy itself, have brought about a revolution in church organizations on this continent. As a matter of fact, the theme of organization always occupies a prominent place in both American and Canadian church histories. How this has come about has been very succinctly explained by Professor Sydney E. Mead in an illuminating article in *Church History* in which he points out that during the upheavals of the Great Awakening the patterns of sectarian religion began to infiltrate the conventional churches and thus "through confusion and compromise" there began a "historical merging of the traditional patterns of 'church' and 'sect', 'right' and 'left' wings, as known in Europe, into a new kind of organization combining features of both plus features growing out of the immediate situation."[25] To this resulting organizational form Mead has applied the term "denominationalism," which he considers a peculiarly American phenomenon and "unlike anything that had preceded it in Christendom."[26] Such being the case there is good and sufficient reason for American church historians to make a fresh review of the European religious scene, so that they may become better acquainted with the origins of a very self-conscious religious ideal which is frequently reiterated in the oft-repeated slogan, "Go to the church of your choice."

CANADIAN VARIATIONS

Since denominationalism is also a Canadian phenomenon, this contemplated revision of European church history may well help the Canadian church historian to set forth Canadian church development more clearly and significantly. And yet he must use this material with caution, for there are variations between the Canadian and American developments which prevent such a radical break with European concepts and methods for the Canadian historian as has been true for the American. For one thing, church history in Canada begins with New France, in which the union of church and state continued for almost a century and a half and was so firmly established that the alliance has partially prevailed in French Canada down to the present day. Under these circumstances it seems quite possible to keep the first half of Canadian church history firmly within the concepts of European historiography, except for the fact that the French-Canadian church did not remain immune to the democratic spirit of the frontier. Outstanding evidence of this is the prominence of lay participation in the councils of the church, which, in the words of Archbishop Roy of Quebec, has led to the formation "of a type of religious grouping to be found nowhere else perhaps but in French Canada."[27]

To this may be added an additional factor, namely, that the Roman Catholic Church in Canada joined with dissenting groups to oppose the British government's attempt to establish the Church of England in Canada. Thus, unwittingly perhaps, the Roman Catholic Church in Canada made its contribution to the ideal of denominationalism and can in some sense fit into the canons of American church historiography. On the other hand, its strongly rooted seventeenth-century concepts, its semi-established position in the Province of Quebec and its consistent emphasis upon loyalty to the ruling authorities in both church and state have made their impact upon the Protestant churches in Canada and give the latter a religious outlook that is not always in accord with Protestant development in the United States. Thus there has been in Canada a religious mood that questions the ultimate desirability of denominationalism and does hanker for greater uniformity of religious expression in the interest of cultural unity. But even beyond cultural unity there has arisen in Canada a spirit of ecumenism with a difference in nuance from that of the United States; the latter's contentment with denominationalism may perhaps be explained by its philosophic acceptance of a pluralistic society which sees catholicity in pluralism, something shared among a number of separate institutions; whereas the Canadian tendency is to see catholicity more in ecumenism—a reality that remains incomplete until it is given some outward expression. The difference may well be explained by the fact that few people came to Canada for sectarian reasons, and that from the beginning of the British era advocates of the indigenization of the church in Canada have made unity one of the planks of their platform. The long series of church unions in Canada, and continuing negotiations, are the historical expression of an ideal that looks beyond American denominationalism as the final "destiny which awaits the whole of the Church Catholic in the future."[28]

PROBLEM OF COMMUNICATION

It seems, then, that the Canadian church historian is challenged to combine the techniques of both the European and American church historians; but his supreme challenge, as it is with any church historian, is to communicate and make relevant to his readers the part that the Canadian church has contributed to the universal history of the church. That does not mean, however, that he overlooks the importance of Canadian church history in understanding the national development of Canada. For it is evident that many of our secular historians miss not a few of the static factors of our cultural development, to say nothing of the poetry and other intangibles which are inseparably bound up with our religious expression. But these are the subordinate responsibilities of the church historian; though without discharging them he would not be doing full justice to his larger task of making the history of the Canadian church relevant to the history of the Catholic church of God. In other words, the historian of the church of Canada has an overriding responsibility to contribute to the writing of a truly universal history of the church.

It is in meeting these two demands, the national and the supra-national, that the problem of communication becomes most acute; for his larger audience he must be somewhat informative as he sets forth the claim to universal significance of church life in Canada with its great variety and novelty; for his smaller audience he must, in a sense, be hortatory as he sets forth the involvement of this activity in the larger life of the church universal.

Above all the church historian, within whatever geographical area he writes, must be sensitively aware of what has been described by Karl Jaspers as an "axial period," lying somewhere between 800 and 200 B.C., when man became "conscious of Being as a whole, of himself and his limitations."[29] It is also with a fairly comprehensive knowledge of the meaningful occurrences of the past—the breath-less history of the last six thousand years, with its significant landmarks of revelation—that the Canadian church historian tries to throw some light upon the church history of his own little cranny of here and now.

NOTES TO CHAPTER ONE

1. Vide Philip Carrington, A Church History for Canadians to 1900 A.D. (To-ronto: General Board of Religious Education, 1946): A history for Canadians that deals mainly with the history of the Church of England. Three chapters out of forty-six are allotted to Canada and the organization of the Anglican Church in Canada. There is a brief paragraph dealing with "other Protestants." In fairness to the author it must be said that the "book is written for the young people of the Church of England in Canada"; nevertheless it is a striking ex-ample of the codicil treatment of "overseas" churches.

2. An extended discussion of this subject is to be found in an article by L. J. Trinterud, "The Task of the American Church Historian," Church History, XXV (March, 1956).

3. Ibid., pp. 3-4.

4. Ibid., p. 4.

5. Such a definition of the church in relation to history is to be found in Karl Barth, The Church and the Political Problem of Our Day (London: Hodder, 1939), p. 5 et seq.

6. Quoted from Barth, op. cit., p. 7.

7. Eusebius, The Ecclesiastical History and the Martyrs of Palestine, trans. Lawlor & Oulton (London: S.P.C.K., 1927), Vol. I, pp. 4 and 14.

8. S. D. Clark, Church and Sect in Canada (Toronto: University of Toronto Press, 1948); C. A. Dawson, Group Settlement: Ethnic Communities in Western Canada (Toronto: Macmillan, 1936) are the most important studies in this field.

9. R. Bultmann, History and Eschatology (Edinburgh: Edinburgh University Press, 1957), p. 122.

10. Ibid.

11. J. McIntyre, *The Christian Doctrine of History* (Edinburgh: Oliver and Boyd, 1957), p. 3. A very interesting discussion of the church historian as a man of faith is to be found in an article by David W. Hay, "The Christian Tradition and the Church Historian" in *Canadian Journal of Theology*, XII, No. 1 (January, 1966), p. 30 *et seq.*

12. Quoted from Jacques Maritain, *On the Philosophy of History* (New York: Scribner, 1957), p. 3.

13. *Vide* R. G. Collingwood, *The Idea of History* (Oxford: Clarendon Press, 1946), p. 257.

14. *Ibid.*, p. 202.

15. Quoted from L. J. Trinterud, *op. cit.*, p. 5.

16. This theory is more fully discussed by Trinterud, *op. cit., passim.*

17. W. W. Sweet, *Religion in Colonial America* (New York: Scribner, 1951), p. vii.

18. Quoted from an article by S. E. Mead, "Professor Sweet's Religion and Culture in America," *Church History*, XXII (March. 1953), p. 45.

19. *Ibid.*, p. 46.

20. Quoted by Mead, *op. cit.*, p. 33, from "Every Dog Has His Day," *The University of Chicago Magazine*, XXXIX (February, 1947), pp. 10 and 11.

21. *Vide* E. H. Harbison, "The 'Meaning of History' and the writing of History," *Church History*, XXI (June, 1952); an interesting discussion of the Christian understanding of history and the influence of modern secular historians on this understanding.

22. *Vide* R. T. Handy, "Survey of Recent Literature: American Church History," *Church History*, XXVII (June, 1958), pp. 161-7; an exhaustive survey of the more recent literature.

23. L. J. Trinterud, *op. cit.*, p. 10.

24. J. H. Nichols, *History of Christianity 1650-1950* (New York: Ronald Press, 1956), p. iii.

25. S. E. Mead, "From Coercion to Persuasion," *Church History*, XXV (December, 1956), p. 336.

26. *Ibid.*, pp. 335-6.

27. M. Roy, *The Parish and Democracy in French Canada* (Toronto: University of Toronto Press, 1950), p. 15.

28. *Vide*, L. J. Trinterud, op. cit., p. 9. The larger context from which the quotation is taken sees a different future for the Church Catholic: "Whatever 'the fissiparous American religiosity' may in fact be, it seems indeed to be that destiny which awaits the whole of the Church Catholic in the future."

29. On the "Axial Period" *vide* K. Jaspers, *The Origin and Goal of History* (London: Routledge, 1953), p. 2: "An axis of world history, if such a thing exists, would have to be discovered empirically, as a fact capable of being accepted as such by all men, Christians included .... It would seem that this axis of history is to be found in the period around 500 B.C., in the spiritual process that occurred between 800 and 200 B.C. It is there that we meet with the most deepcut dividing line in history. Man, as we know him today, came into being. For short we may style this the 'Axial Period.' "

TWO

The Great Discovery

Before the prospect of interplanatory exploration loomed upon the horizon, writers on discovery were inclined to stress the singularity of Columbus' first voyage to America. Today we hesitate before saying that "nothing like it can ever be done again."[1] But even if the unprecedented character of this voyage into the outer space of the medieval world should be matched or overshadowed by a voyage into the outer space of the contemporary world, the dynamic effect of the great discovery of the fifteenth century will still remain written large on the pages of history, and historians will continue to trace its influence in all departments of life: in trade and commerce, in political and social development and in church reform.

DISCOVERY AND REFORMATION

The connection between the discovery of America in the fifteenth century and the religious reformations of the sixteenth century may not at first sight appear obvious, and must to a large extent be argued from chronology. Yet when it is recalled that it was only twenty-five years after Columbus' first voyage to the West Indies that Martin Luther nailed his ninety-five theses to the church door at Wittenberg, and only twenty-five years later that Paul III issued a bull which led to the assembling of the Council of Trent and thus set in motion a counter-reformation, it does seem highly probable that the former event had some bearing upon the two latter. It is true that there had been many attempts to reform the church before the discovery of America—John Wycliffe and John Huss both had anticipated Luther's defiance of the papacy; the great reforming councils of the fifteenth century were as keen as that at Trent to strengthen the church to meet the attacks of its critics and enemies —but these earlier reformers and councils failed in their objectives,

11

whereas the latter succeeded beyond all expectation.[2] There would seem, therefore, to be some ground for arguing that the sixteenth-century achievement was due to the great stimulus administered to the human psyche by the amazing discovery of a new world.

The stimulation was at first perceived in the form of a shock; and the church's primary reaction was, in conservative quarters at least, a warning against prying into the forbidden secrets of the universe. Explorers were bluntly told that there were better things to do than to waste one's time trying to grasp such complex knowledge as exploration demanded. Sebastian Brant, in his famous satire *Das Narrenschiff*, published two years after Columbus' initial voyage, pours scorn on "man's folly in trying to know so large a subject as the earth when he can hardly know himself." Sardonically he asks,

> Why should we humans seek to be
> More than we are in verity?

to which he adds,

> Some have explored a foreign land
> But not themselves can understand.[3]

This outburst was a reflection of the spirit that distinguished the medieval from the modern world; the former regarded the life of contemplation or monastic retreat as the ideal, whereas the latter has chosen the life of action directed to the world around it. The choice had already been made by the humanists, of whom Brant was one—though it would appear almost unwillingly, for he still had a nostalgia for the medieval world. But his very vehemence in denouncing fools seeking a fool's paradise in an unknown world led him to rebuke many of the evils within the churches, since he felt that these had created the restless spirit which indulged in exploration. Because of its author's ambivalence, the *Narrenschiff*, which was supposed to be a defence of the good old days, has been described as "a most effective preparation for the Protestant Reformation."[4]

Brant had many sympathizers in his last-ditch stand against the new trend. More than a decade after his own lament a chaplain of the College of Ottery St. Mary in Devonshire, Alexander Barclay, writes in his *Ship of Fools,* in words reminiscent of Brant:

> . . . And so this fole castyth his wyt so wyde
> To know eche londe under the fyrament
> That thereabout in vayne his tyme is spent . . .[5]

Even more shocking to conservative theologians than the appearance of the activist spirit was the information that these newly discovered lands were inhabited by weird savage folk, thus giving credence to medieval speculation about an antipodal world peopled by strange human beings who shaded off into "Gorgons, hydras, and chimeras dire."[6] St. Augustine in the fifth century had raised a question about the theological position of semi-human creatures, but decided its solution could wait until such creatures were discovered. The responsible church leaders of the Middle Ages went further than St. Augustine: they held that such speculation itself was wrong and refused to give any credence to the existence of beings, human or semi-human, beyond the reach of Christ's command to "make disciples of all nations."[7] When Portuguese sailors, returning from voyages down the coast of Africa, first announced the existence of a hitherto unknown race of men and women, many churchmen still disbelieved, but after the discovery of America this was no longer possible, and so the church was compelled to reinterpret its theology in the light of new knowledge.

Admission of the existence of an antipodal people was perhaps less of a shock to orthodox churchmen than the admission that the world was spherical in shape. According to medieval conceptions no such flood as that described in the seventh chapter of Genesis could possibly have occurred on a globular earth; in defence, therefore, of the truth of the Scriptures it was necessary to maintain the popular view that the earth was a rectangular plane. Although Ptolemy's spherical theory of the universe was well known among the learned, including many clergymen, yet it was not officially approved by the church. It was inclined to side with Cosmas Indicopleustes, a monk of Alexandria and a self-proclaimed Christian geographer, who maintained in opposition to Ptolemy that the inhabited lands of the earth were in the centre of the floor of the universe, "surrounded on all sides by a great ocean." It was dangerous to sail for any distance into this limitless sea, even though Cosmas felt inclined to concede that in some far corner beyond the ocean "is the Paradise from which Adam and Eve were expelled."[8] This was a concession hardly likely to encourage exploration—at least until it was possible to retain one's sense of direction in the vast ocean lying between Europe and Paradise. When, at last, by the invention of the compass the ocean became more navigable there was considerable hesitancy on the part of mariners in using this new guide lest, like Roger Bacon, they be condemned as magicians.[9]

All these theological objections to exploration were, to the spirit of the time, real enough; and those who urged them were in many cases sincerely intent on safeguarding religious faith. When it was finally brought home to these churchmen that their negative attitude could no longer be maintained, there must have intervened a period of reappraisal such as had often been imposed upon theologians after the break-down of established philosophies or conventional cosmologies. We can only speculate as to the outcome, but it seems not improbable that these religiously concerned people began to search diligently for something to replace the old values and securities of the Middle Ages. It may well be that these conservative churchmen by their very concern for the abiding realities of the medieval world contributed more to the reform movements of the sixteenth century than those ecclesiastics who enthusiastically welcomed the new science and the discoveries of the explorers with little regard for the church's doctrinal embarrassments.

ECCLESIASTICAL INITIATIVE IN EXPLORATION

On the other side in this issue were many churchmen, some in very high office, who gladly welcomed the new knowledge that made discovery possible. Nor were they by any means startled by the sudden discovery of the long-rejected antipodal world. Some of them were troubled about the cultural isolation of Christian Europe in the Middle Ages; on the Iberian Peninsula, where they were in contact with the Muslim East, cultural contacts were made mainly as Hendrick Kraemer points out, "on the initiative and out of the *curiosité* of the European Westerners."[10] In this curiosity there was an element of dynamism—perhaps the result of a sense of incompleteness following the separation from Byzantium?—that always sought to break out of this isolation and to establish contacts with, and even beyond, Islam. This dynamism was complex in its expression. One motive—represented by the Crusades and in a different way by St. Francis of Assisi—was expansive and missionary, springing from a confidence in European and Christian values and from a desire to export them; the other was a desire to let some fresh air into the stuffy atmosphere of Europe. Christopher Dawson has pointed out that Europe was the scene of a constant series of rebirths, each the result of some fresh contact with the outside, notably with antiquity as preserved by Muslim scholars. He deprecates the fact that in our "current methods of teaching history" the names of the great missionaries who explored in far lands take a secondary place to the geographical explorers, or are ignored altogether.[11] Nor should we forget the names of prominent churchmen, some in very high office, who helped to make discoveries possible. It was a cardinal of the Roman Church, Pierre d'Ailly (1350-1420), the author of a treatise on geography, *Imago Mundi*,[12] who convinced Columbus that it was possible to sail across the Atlantic on a continuous voyage that would ultimately lead him to the Indies. It was none other than the Grand Master of the Order of Christ, Henry the Navigator, who determined with all the help that science could supply to know what might lie beyond earth's remotest bounds. To this end he secured funds from his order "for the worthy purpose of advancing the interests of science, converting the heathen and winning a commercial empire for Portugal."[13]

Great credit for contributing to the discovery of America must be given to the prior of a Franciscan monastery, Juan Perez, for his championship of what were generally regarded as the chimerical views of Christopher Columbus. In the quiet retreat of Father Perez' monastery at Palos, Columbus finally gained a genuine hearing for his plan to reach the Indies by sailing westward across the Atlantic. Furthermore, it was the monks at Palos who arranged an all-important gathering of church dignitaries at Granada where Mendoza, the Archbishop of Toledo and Primate of Spain, was induced to use his powerful influence to persuade Queen Isabella to provide the ships and men for Columbus' projected voyage.[14]

All this vigorous support by the clergy of apparently chimerical schemes is explained by the fact that Columbus was a man of mystical vision and always presented his project as part of a divine plan "for enlarging the bounds of Christendom."[15] When, finally, through his efforts a new inhabited world was brought into view, the church in Spain by its identification with Columbus' project was spiritually prepared, as it were, to embark upon a great missionary campaign to bring these new people within the Christian fold. It was also inclined to agree with the prevalent Spanish opinion that the discovery was a reward to Spain for its vigorous support of the Christian cause. This general opinion was clearly expressed by one of the most popular poets of the day, Giuliano Dati, who after due thanks "to the illustrious discoverer Columbus," reserved the "greater thanks to the supreme God, who is making new realms to be conquered for thee [Spain] and for Himself and vouchsafes to thee to be at once strong and pious."[16]

No longer were there any troublesome questions about the improbability of God's leaving a people separated for centuries from the means of salvation; no longer was there fear of penetrating into mysteries beyond human understanding; from pious monarchs down to humble cabin-boys all theological doubts were dispelled by the exhilarating thought that God had been holding in reserve new worlds to conquer for the kingdom that served him best. Both Isabella and Ferdinand were certain that Columbus' discovery was God's reward to them for the capture of Granada, the last Islamic stronghold in western Europe, as well as for the expulsion of the Jews from Spain and for the harsh measures they had taken to extirpate heresy. And with this view conquistador and missionary were in hearty agreement as they prepared to exploit and convert the new-found lands and peoples.

UTOPIAN VISIONS

The exuberant mood which led to the immediate colonization of the barbaric world by Europeans could not be confined to the Iberian Peninsula; in a very brief time it spread across western Europe and fired men's ambitions to perfect a new and better future for all mankind. This in turn led to more daring thinking and a greater freedom of expression than was customary in medieval Europe.

The era that preceded the discovery of America seems to have been very wary of new ideas, and would have resented the suggestion:

> There are more things in heaven and earth, Horatio,
> Than are dreamt of in your philosophy.[17]

Roger Bacon's fanciful endeavour to outline a better future led to years of imprisonment, and Petrarch's attempt to enlarge the intellectual horizon of his time gained for him the title of wizard. But with a new world of wonders being proclaimed by such responsible reporters as Peter Martyr of *De Orbe Novo* fame, of Richard Eden in his *Decades*,[18] it became manifestly impossible to prevent men from dreaming dreams and seeing visions of a new and better society than mankind had ever envisaged before. The challenge was first accepted by Sir Thomas More, who in writing *Utopia* started a vogue of imaginary "brave new worlds" that has continued down to our own time. "Utopia," or "no-where place," was suggested to More while reading a little book called *Cosmographiae Introductio*, which described the four voyages of Amerigo Vespucci. More selects one of the characters in this book to serve as the spokesman for a new world order. The narrator tells us that "among Utopians all things being common, every man hath abundance of everything . . . " and that he holds "well with Plato . . . that all men should have and enjoy

equal positions of wealth and commodities. . . . For where every
man, under certain titles and pretences, draineth and plucketh to
himself as much as he can, so that a few divide among themselves
all the whole riches . . . there to the residual is left lack and
poverty."[19] As one reader of *Utopia* has exclaimed, this "is almost
the voice of Karl Marx. . . . It remains as contemporary as a planned
economy and the welfare state."[20]

What is even more surprising is that More, a loyal son of the
medieval church, should predict the spirit of modern day sectarianism, since in Utopia religion is voluntary and "no prayers be
used (in church) but such as every man may boldly pronounce without offending any sect."[21] Las Casas, the famous Spanish missionary,
also indulged in utopian visions, dreaming "of an ideal colony,
peopled by perfect Christians labouring for the conversion of model
Indians,"[22] a dream partly realized in the Jesuit colony of Paraguay.
A consequence of these dreams was the founding of new religious
orders dedicated to foreign missions among far-away peoples; another was the attempt to create in the forests of the New World new
Zions based upon the principles of reformed or "purified" churches.[23]

In the same category as utopiansim was a tendency on the part
of the early explorers and missionaries to idealize the American
Indian. It seems fair to say that this Indian of fancy's creation has
had an even more revolutionary influence than utopian visions upon
Western civilization. A mythical Indian first began to take form
through Columbus' desire to impress the importance of his discoveries upon the Spanish sovereigns. In trying to do so he described
the primitives of Cuba as "very gentle, without knowledge of evil,
neither killing nor stealing. . . . In all the world there is not a better
people or a better country; they love their neighbours as themselves
and they have the sweetest and gentlest way of speaking in the
world and always with a smile."[24] With even more fervour Las
Casas declared: "All these infinite peoples were created by God and
most simple of all others, without malice or duplicity, most obedient
and faithful to their rulers, whom they serve; the most humble,
patient, loving, peaceful and docile people, without contentions or
tumults; neither factious nor quarrelsome, without hatred or desire
for revenge more than any people in the world."[25]

Reports like these led not only to the writing of fanciful utopias,
but also to serious and semi-serious books on political economy.
Rousseau's *Le Contrat Social*,[26] the textbook of the French Revolution, drew its inspiration from *le bon sauvage;* this is also partly true

of Chateaubriand's *Génie du Christianisme* which contributed so much to the romantic movement of the nineteenth century, a movement which gave to Christianity the greatest territorial expansion in all its long history.[27]

AN OPEN FRONTIER

Such were the contributions of the idealists and dreamers to the thought and culture of modern Europe. But there was also the contribution of entrepreneurs and shopkeepers. Their opportunity came through what has been designated as the "open frontier."[28]

One of the most significant facts about fifteenth-century Europe was its fortress-like existence; on one side were the Turks, on the other the Barbary pirates. Within this beleaguered fortress, comprising an area of about three and three-quarter million square miles, life was static, with well-defined classes, and a population of some 100 million people was continually pressing on the means of subsistence.[29] Although the old manorial economy had been greatly threatened by the sudden depopulation brought about by the Black Death, yet it was still being buttressed by harsh legislation which prohibited artisans from moving about. Then came the miracle: a way of escape from the rigid caste system was opened up by the discovery of a New World. The decline of the manorial system was now greatly hastened by the expanded trade of the Atlantic powers that followed shortly upon the discoveries of the mariners; and this in turn helped the yeomanry and peasants to get out of the hands of their overlords, as they moved steadily into the world of shops and warehouses and began to develop "a passion for bourgeois comfort."[30] It was not long before the shopkeepers struck upon the idea of uniting their savings in great corporations for the exploration of new-found lands. The stockholders, however, were not shopkeepers only but came from the most diverse groups of society. Thus was created a new fraternity in which class barriers began to disappear. In the London company incorporated to develop Virginia there were "besides earls, bishops, knights and gentlemen, plain commoners, merchants, tailors, stationers, shoemakers, etc. and two women."[31]

Lure of profit no doubt played the dominant role in creating this unusual fraternity; yet there was also mixed with the profit motive a spirit of service, directed either towards the welfare of the aborigines in the new world, or towards national interests in the old. So sincerely was it believed that a joint-stock company might serve a beneficent purpose that shares in common stock were actually advertised from the pulpits of the churches in England. "Before it was anything else," says one student of the Virginia Company's records, "the Virginia Company was a Christian enterprise."[32] Certainly the Massachusetts Bay Company regarded its spiritual purpose as primary, even though the appetite for profits grew with increasing dividends, and Bible and ledger became inextricably commingled in the exploitation of the New World.

Accordingly, there arose in the age of discovery a more dynamic imperialism than mankind had yet witnessed. A famous German economist, Sombart, has tried to explain the dynamic of this new imperialism by reducing it "to the terms of the everlasting struggle among human societies over feeding places on the wide surface of the earth and over the distribution of the world's natural resources."[33] The Beards in their justly famous history, The Rise of American Civilization, though much impressed by the Sombart thesis, make the reservation that "the story of human migration cannot all be told in the terms of commerce, profits, conquest and exploration."[34] Apart from the Roman Catholic missions and the Calvinistic belief in destiny, both of which added new forces to the development of Western imperialism, there was the tremendous uplift of the open frontier ever beckoning adventurous souls forward to the land of Eldorado. Eldorado, however, was a lodestar that attracted far more than mere gold-seekers and those in search of perpetual youth. As already observed, it attracted those concerned with new and better world orders and reformed churches while even those who stayed at home could not fail to feel the contagion of the optimism of those who were venturing forth with great expectations; this very spirit of optimism and feeling of freedom gave to Western civilization a dynamic quality that has only recently begun to wane.[35]

MISSIONARY ENTERPRISES

In the field of religion this new quality became most evident in missionary enterprises. At the time of the discovery of America missionary work had about come to an end; Europe, with the exception of Lapland, had been evangelized and religious orders with missionary motives seemed doomed to extinction. Then came the challenge of the New World, and an amazing response on the part of the medieval church. At a time when the papacy was under most corrupt leadership and was soon to be shaken to its depths by the Protestant revolt it proceeded almost at once to embark upon a great missionary adventure. The dates speak for themselves. As early as

May, 1493, a department of Indian affairs was set up with Juan Rod-
riguez de Fonseca, the Archdeacon of Seville, at its head. On September 6 in the same year the papacy issued a bull, *Dudum siquidem
omnes*, calling attention to the need for missionary effort to justify
the occupation of the new country by Europeans. To superintend
missionary work, a Franciscan friar, Bernardo Bayle, was selected
by the pope and given the title of Apostolic Vicar for the Indies.[36] In
1524 there was organized the Council of the Indies, one of whose
most outstanding members was Bartholomew de Las Casas; another
was the chronicler, Peter Martyr, whose writings kept a large reading public in Europe acutely conscious of the larger world in which
they now lived.[37]

Such a vigorous response to the challenge of America was not
made without some preparation. Discoveries in the thirteenth century, and particularly the voyages of the Polos, had given new
currency to a "religious utopia of the *Regnum Dei* . . . an abstract
ideal of the mystics of ancient Europe,"[38] which had for centuries
been part of the folklore of medieval Europe. It was this ideal that
had imbued men like Raymond Lull with a desire to convert the
Asian peoples who were becoming more intimately known to Western Europe.[39] Columbus was not unaware of this missionary urge;
moreover, he had the conversion of the Indies in mind even while
seeking a sponsor for his projected voyage across the Atlantic.

The spiritual Franciscans were, from the first word of discovery,
ready to proceed to the New World as were also other mendicant
orders. Nor was it long before new orders arose, particularly adapted
to frontier outpost conditions. In these first days the Roman Catholic
Church far outdistanced the Protestant churches, partly because the
latter were long delayed through controversy and irresolution in
working out a philosophy of missions, and partly because the challenge of the Reformation forced the Roman Catholic states "to
develop the missionary state as an answer to this threat."[40]

The ecclesiastical demands of the New World became so pressing
in the seventeenth century as to compel Pope Gregory XV to create
the *Congregatio de propaganda fide* (1622);[41] under its auspices col-
leges were set up in the Americas to train missionaries for work both
at home and abroad. This new activity led to much coming and going
in church circles; councils were frequently summoned to deal with
the transformation in religious institutions and unusual experiments
in religious expression. These transformations and experiments must
be given a large place in any study of the religious background of the
churches of the Americas, including Canada.

NOTES TO CHAPTER TWO

1. Vide John Fiske, *The Discovery of America* (Boston: Houghton, Mifflin, 1892), Vol. I, p. 446: "The first voyage of Columbus is thus a unique event in the history of mankind. Nothing like it was ever done before, and nothing like it can ever be done again"; also A. P. Newton, *The Great Age of Discovery* (London: University of London Press, 1932), p. 41 *et seq.*; J. B. Brebner, *The Explorers of North America* (London: Black, 1933), p. 3. Brebner does admit the possibility of Columbus' discovery being outranked: "Unless mankind is to embark some day on interplanetary exploration, there can never be a geographical adventure like the discovery and exploration of the Americas."

2. On the world-historical significance of the "Ninety-Five Theses" *vide* H. Bornkamm, *Luther's World of Thought*, trans. M. H. Bertram (St. Louis: Concordia, 1958), pp. 36-54; on the unusual dynamism of the Council of Trent *vide* R. Aubert, *Historical Problems of Church Renewal* (Concilium", Vol. VII [Glen Rock, N.J.: Paulist Press, 1965]), pp. 69-87.

3. Quoted by F. T. McCann, *English Discovery of America to 1585* (New York: Kings Crown Press, 1952), pp. 73-4.

4. "Brant, Sebastian," *Encyclopedia Britannica*, 14th ed.; Vol. IV, p. 38.

5. Quoted by F. T. McCann, *op. cit.*, p. 79.

6. J. Fiske, *op. cit.*, Vol I, pp. 311-2.

7. Matt. 29: 19. Some Irish monks who abandoned Iceland in the ninth century because they would not live there with heathens must have had a shrewd suspicion that there were strange people in the far west who had not heard Christ's message; *vide* Gwyn Jones, *The Norse Atlantic Saga* (New York: Oxford University Press, 1964), pp. 8-9.

8. Cosmas' work is entitled "Topographia Christiana"; text in J. P. Migne, *Patrologia Graeca* (Paris: Migne, 1909), Vol. 88, pp. 9-476. (*Cosmas Indicopleustes* means "Cosmas who sailed to India"); *vide* J. Fiske, *op. cit.*, Vol. I, p. 265.

9. *Vide* J. Fiske, *op. cit.*, p. 314.

10. Hendrik Kraemer, *World Cultures and World Religions* (London: Lutterworth, 1960), p. 32.

11. *Vide* Christopher Dawson, *The Movement of World Revolution* (New York: Sheed and Ward, 1959), pp. 10-1.

12. *Vide* S. E. Morison, *Admiral of the Ocean Sea* (Boston: Little, Brown, 1942), p. 93.

13. J. Fiske, *op. cit.*, Vol I, p. 320.

14. *Ibid.*, p. 413.

15. *Ibid.*, p. 416.

16. *Ibid.*, p. 450.

17. Shakespeare, *Hamlet*, Act I, Scene 5.

18. *Vide* Pietro Martire d'Anghiera, *De Orbe Novo*, etc., French trans. Paul Gaffarel (Paris: Leroux, 1907); R. Eden, *The Decades of the Newe Worlde*, ed. Edward Arber (Birmingham: Turnbull, Spears, 1885).

19. More, *Utopia* (New York: Dutton, 1951), p. 44.

20. Will Durant, *The Story of Civilization*, Part VI: "The Reformation" (New York: Simon and Schuster, 1957), p. 555.

21. Quoted by Will Durant, *op. cit.*, p. 554.

22. Quoted by F. A. MacNutt, *Bartholomew de Las Casas* (New York and London: Putnam, 1909), p. vi.

23. *Vide* K. S. Latourette on "The Contribution of the Religion of the Colonial Period to the Ideals and Life of the United States," found in *History of Religion in the New World during Colonial Times* (Washington, D.C.: Conference on the History of Religion in the New World during Colonial Times, 1958), pp. 4-19.

24. F. A. MacNutt, *op. cit.*, p. 19.

25. *Ibid.*

26. *Vide* Jean Jacques Rousseau, *Du Contrat Social* (Paris: Gallimard, 1964), Bk. IV.

27. *Vide* K. S. Latourette, *A History of the Expansion of Christianity* (New York and London: Harper, 1941), Vol. IV, Chap. I.

28. On the influence of the frontier see F. J. Turner, *Rise of the New West* (New York: Harper, 1906), *passim*.

29. *Vide* W. P. Webb, *The Great Frontier* (Boston: Houghton, Mifflin, 1932), p. 142; on the static "conception of society in the Middle Ages" *vide* J. Huizinga, *The Waning of the Middle Ages* (London: Arnold, 1924), pp. 48-55.

30. Charles and Mary Beard, *The Rise of American Civilization* (New York: Macmillan, 1933), p. 20.

31. *Ibid.*, p. 27.

32. A. L. Maycock, *Nicholas Ferrar of Little Gidding* (London: S.P.C.K., 1938), p. 87, speaking of some of the directors of the Virginia Company, says: "To have neglected the spiritual or pastoral aspect of their work in Virginia would have been a gross and sinful violation of their trust and a grave misuse of their authority. To the truth of this there is ample witness in the Court Books."

33. Quoted by C. and M. Beard, *op. cit.*, p. 5.

34. *Ibid.*, p. 8.

35. On the genesis of modern dynamism, *vide* W. P. Webb, *op. cit.*, p. 140 *et seq.*

36. J. Fiske, *op. cit.*, Vol. I, pp. 460-2.

37. A. P. Newton, *op. cit.*, p. 99, says: Peter Martyr (1457-1526), "fulfilled a purpose similar to that of the foreign correspondents of a great newspaper today."

38. *Vide* Nicolau D'Olwer, "Comments on Evangelization of the New World" found in *History of Religion*, etc., *op. cit.*, p. 66. On the kingdom of God and history *vide* C. Dawson, *The Dynamics of World History*, ed. J. J. Malloy (London: Sheed and Ward, 1957), pp. 279-86.

39. *Vide* S. M. Zwemer, *Raymond Lull, First Missionary to the Moslems* (New York and London: Funk and Wagnalls, 1902), *passim*.

40. *Ibid.*, p. 50.

41. For the origins of the Propaganda Congregation, *vide* *The Catholic Encyclopedia* (New York: The Encyclopedia Press, 1907-22), Vol. XII, p. 456 *et seq.*

THREE

The Religious Background of New France

The seventeenth century was the great age of Catholic revival in France. If this is a most significant fact to keep in mind for any understanding of French history in this era,[1] it is doubly important for New France, since it was the greatest single impetus for later colonization and the prime factor in developing the nature and quality of France's American colonies. Catholic revival, however, was not unique to France but was part of a great religious stirring throughout Europe that is generally designated as the Counter-Reformation. Nor indeed can the French revival be dissociated from the Protestant Reformation, the Renaissance, or the discovery of America itself. It is the purpose of this chapter to make a study of certain specific tendencies within this upsurge of religious life in seventeenth-century France and to note what influence they had upon the religious and cultural development of New France. Before doing so it will be helpful in the understanding of a complicated religious phenomenon to seek the origins of many aspects of the French revival in earlier reform movements within the ancient Catholic Church.[2]

EFFECTIVE GRACE

Such an investigation could well carry us back several centuries in church history, for even in the darkest ages of Christendom the spirit of revival and reform was never wholly dormant. To keep this review within manageable proportions we shall look no further back than the fifteenth century. During this century, when ecclesiastical life was almost completely secularized, the more thoughtful prelates were already deeply concerned over the lack of spiritual direction for troubled souls. " 'What a sight,' they exclaim, 'for a Christian as he wanders through Christendom, this desolation of the church; all the pastors have abandoned their flocks; they are all handed over to hirelings!' "[3]

Among the most tireless advocates for reform during this bleak period were the mystics. For them what mattered supremely in the Christian life was not the mere fine-spun speculation of the school-men but holy living; and they sought to achieve their goal through an intensified devotion to God, best exemplified in a loosely organized order known as the Brethren of the Common Life.[4] One outstanding production of this movement of devotion was *The Imitation of Christ* written by Thomas à Kempis, somewhere be-tween 1420 and 1425. This book set forth the theme that was to dominate the religious controversies of the sixteenth century and has never yet ceased to trouble the theological world. "O Lord," Thomas à Kempis prayed, "I stand in need of yet greater grace, if I ought to reach that pitch, where neither man nor any other creature shall be hindrance unto me."[5] How to attain that effective grace or how to be justified before God was the pre-eminent concern of the Protestant Reformation. But it was very much a concern of the leaders of the Counter-Reformation as well, particularly of a group of men who had founded at Rome during the reign of Leo X an Oratory of Divine Love, dedicated to holy living—this at a time when it was fashionable in church circles "to question the truths of Chris-tianity and to scoff at them."[6] Among the members of the Oratory were several priests who were later to become renowned in Euro-pean church life, such men as Cajetan of Thiene, Peter Caraffa, and Reginald Pole. Their purpose was very similar to that of their great contemporaries in the Protestant world, Luther, Zwingli, Calvin and Melanchthon—"the renovation of the doctrine and faith of the church"—and they were by no means shocked by the Lutheran doctrine of justification.[7]

Such widespread preoccupation with the doctrine of justification at this time is all the more remarkable for the fact that controversy on the subject had occurred only infrequently among the schoolmen; but now, as Ranke points out, it was suddenly to "captivate and en-gross an age, and challenge the activity of all minds that belonged to it." The explanation for this intense interest in grace, as Ranke rightly observes, was a reaction against "the secularization of the ecclesiastical order, which had almost forgotten the immediate rela-tion of man to God."[8]

Unfortunately, the members of the Oratory of Divine Love and the followers of Luther were to divide over the question as to the best means to attain sufficient grace; Luther on the basis of his conception of "justification by faith alone" saw no inevitable need for the priesthood;[9] the men of the Oratory sought to make the church more conscious of its supernatural function of mediating grace by a reform of the priesthood. To this end Cajetan of Thiene and Peter Caraffa jointly founded the Institute of the Theatines to train a more spiritually minded clergy who would take their sacerdotal functions seriously; they emphasized strongly devotional exercises accompanied by acts of mercy.[10] Orders of a similar nature such as the Somaschi, the Barnabites and the Oratorians began to spring up all over Italy. These in turn had a stimulating effect upon the long-established religious communities; within the Franciscans there emerged the Capuchins, with their pointed hood as a sign of their stricter adherence to the ideals of St. Francis, and the Recollets, with a strong emphasis upon interior reflection. A new element was added to this reform by Philip Neri, who in 1564 founded the Congregation of the Oratory, not only to deepen the spiritual life of the priesthood but also to strengthen its intellectual acumen.[11]

Concurrently with this revival of the religious life among the male orders was a renewed interest in religious revival among the female orders. In 1542 appeared the Capuchines based upon the model of the Poor Clares. Earlier (1535) Angela Merici founded the Ursulines, an order that was destined to play an unusually significant role in the religious development of French Canada. Its primary activity, the instruction of young girls, was frequently supplemented by deeds of mercy to the sick and indigent.[12]

Female orders played an important part in reviving the religious life of Spain, thanks above all to the vigorous zeal of St. Teresa of Jesus. In 1562 she brought the Carmelite convent at Avila back to its original austerity. St. Teresa lived during the "golden age of mysticism in Spain,"[13] and much of her reforming zeal is characterized by a strong sense of divine direction. She drew her inspiration from the mystical giants of the time, particularly St. Peter of Alcantara who in 1555 originated the Discalced or Barefoot reform of the Franciscan Order, and St. John of the Cross whose "incomparable lyrics," says E. A. Peers, "are among the choicest treasures of all seekers everywhere after reality."[14]

Closely associated with the golden age of mysticism in Spain was the rise of the Society of Jesus, which was to give substance and form to the Counter-Reformation. The life story of its founder, St. Ignatius Loyola, is too well known to be touched upon here; suffice it to say that his *Spiritual Exercises*, first published in Latin in 1548, sparked the most far-reaching reform in all Christendom.[15] Although

the Exercises owe much to Spanish mysticism they were not unin-
fluenced by earlier reform movements in Italy. During a period of
residence at the monastery of the Theatines in Venice, Loyola beheld
"an order of priests zealously and strictly devoting themselves to
duties properly clerical."[16] At this time he was contemplating founding an order of knights-errant for God and with the example of the
Theatines before him he resolved that, through ascetic practices, his
contemplated order should become essentially spiritual; nevertheless, he also felt that it would be possible to combine the ascetic life
with "the utmost wordly shrewdness."[17] Later, when he and his little
band of followers went to Rome to offer their services to the pope,
he was to incorporate another important element into his discipline
—a detachment from wealth.

It happened during his visit to Rome that a Reform Commission
set up by Paul III in 1536, with instructions to deal frankly with the
prevailing evils within the church, was reporting on its work to the
pope. Among its members were many eminent ecclesiastics, who
stated frankly that the great menace to the church was not clerical
immorality, as so many reformers had maintained, but the temptations of excessive wealth. This report made a vivid impression upon
Loyola and his companions, and freedom from wordly possessions
became a primary condition for membership in the Society of Jesus.[18]
Another observation of this commission, that the church was greatly
in need of an educated clergy, led Loyola to seek also to better his
own education by enrolling at the Sorbonne in Paris in 1528. Here
he learned how much the authority of the church had been undermined by the philosophic attack of the nominalists upon medieval
doctrine, and he therefore resolved to put an end to gnawing doubt
by seeking a clear and rigid definition of the church's faith, an objective finally achieved by his followers at the Council of Trent.[19]

These then were the dominating principles of a society that was
destined to stop the onward sweep of Protestanism in Europe, and
was also destined to contribute much to the formation of the religious
life of Latin America and French Canada.

FRENCH CALVINISM

There was considerable delay, however, before France committed
the serious responsibility for missionary work in the New World to
the Society of Jesus. The cause of the delay was the difficulty she
had in deciding which variety of reform she would accept; the reason
for her perplexity has been well expressed by an eminent French his-

torian Henri Martin, who "has depicted the three rival systems, Rome, the Renaissance, the Reformation, which were presented to the choice of France, and were represented in three individuals, who happened to be together for a moment in Paris—Calvin, Rabelais, Loyola."[20] The choice to all intents and purposes had been made in 1515 when Francis I signed a concordat with Leo X; but it was by no means a firm choice, for the main issue of the great religious debate in the sixteenth century, the place of grace in the scheme of salvation, had not yet been settled to the satisfaction of the religiously concerned. And it was to continue to disturb the Church of France down to the Revolution.

Calvinism was a product of the French mind, but even before John Calvin had produced his solution of the problem of grace in the *Institutes* Jacques Lefèvre, an honoured humanist at the University of Paris, was teaching a doctrine of "gratuitous justification" similar in content to Luther's.[21] One of his pupils, Briçonnet, Bishop of Meaux, gave encouragement to an evangelistic revival in his diocese that had been stimulated by the warm-hearted teachings of Lefèvre. For a time "it seemed as if Meaux aspired to become another Wittenberg."[22] The Sorbonne, however, decided otherwise; in 1521 its theologians condemned Luther and all his works. This caused Briçonnet to withdraw his support of the evangelistic movement even to the extent of acquiescing in the persecution of the Protestants in his diocese.[23]

The defection of Briçonnet did not completely overwhelm the new movement, for Calvinism came along to give it a fresh impulse, and it also had acquired powerful supporters in very exalted circles so that for a time it was in a fair way to establishing a permanent enclave within the French nation.[24] Furthermore, a variation of Calvinism perhaps even more appealing to the French mind had appeared in 1555 with the publication of *Dialectique* by Pierre de la Ramée, whose new method of logic seemed to offer "liberation from the gloomy cave of scholastic metaphysics." Ramée has been credited by some American church historians with providing the foundation of New England culture.[25] The *Dialectique* had a brief career in France, as the fearful massacre on St. Bartholomew's day (1572) included Pierre de la Ramée among its victims, and the Calvinists, or Huguenots as they were called in France, from now on adhered even more firmly to the uncompromising dogmas of Calvin. Since the Huguenots were as Pierre Joudra suggests "people of the cities,"[26] artisans of every type over whom it was difficult to keep strict surveillance, they long continued to play a prominent role in the

commercial life of France and to keep alive within the French church
the haunting problem of man's relation to God, which was again
raised in a more acute form in a later century by the Jansenists and
the Quietists.[27]

A MYSTICAL INVASION

Thus it was to a situation of religious violence and intellectual conflict that the Catholic revival, whose origins we have traced in Italy
and Spain, came to France. It came in the form of a mystical invasion,
which has been set forth in great detail by Henri Bremond in his
literary history of religious sentiment in France, an indispensible
guide for this very confused period of religious controversy.[28] According to Bremond the way for mysticism was prepared by the
"devout humanists" of the sixteenth century. Among these are
included several Jesuits who, despite Loyola's coolness towards
many leading humanists such as Erasmus,[29] were according to
Bremond true Hellenists; but adds that they were "more speculative
than practical, more aristocratic than popular: in that they sought
the true and beautiful rather than the holy, addressing themselves to
an elite rather than the populace."[30] In France Bremond finds that
this esoteric doctrine was transformed into a more comprehensive
religion and at the same time stimulated a mystical development that
did much to further the missionary consciousness of the French
church.[31]

François de Sales is given the credit for bringing the devout
humanism of the sixteenth-century Jesuits down to earth. This was
achieved partly by the genius of his personality, but also by his
famous book of devotion, Introduction à la vie dévote, which put, as
it were, "the whole Christian Renaissance at the door of the most
humble."[32] The result was a phenomenal outburst of pious speculation in which mysticism played a prominent role.

One of the key figures in this movement was Pierre Coton, a leading Jesuit who resolved to turn this mystical piety into practical
channels for the glory of the Catholic Church both at home and in
the missionary field. Born in 1564 in Neronde, an area much troubled
by religious wars, he had been taught by his father to shun the "twin
plagues" of Calvinism and Jesuitism.[33] Somehow he overcame his
parent's mistrust of the Jesuits, for ultimately he became a prominent
member of the Society of Jesus and was given the important task of
convincing Henry IV, a former Huguenot, that the Jesuits had the
good of France at heart. So brilliantly did he succeed that he himself

became Henry's most trusted counsellor and collaborator, as well as the director of the earliest missions to New France. Nor is it surprising that the king who promulgated an edict of toleration for the Huguenots should have chosen Coton as his spiritual adviser, as the latter after his admission to the Society of Jesus remained liberal in outlook and was "sometimes more or less suspect to his friends."[34]

It was through the confessional that Father Coton exercised a unique control over the mystical movement, which frequently seemed to be getting out of hand. One of the most notable members of the movement, Marie de Valence, sought his advice about her ecstatic experiences and so impressed Father Coton with her profound religious insight that he persuaded her to move to Paris for the purpose of sharing her impressions with the devout of that city. Thus there arose in Paris a loosely organized community of contemplatives, among them Madame Acarie whose salon became the meeting place of the mystics. The most influential member of the group, from a political point of view, was the chancellor of France, M. de Marillac, who was often able to give powerful aid in practical matters. From the more subtle world of theology came Pierre de Bérulle, who has been credited with the spiritual education of some of the most notable of French theologians, including Vincent de Paul, Jean-Jacques Olier, and the towering Bossuet himself.[35]

It was Bérulle who first perceived that the movement might be heading in the direction of Quietism and took measures to forestall such a development. With the help of Chancellor de Marillac he made it possible for Madame Acarie to go to Spain to seek out one of St. Teresa's most gifted pupils, Anne of Jesus, and persuade her to bring some Spanish Carmelites to France and set up a convent as a standard for all mystics to emulate. Madame Acarie succeeded brilliantly in her mission, with the result that French mysticism was brought under a Spanish discipline; according to Bremond it was purged of its "ferment of pantheism and moral indifferences."[36]

Bérulle also provided the movement with a method of meditation which differed sharply from the Ignatian. The latter is a disciplined method which has for its goal the perfection of the individual; the Berullian was based upon the assumption that the interior life is for God and his glory; in the words of Bremond, "Saint Ignatius formed moralists and ascetics, while Bérulle formed worshippers."[37]

The most illustrious of the worshippers was St. Vincent de Paul, who in preparing a rule for the Daughters of Charity made theocentrism its most outstanding characteristic: the daughters were not only to be ready to respond immediately to the call of the needy and unfortunate, but also must at all times be "*en rapport* with the Holy Trinity."[38] Many of these daughters carried the Berullian method of devotion to the New World; by the sincerity of their works of mercy, free from the taint of "egotistic obsessions," they made the name of St. Vincent de Paul one of the most revered in French Canada. Berullian influence did not reach the New World through the Daughters of Charity and St. Vincent de Paul alone: another brilliant pupil of Bérulle was Jean-Jacques Olier, the founder of the Order of St. Sulpice, which was to become a serious rival to the Jesuits for the spiritual leadership of New France. Olier, after a crisis of despair, became the Berullian *par excellence*. He felt it was his particular mission to bring his master's method of devotion within the reach of the ordinary member of the church; he did this with so much fervour and richness of imagination that a philosophy "at first a little difficult becomes accessible and persuasive to the mediocre reader."[39]

It is against such a background of movement and personality that the religious life of the early settlements in New France must be perceived. But it would hardly be a true picture of the movement to see it all in glowing colours. Unfortunately the Catholic revival itself was shot through with violent religious controversy that was to have an inhibiting effect upon its overseas expansion. One brutal method for the suppression of controversy was the Inquisition which was early introduced into Spanish America. No such untoward event happened in New France. Nevertheless there was among the early missionaries to Canada a spirit of apprehension towards new ideas and independent judgments, resulting in a very close surveillance of the religious development of the colony. In the allocation and *mandements* of the religious authorities in New France there is a constant echo of the struggle over Jansenism in the Old World as well as overtones of the violent suppression of Quietism, both of which were closely intertwined with a constitutional debate over Gallicanism. Consequently a review of the religious background of the French-Canadian church would not be complete without some reference to these three controversial matters.

JANSENISM, QUIETISM AND GALLICANISM

In order of importance Jansenism comes first. It takes its name from a Louvain professor, Cornelius Jansen, whose posthumous work, *Augustinus* (1640), raised a storm of protest in the Society of Jesus.[40] Jansen and his followers early had protested against a form of popular religion directed by the Jesuits through the confessional, based upon a method of casuistry that was to be ridiculed by Pascal in his *Provincial Letters*.[41] The Jansenists asserted that this religion was anything but evangelical, since it varied between pious little devotions and a natural moralistic theology of stoical sufficiency. Against this rather mechanical religion the Jansenists urged that experience, not reason, must be the final guide for the spiritual life; the *Augustinus*, like Calvin's *Institutes*, also stressed the utter helplessness of man in trying to lead the good life and his consequent dependence upon grace.[42] No amount of church-going, said the Jansenists, can save a man unless the love of God is in him; this love he cannot find in himself; it depends completely upon "conversion"— the gift of God.

At this point the Jesuits laid the charge of heresy. The Jansenists' emphasis upon "conversion" had for them all the defects of the Calvinistic doctrine of predestination—a man could do nothing towards his own salvation. Jansen denied the charge, since he held that God may always grant his gift of conversion, and this he felt modified Calvin's grim determinism.

Nevertheless the Jesuits were determined to secure papal condemnation of the *Augustinus* and, indirectly, of the Jansenists, but their task was complicated by the fact that both Jansen and his followers vehemently affirmed their loyalty to the Roman See.[43] It was not until 1713, with the publication of the bull, *Unigenitus*,[44] that Jansenism was finally outlawed in France; but only to recur in the even more dangerous guise of Quietism, or so the Jesuits thought.

The chief apostle of Quietism was a Spaniard, Miguel de Molinos, who in 1675 published the *Guida Spirituale*[45] which became the textbook of the movement. One of the most famous disciples of Molinos was Madame Guyon, who carried the mystical doctrines of the *Guida* to the French court and found a most enthusiastic supporter in the person of François de Salignac de La Mothe Fénelon, the Archbishop of Cambrai.[46] Fénelon was greatly charmed by the *Guida Spirituale*, but the Jesuits found in the book many of the "errors" of the *Augustinus* and in this they were supported by Bossuet. A modern student of the controversy, Ronald Knox, agrees with the Jesuit analysis: "Quietism," he says, "was the natural outcome of Jansenism, a translation of its theories into practice," and he regards Molinos' assurance that "God will work out his justification in us as long as we freely give our consent by means of resignation,"[47] as being the ultimate goal of Jansenism, however much the Jansenists might repudiate Quietism.

Be that as it may, the Jesuits regarded Quietism as being still another threat to the spiritual authority of the church, since the
Quietists even more than the Jansenists dispensed with any mediator
between man and God. It was at the instigation of a leading Jesuit,
Father de La Chaise, the king's confessor, that Louis XIV took action
against the movement by locking up Madame Guyon in the Bastille
and banishing Fénelon to his diocese of Cambrai.[48]

Not without fierce opposition, the Jesuits succeeded in overcoming
their opponents; there were times when it appeared as if they themselves might be outlawed from France, as indeed they were in the
following century, because of their mistrust of Gallicanism. With
few exceptions the Jesuits were ultramontanists, arguing that ecclesiastical interests were primary, and that the final voice in disputed
matters between church and state must be that of the pope.[49] On this
point Louis XIV took Bossuet for his mentor: the latter became the
powerful spokesman for Gallicanism, which he succinctly formulated
in a famous *Declaration of the French Clergy*.

Gallicanism, however, was no new factor intruded into the church
by Louis XIV. In the fourteenth century Philip the Fair had asserted
the power of the monarchy in the relations of church and state; this
was political Gallicanism. But in the seventeenth century there was
added by Edmond Richer, a doctor of the Sorbonne, what might be
called theological Gallicanism, namely, that the church's infallible
authority resided not only with the pope, but with the pope in collaboration with the bishops. In the *Declaration*, issued by the clergy
in 1682, Bossuet combined political and theological Gallicanism.
Besides reaffirming Richer's assertion that the infallibility of the
church belongs to bishops and pope jointly, he also asserted that
the temporal authority of kings is independent of the pope, that a
General Council is superior to popes and that the ancient liberties
of the Gallican church are sacred. What he was really attempting
was to create a strong national church which would give stability
and strength to the absolute monarchy of France. As part of this
ideal he hoped to have all Frenchmen owe allegiance to one constitutional church. It was necessary then that the dissenting churches in
France be induced to return to the established church of France. To
facilitate this return Bossuet sought to soften somewhat the rigidities
of Roman doctrine. His great work, *Exposition de la doctrine catholique,* was so moderate in tone that he was accused "of having
fraudulently watered down the Roman doctrines to suit a Protestant
taste."[50] Another of his works, *The History of the Variations of the
Protestant Churches,* went even further in this direction, since he

sought to prove that variation was not necessarily an indication of doctrinal error.[51]

All this was shocking to the Jesuits, who adhered to a rigid definition of doctrine, and they saw Gallicanism, as presented by Bossuet, as one of the major causes for an unjustified flirting with Protestanism. They were now confirmed in their conviction that only a strongly centralized church and a powerful papacy could save Christian Europe from slipping into irretrievable error. It is small wonder then that when the Jesuits achieved supremacy in New France they not only took good care, as far as in them lay, to keep out Jansenists and Quietists but also reversed Gallicanism to such an extent that the civil power came close to subjection to the spiritual. In point of fact the church in Canada from the first displayed a concern with political and social development that left little room for lay initiative in the fields of political and social science.[52]

THE ENLIGHTENMENT

This close watch over the religious life of French Canada was to have a profound effect upon the cultural life of the colony. For one thing the Jesuit suspicion of Jansenism and other dissenting movements in France prevented New France from sharing in a scientific revival in Europe heralded by such giants as Kepler, Galileo, Newton and Descartes. In the natural order of events one would expect the work of these men to be included in a review of the religious background of French Canada, as it undoubtedly must be in any review of the religious background of New England.[53] In Europe itself, theological thought was greatly stimulated by what has been described as "the downfall of Aristotle and Ptolemy."[54] Both Pascal and Bossuet attempted to meet the challenge to church doctrine of the Copernican revolution, but none of this preliminary work for a new apologetic found its way into the libraries of French-Canadian seminaries; nor did anything of the spirit of doubt and inquiry of Montaigne or Descartes.

When the scientific revival had transformed itself into the Age of Enlightenment the latter received no comprehension in New France, and without the Enlightenment the French Revolution was an inconceivable event which culturally alienated New France from old France. Additional factors helped to prepare the way for such an alienation: one was the fact, as Professor Philippe Garigue has emphasized, that the French who migrated to Canada in the seventeenth century "brought little if anything of the social institutions of peasant France" with them. And what has turned out to be a very close-knit and well integrated society began almost without design "as a series of trade and missionary posts which grew into towns."[55] Rural French Canada came later as an extension of these towns, so there never has been any great cultural differentiation between town and countryside in French Canada as there is in France. Other factors —such as a strong central administration in both church and state, the centrality of the church building around which the village grew with its *fabrique*, or church council, of elected persons—have created a society which has little counterpart either in France or in North America. Such a unique social structure isolated in one corner of North America has inevitably given rise to several conflicting views as to its origin and as to what may be its fate as it tries to make its adjustments to large-scale industrialization.[56] Although there are sharp differences of opinion in this debate all schools of thought are in agreement that the church played a decisive role in the formation of the French-Canadian society; consequently, a study of the religious development of New France is inextricably entangled with its political and social development as well. It began, however, as a missionary project inspired by the Catholic revival of seventeenth-century France among the aborigines of North America; and so in the following chapter the Canadian Indian, who has played an unusually prominent role in the formation of the French-Canadian church, will be our primary consideration.

NOTES TO CHAPTER THREE

1. *Vide* E. Lavisse, *Histoire de France* (Paris: Colin, 1905), Vol. III, Chap. I, p. 88: "Négliger les choses religieuses du XVIIe siècle ou les estimer petitement, c'est ne pas comprendre l'histoire de ce siècle, c'est ne pas le sentir."

2. For a balanced definition of the Counter-Reformation and its relation to the Protestant Reformation *vide* A. Fliche and Victor Martin, eds., *Histoire de l'Eglise depuis les Origines jusqu'à Nos Jours* (Paris: Bloud & Guy, 1945), Vol. XVIII, "Après le Concile de Trente; la Restauration catholique 1563-1648" par Leopold Willaert, pp. 15-23.

3. L. von Ranke, *A History of the Papacy Political and Ecclesiastical in the Sixteenth and Seventeenth Centuries*, trans. J. E. M. D'Aubigné (Glasgow: Blackie, 1855), Vol. I, p. 53; *vide* also Pierre Janelle, *The Catholic Reformation* (Milwaukee: Bruce, 1948); Chap. I, pp. 1-19, deal with "Anarchy, the Disease within the Church."

4. A good account of the origin of the Brethren of the Common Life is to be found in E. J. Ives, *The Message of Thomas à Kempis* (London: S.C.M., 1922).

5. Thomas à Kempis, *Of the Imitation of Christ* (Oxford: Oxford University Press, 1920), p. 128.

6. L. Ranke, *op. cit.*, Vol. I, p. 104.

7. As late as 1541 Paul III on the advice of a group of reforming cardinals sent Gaspar Contaraini to the Colloquy of Ratisbon to discuss prospects of

reunion; agreement on justification was reached, but political rivalries frustrated the Colloquy. *Vide* B. J. Kidd, ed., *Documents Illustrative of the Continental Reformation* (Oxford: Clarendon Press, 1911), pp. 340-5.

8. L. Ranke, *op. cit.*, p. 107.

9. *Vide* J. Pelikan and H. T. Lehmann eds., *Luther's Works* (St. Louis: Concordia, 1958), Vol. XL, "Church and Ministry" Chap. II. "Thus no other sacrifice remains for our sins than his, and by putting our trust together in it, we are saved from sin without any merits or works of our own," p. 14.

10. Fliche et Martin, *op. cit.*, Vol. XVIII, Chap. II, "Nouveaux Ordres Masculins, les Congrégations, Les Compagnies de Prêtres," pp. 127-44.

11. A brief account in English of the rise of these orders is to be found in B. J. Kidd, *The Counter-Reformation 1550-1600* (London: S.P.C.K., 1933), pp. 9-22.

12. Fliche et Martin, *op. cit.*, Vol. XVIII, Chap. III, "Ordres et Groupements Feminins," pp. 145-62.

13. On "The Golden Age of Spanish Mysticism" *vide* E. A. Peers, *Studies of the Spanish Mystics* (London: S.P.C.K., 1927-30), Vol. II, p. 3 *et seq.*

14. *Ibid.*, Vol. I, p. 288.

15. P. Janelle says, "The *Spiritual Exercises* are at the root of all the surprising results obtained by the Society of Jesus." *op. cit.*, p. 125.

16. L. Ranke, *op. cit.*, Vol. I, p. 146.

17. *Ibid.*, Vol. I, p. 149.

18. For emphasis upon poverty *vide* P. Janelle, *op. cit.*, pp. 131-32.

19. James Lainez and Alphonsus Salmeron, Loyola's colleagues, "who, as papal theologians" at the Council of Trent, "took precedence over the rest." *Vide* H. Jedin, *A History of the Council of Trent*, trans. E. Graf (London: Nelson, 1957-61), Vol. II, p. 134.

20. G. P. Fisher, *The Reformation* (New York: Scribner, 1916), p. 215.

21. *Ibid.*, p. 210.

22. On *Le Cercle de Meaux vide* Fliche et Martin, *op. cit.*, Vol. XVI, p. 133 *et seq.*

23. *Ibid.*, Vol. XVI, p. 167 *et seq.*

24. *Vide* F. P. G. and De Witt Guizot, *The History of France from the Earliest Times to 1848*, trans. R. Black (New York: Collier, 1898), Vol. III, p. 440 *et seq.*

25. *Vide* Perry Miller and T. H. Johnson, *The Puritans* (New York: American Book Co., 1938), pp. 28-40. Concerning Ramée they write, "He put into the hands of Protestant divines and scholars dialectical spears with which they could pierce the metaphysical armour of the Catholic champions."

26. Fliche et Martin, eds. *op. cit.*, Vol. XVI, p. 267.

27. *Vide infra*, pp. 30-32.

28. H. Bremond, *Histoire littéraire du sentiment religieux en France* (Paris: Bloud et Guy, 1916-33, 11 vols.), Vols. I, II and III have been translated into English by K. L. Montgomery (New York: Macmillan, 1928-36).

29. *Vide* H. Jedin *op. cit.*, Vol. I, p. 160, on "why the leaders of the Catholic reform, headed by St. Ignatius Loyola declined to accept Erasmus as an educator."

30. H. Bremond, *op. cit.*, Vol. I, p. 17.

31. *Ibid.*, Vol. I, p. 71.

32. *Ibid.*, Vol. I, p. 72.

33. *Ibid.*, Vol. II, p. 77.

34. *Ibid.*, Vol. II, pp. 83-96.

35. *Ibid.*, Vol. II, p. 265.

36. *Ibid.*, Vol. II, p. 311.

37. *Ibid.*, Vol. III, p. 114; *vide* also P. Janelle *op. cit.*, p. 125. Janelle says, "The whole trend of St. Ignatius' teaching is directed towards strengthening the will."

38. H. Bremond, *op. cit.*, Vol. III, p. 251.

39. *Ibid.*, Vol. III, p. 461.

40. On the *Augustinus*, *vide*, J. M. Neale, *A History of the So-Called Jansenist Church of Holland* (Oxford: Parker, 1858), p. 11 *et seq.*

41. *Vide* esp. the ninth letter, Pascal, *Les Provinciales* (*Texte de 1656-7*, Paris: Flammarion, n.d.), pp. 125-42.

42. *Vide* Calvin's "Antidote to the Sixth Session" of the Council of Trent on Justification, found in *Tracts and Treatises in Defence of the Reformed Faith* by John Calvin, trans. Henry Beveridge (Edinburgh: Oliver and Boyd, 1958), Vol. III, p. 108.

43. J. Forget writes in *The Catholic Encyclopedia* (New York: The Encyclopedia Press, 1907-22), Vol. VIII, p. 287, "... Jansenius although he gave his name to a heresy was not himself a heretic, but lived and died in the bosom of the Church." *Vide* also Fliche et Martin, *op. cit.*, 1*ère* partie, for discussion of Jansenism in France, pp. 193-211.

44. *Ibid.*, p. 215 *et seq.*

45. A book still treasured by the Society of Friends; *vide The Spiritual Guide* (written by Dr. Michael de Molinos, translated from the Italian copy at Venice, 1685; printed in London: Hodder, 1928).

46. *Vide Le Quiétisme en France* in Fliche et Martin, *op. cit.*, Vol. XIX, Part I, p. 168 *et seq.*

47. R. A. Knox, *Enthusiasm* (New York: Oxford University Press, 1950), p. 232.

48. *Vide* Fénelon, *Pious Reflections* (London: Houlston, 1839), p. xv.

49. *Vide* article on the Gallican Church by Viscount St. Cyres in *The Cambridge Modern History*, Vol. V, esp. p. 75; also *Le Gallicanisme* in Fliche et Martin, *op. cit.*, Vol. XVIII, p. 367 *et seq.*

50. St. Cyres, *op. cit.*, p. 86.

51. *Vide* J. B. Bossuet, *The History of the Variations of the Protestant Church* (2 vols., New York: Sadlier, 1845), esp. Vol. II, p. 314.

52. *Vide* Fliche et Martin *op. cit.*, Vol. XIX; 2e partie, "Les luttes politiques et doctrinales aux xviie et xviiie siècles": "Tout le tintamarre des querelles gallicanes, jansénistes, quiétistes qui remplit l'histoire de l'Eglise de France disparaît au Canada," p. 584.

53. *Ibid.*, p. 585, "L'atmosphere canadienne était practiquement imperméable à la propagande philosophique: les paysans canadiens avaient autre chose à faire que de savourer l'ironie voltairienne ..."; for New England *vide* Miller and Johnson, *op. cit.*, pp. 732-5.

54. H. Butterfield, *The Origins of Modern Science* (London: G. Bell, 1949), p. 48 *et seq.*

55. *Vide* "Change and Continuity in Rural French Canada" by Philippe Garigue, reprinted from *Culture* (Quebec), XVIII (décembre, 1957), pp. 379-92, found in *French Canadian Society*, ed. Rioux and Martin (Toronto: McClelland and Stewart, 1964), Vol. I, p. 125.

56. A critical review of the various theories of the social evolution of French Canada is given by Hubert Guindon in an article, "The Social Evolution of Quebec Reconsidered" reprinted from *The Canadian Journal of Economics and Political Science*, XXVI (November, 1960), pp. 533-51, in *French Canadian Society*, pp. 137-61. Guindon takes issue with Philippe Garigue's attack on the Chicago School analysis of French Canada. The Chicago School view has been persuasively set forth in E. C. Hughes, *French Canada in Transition* (London: Routledge and Kegan Paul, 1946), *passim.*

FOUR

The Challenge of the Aborigine

The aboriginal population of Canada at the time of the first white settlements was about two hundred and twenty thousand; today it is in the vicinity of one hundred and ninety-two thousand.[1] These figures themselves are vivid testimony to the fact that the Indians in Canada, as in other parts of America, have suffered fearfully under white domination. Despite all the hopeful plans of governmental agencies for their preservation and improvement there is as yet little evidence that the Indian is on the way to full citizenship in Canadian national life.[2] It is customary to regard the sad plight of the Indian in North America as due to the intolerance of the civilized world towards a primitive people, or at least as due to the failure of civilized groups to protect and train backward races "until they can bridge the gap between the old conditions and the new."[3] However much that may be true of the Spanish and English colonizers it cannot be said of the French, who were willing and anxious to receive the Indian into their own civilization, particularly in the seventeenth century; consequently, we must look for other reasons than intolerance and impatience to explain the failure of France to transform the Indian of Canada into a mellowed citizen. Part of the answer to this vexing problem in Canadian national life may be learned from a study of the French missions to Canada, for there is little doubt that French missionaries came to North America with a genuine interest in the moral and spiritual welfare of the original inhabitants of this continent.[4]

EARLY MISSIONS

The primary stimulus behind this zeal for the welfare of the Indians can be traced to the Catholic revival in seventeenth-century France. Previously the challenge of the Indian to the Christian conscience was largely ignored by the French church, even though

Norman and Breton fishermen were constantly returning from expeditions to American shores with amazing tales about the savage inhabitants of the New World. As early as 1508 a Dieppe pilot, Thomas Aubert, had brought a few Indians to France but failed to stimulate much interest in his strange captives.[5]

It was almost three decades later that Francis I was moved to send Jacques Cartier on a voyage of exploration in "the hope of winning imperial domains and golden riches in America."[6] Cartier's voyages did little to encourage the hope of riches. On his return from his second voyage, however, he had with him several Indians, among them a chief by the name of Donnacona. On this occasion the people of France displayed an unusual interest in Cartier's captives and also in the prospects of creating in the New World a Catholic empire based upon an aboriginal foundation.[7] This interest was no doubt greatly stimulated by Cartier's own published account of his voyage in which he urged "that as the king of Spain had spread the gospel to Spanish America, so should the French in other and unknown infidel regions."[8]

The suggestion caught the fancy of the French king who had been much impressed by the simplicity of the Indians whom Cartier had taken to his court; particularly was he affected favourably by the courtly bearing of Chief Donnacona. Francis now decided that the conversion of the Indians was a task well worthy of his support; consequently, in 1541, he named Jean-François de La Rocque, Sieur de Roberval, viceroy and lieutenant-general in Canada and provided him with a subsidy to found a colony in the midst of the natives. In his own words the purpose of the colony was "to attain better our announced intention and to do something pleasing to God, our creator and redeemer, and which may be to the augmentation of his holy and sacred name and of our mother Holy Catholic Church of whom we are called and named first son."[9]

Under this new arrangement Cartier became Sieur de Roberval's captain-general to cooperate in the task of founding a colony. The joint endeavour was far from harmonious and the colonists, mostly "jail-birds," brought out against their wills, soon found their way back to France. After the failure of this initial attempt at colonization in Canada little is heard about the conversion of the Indians until Samuel de Champlain appears upon the scene in 1603. During a voyage up the St. Lawrence he came to know the Indians intimately and resolved to do all in his power to persuade churchmen in France "to devise some means of bringing them the knowledge of God."[10]

This zeal for the conversion of the Indians was embodied in a charter granted the same year to Pierre du Gua, Sieur de Monts, for the exclusive privilege of the fur trade in territories claimed by France in North America. By this charter Henry IV hoped to achieve several things: first and foremost he wanted a colony to be representative of his person in the New World; also he was looking for an outlet for the commercial enterprises of the Huguenots; and there seems little doubt that he inherited Francis I's romantic desire to embrace the aboriginal population within a French Catholic empire. Or, as one student of the period has aptly expressed it, he, like Francis and Cartier, "had given to imperialism the motivation of religion as well as economic and territorial conquest—a combination that characterized French policy in Canada until 1760."[11]

Although the charter allowed the Huguenots to emigrate to the contemplated colony and to take ministers along with them, the conversion of the Indians was to remain exclusively with the Roman Catholic Church. The Huguenot merchants, who were chiefly responsible for financing the first colony in Acadia, were not greatly pleased with the religious terms of the charter, but a small gesture to fulfil the terms was made by Baron de Poutrincourt, who had taken over De Monts' interest in Acadia, when he brought out in 1610 a secular priest, Jessé Fléché. The latter baptized about twenty-five Micmacs without giving them much previous instruction — among them a famous chieftain, Membertou, who seems in time to have become a devoted Christian.[12] Fléché soon disappeared from the scene to be replaced the following year by a Jesuit mission.

It was through the intercession of Father Coton, the king's confessor, that Henry IV decided to put the Acadian mission under the direction of the Jesuits; this was the beginning of an alliance between the French monarchy and the Society of Jesus that was to have fateful consequences for the cultural and social development of New France. It also represented a mood on the part of the king to bring the vast territory of Canada firmly into the kingdom of France. As Parkman so succinctly expressed it, "Policy and military power leaned on the missions as their main support, the grand instrument of their extension."[13]

Many obstacles were placed in the way of the Jesuits before they reached America, particularly by the Huguenot merchants; but successive French governments continued to rely upon the Society of Jesus as their main arm in the creation of a French Catholic empire in the New World. The Jesuits, for their part, gave loyal and vigorous support to France's imperial and commercial interests but never

failed to keep to the fore their chief concern, the spiritual transformation of the aborigines, so that they might enter into the main
stream of Catholic Christendom. With this object in view they
persuaded members of the high aristocracy to patronize their
missions in a most spectacular fashion.[14]

Under Jesuit leadership France developed a policy toward the
aborigines of America that always remained far wiser and kindlier
than any of her European rivals. No higher tribute has been paid to
this policy than that given by Francis Parkman, not always a kindly
critic of either France or the Jesuits: "Spanish civilization crushed
the Indian; English civilization scorned and neglected him; French
civilization embraced and cherished him."[15]

INDIAN ORIGINS

Who were these Indians upon whom was expended for a century
or more the full force of the Catholic revival in France? Whence did
they come and what was their cultural condition at the time of the
arrival of the white man in Canada? These and some allied questions
will be the principal concern of this chapter.

To these questions we find that our chief authorities give varying
answers, but on one important point there is universal agreement,
namely that the Indians are not indigenous to America. Like all the
rest of us, they must trace their ancestry back to the Old World.
There is also a fairly substantial agreement, with a few dissenters,
that they came to America by way of the Bering Strait within the
Pleistocene or glacial epoch, somewhere between ten or fifteen
thousand years ago, probably not all at one time but over a long
period, thousands of years rather than centuries.[16] It is also generally agreed that they are of Mongoloid stock, from eastern Asia;
but because of the great variety of types to be found throughout the
New World, there are advocates of several possible original homes,
varying from Asia Minor to China and the Melanesian Archipelago.
There are even advocates who regard Africa as the original home of
the Amerindian.[17] This inference is due to traces of Caucasian and
even of Australoid elements among the Indians; but, regardless of
their origin, "they undoubtedly in time became Mongolian."[18] The
variety of types can well be explained by the great length of time
between the first and last waves of immigration and the subsequent
geographical isolation provided by the vast empty spaces of America.
Differences of type may well have begun to emerge in Asia after the
present American branch had broken away from its parent stock.

But wherever the original home in the Old World may have been there appears to have occurred a very definite cultural break from the homeland after the Indians arrived in America either by way of an isthmus across the Bering Sea or in small boats across the Strait. If by the latter it may well be, as has been suggested, the Bering Strait acted as a "cultural sieve"[19] compelling the Indians to start afresh on this continent. From this fresh start new and distinct types began to emerge, but despite the variety of types there is strong evidence pointing to one parent stock in the Old World. This is most visibly seen in the common character of the physical organization of the Amerindians; it is also apparent in the similar construction of their languages.[20]

It was the variety, not the uniformity, that most impressed the first European visitors to these shores, particularly the great contrasts in cultural development. This variety has been vividly set forth by Waldo Frank: running the gamut, as he phrases it, "from Carib whose sole culture was war, and Amazonian whose sole science was survival in the jungle, to lofty Mayan and Toltec and to the communistic state of the Incas, esthetically inferior to Mexico but far advanced in social institutions."[21] It would be a mistake, however, to become so preoccupied with the variations as to overlook the impressive fact that our Canadian Indians are part of one common stock extending from Alaska to Patagonia; and in trying to estimate their prospects it is helpful to know how this stock has fared in other parts of America during the process of Westernization. It also seems necessary to pursue our study with the thought in mind that the inhabitants of the New World were within the providence of God during the millenia they were isolated from the Old World, and that there was a better destiny awaiting them than that which they have been able to achieve under white dominance.[22]

PHYSIOGRAPHIC FACTORS

Keeping in mind then the general uniformity of Indian stock, it is interesting to note how much the physiographic features of Canada have placed their impress on the social and cultural development of the Indians as well as upon the white stock that has been relentlessly replacing them. In point of fact it is these physiographic factors that provide the most useful basis for classifying the various cultural groups that were in possession of this vast territory before the white man's arrival. In the sixteenth century, for example, there were over fifty distinct cultural groups of Indians in Canada, speaking their own separate languages or dialects and possessing their own peculiar customs and religions. At first sight it would appear that we have in these groups a primary basis for classification along either tribal or linguistic lines; but neither of these usually distinguishing factors will serve for a detailed description of the Canadian aborigines. The migratory habits of the Indians, the practice of adopting alien prisoners into victorious tribes, have fearfully mixed formerly widely separated groups. The term "tribe," itself, is a highly unsatisfactory designation for the various political units to be found across Canada. Political life was seldom organized on so definite a basis as a tribe; rather, there were numerous subdivisions or bands, each with their own local chiefs or leaders. A linguistic basis is even more unsatisfactory for the purposes of classification since it would require us to join together widely separated tribes like the Micmacs and Blackfoot, who speak similar dialects but are separated by two thousand miles of land and have very different social customs; furthermore, they were in complete ignorance of one another's existence until fairly modern times.[23]

In view of the obstacles to either a tribal or linguistic classification, anthropologists have now accepted a territorial basis as the best method of sorting out the diverse political and cultural units inhabiting Canada at the time of European invasion.[24] The first such unit to come under European observation comprised the nomads of the enormous wooded area of the Atlantic provinces, Ontario, Quebec and Manitoba. This extensive area was roamed over by Algonkians, split up into various bands, known as Micmacs, Naskapi, Objibwa, Beothuk and other lesser bands. They were quite proficient in the use of birch bark, and practised a seasonal economy of hunting and fishing. They had a very immature political structure, in which religion played a minor role.

Another cultural group which early came under the observation of French explorers was that of the Iroquoian-speaking tribes inhabiting the agricultural area of southern Ontario and Quebec. Through the annual reports of the Jesuit missionaries, now generally known as the *Jesuit Relations*,[25] the names of the various units of these sedentary Indians became almost household words in seventeenth-century France. The best known were the Hurons and the Iroquois; almost equally well known were the Neutrals, Eries and the Tobacco Nation. These designations, however, hardly begin to exhaust the various subdivisions of the Iroquoians. Their sociopolitical structure was more complex than the Algonkians, due to the fact that they had emerged from the nomadic state and were practising an intensive horticulture.

European explorers, fairly early, came in contact with a third cultural area, the arctic region, extending from the shore of the Bering Strait eastward to Greenland. This region was occupied by small bands of Eskimos, whose ingenuity in tool making and in the science of survival in a most inhospitable setting has long been a source of amazement to northern explorers.[26] Because of its extremely cold temperature the arctic region was little disturbed by white men until modern days.

Another cultural area long inaccessible to white settlers was the open prairie of what is now Western Canada and Western United States inhabited by the Plains Indians. On the Canadian side were the Blackfoot, Sarcee and the Assiniboine. Before their discovery they had acquired horses from Mexico and had become mounted hunters with an advanced economy based upon the bison, within the framework of a meticulous social and religious ritual.

In the northern forest regions extending from the Yukon through the Northwest Territories, northern Alberta and Saskatchewan was another hunting group, depending upon the caribou for livelihood. These were Athapaskan-speaking bands, very loosely organized politically, and weak both materially and in cultural attainments. For this reason they tended to be influenced by the tribes of the prairies, the arctic and the west coast. The latter probably exerted the greatest influence, as they were the most advanced cultural groups in Canada. Like the Iroquoian, these bands consisting of the Tlinkit, Tsimshian, Haida, Kwakiutl, Bella Coola, Nootka and the Coast Salish lived for the most part in village units, depending upon fish for food. Although they were known early in the age of discovery to explorers and traders on the west coast, their conversion to Christianity had to wait until the quickening of the missionary spirit in the nineteenth century. The same is true also of their nearest neighbours, the aborigines of the intermontane region of southern British Columbia. These were the Interior Salish, the Athapaskan and the Kootenay. Because of the extremes of temperature in these deep gorges, the cultural development of these Indians was greatly retarded; consequently, their tribal affiliations were weak and they were constantly prey to their more advanced Pacific coast neighbours.[27]

It can readily be seen that cultural variations in the seven regions indicated above were due, for the most part, to physiographic factors. In other words, the aborigines had worked out a delicate ecological balance with "the forest, the plain, the desert, the waters and the animal life"[28] of their allotted territory. An inevitable result of the white man's intrusion into these preserves was the upsetting of a balance that had been achieved by trial and error over the centuries—with dire consequences both to the Indian's societies and to his life power. Thus the Indian has become a stranger in his own homeland; some of them "feel that their race is run and calmly, rather mournfully, await the end."[29]

PSYCHOLOGICAL MATURITY

Little of this latter-day tragedy was evident when French and Indian first met in Canada. On the contrary it appeared as if the two stocks might well complement one another to the advantage of both. The French had brought with them useful iron-age tools which did much to lighten the everyday toil of the stone-age Indians and these the latter gladly accepted. The Indian for his part had much to offer: he taught the white man how to find his way through the dense forest and over the never ending plains; how to grow many varieties of foods, hitherto unknown to the Europeans; and how to survive the rigours of the climatic extremes. Not the least of the aborigine's contribution to the welfare of the European was an example of equanimity in the face of the awe and terror of trackless forests, unbroken prairies and dreary wastelands.[30]

Because of his ingenuity, with limited resources, in creating useful artifacts and because of his psychological maturity the Indian was highly esteemed by the first white settlers in Canada; nor did these settlers ever regard the Indians "as in any way mentally inferior to themselves."[31] This has been amply demonstrated by Frederick Johnson in an admirable study, *Man in Northeastern North America*. One of his chief sources, the *Jesuit Relations*, from which he quotes copiously, bears witness to the fact that the Indians "nearly all show more intelligence in their business . . . than do the shrewdest merchants in France."[32] All the early visitors to New France were greatly impressed by the fortitude and tranquillity of the Indians. The historian of the Recollet missions to Canada lays particular emphasis upon this aspect of Indian social development; he writes, "They have patience enough in their sickness to put Christians to confusion. . . . It is necessary, they say, to live without annoyance and disquiet, to be content with that which one has, and to endure with constancy the misfortunes of nature because the sun, or he who has made and governs all, orders it thus."[33]

The many marriages that occurred between the French and the aborigines with both Church and State approval are strong evidence of the spirit of equality that existed among the old settlers and the new. The Franciscans for their part welcomed this inter-racial contact as the most immediate way of converting the Indians to Christianity; the Jesuits were inclined to keep the Indians segregated from the whites, but this was to prevent them from being infected by the Europeans' vices rather than the other way round.[34] For a time it appeared that racial intermarriage would produce a new and unique people both in Acadia and in the St. Lawrence Valley, but the intermixture for the most part simply meant the absorption of the Indian into the white race; consequently, the Indians of these areas have largely disappeared as a distinct group. According to one student of the aboriginal problem they were the most fortunate Indians in Canada.[35] Such a solution to the Indian problem was only possible during the first two centuries of settlement when illiteracy was quite general in Europe and the contrast between the two groups was not as great as it is at present.[36]

CULTURAL DEVELOPMENT

But even in those earlier days when miscegenation was quite common, many of the factors that have reduced the Indian to his present unhappy status in Canadian society were only too evident. The most obvious of these were the diseases brought in by the white men and to which the Indians for centuries have been helpless prey. Even more devastating, however, have been the psychological factors, arising out of the great chasm between the culture and the religion of the Indians and those of the Europeans. Since culture is made up of elements passed down through many centuries of trial and error, a sudden meeting of two diverse cultures must inevitably bring on a cultural warfare;[37] and a cultural defeat, it is now recognised, is far more disastrous for the defeated party than any military reverse, for it means the destruction of intricate forms that have probably taken thousands of years to perfect. It was such a cultural defeat that destroyed the life power of the Canadian Indians and has made it almost impossible to revindicate them. This is not true of Mexico and certain parts of South America where the revindication of the Indian is going on apace; but fortunately for the Indians of these countries their culture was far more advanced than in Canada and consequently they were able to put up a strong defence against the European attack.[38]

But it was not so in Canada, where the Indian at the time of the discovery of America had only recently emerged from the Pleistocene age, when man had first invented tools. Nevertheless he seems to have been making rapid progress in perfecting his tools and was beginning to add to his utensils a certain amount of form and colour, which is an important step in the perilous climb to civilized living. He had also shown great inventiveness in the formation of human societies; but his most amazing feat was in the realm of important food-stuffs, particularly his development of "hybrid" corns, which "remains one of the most difficult and important achievements in genetics to this date."[39] It is perhaps a sweeping claim to credit this achievement to the Canadian Indian, but at least the Indians of Canada were enjoying American cereals before the arrival of the white man, good evidence that when one branch of the Amerindians made an important achievement it was only a matter of time before it was the common possession of all.[40] Indeed if we are to gain a true perspective of the cultural prospect of the Canadian Indians before the white man set a terminus to endemic progress we must view it against the background of the total pre-Columbian development of man in the New World. For apart from the uniform character of Indian stock and the common possession of many staples of diet, indicating a close association of all the various tribes in some extremely remote prehistoric age, there is convincing evidence that the Indians, even at the time of Columbus' arrival, were proceeding along a common pattern of development. Such being the case, it is reasonable to conclude that there was a better destiny awaiting the Canadian Indian than he has been able to achieve within the framework of Western civilization.

True, there is little evidence of a common *Weltanschauung* among the hundreds of distinct societies, unless a rather universal sense of "cosmic consciousness"[41] may be regarded as such; but similar elements in all Indian dances, as well as many common ceremonial practices do indicate some kind of subtle communication of notions throughout the Americas. A serious obstacle in articulating these notions or perceptions into a common world view even among the more advanced societies was the lack of an alphabet; but there are indications that even this medium for communication of ideas was to become available to the Indians in a not-too-remote future. Sign writing, at least, was making great progress among the more advanced Indians. In Canada it was limited to carving an arrow-head on the bark of a tree to indicate the direction of a march, supplemented occasionally by a few signs to convey the success or failure of an expedition. Further south, however, a notable advance in written communication had been achieved. The unearthing of Uxmal, "one of the major archaeological sites in Mexico,"[42] reveals buildings with hieroglyphs that may reach back some two thousand years. Before the great break in Mayan civilization, a rough outline of

Mayan history, both oral and in hieroglyphs, was reduced to writing in Latin script; scholars today would like very much to know the original behind the script, but unfortunately an early Franciscan monk who went to Yucatan believed that the most effective way to eliminate paganism in his mission was to destroy Mayan books, so that only three survived and these are very imperfectly understood.[43] The Aztecs also had acquired several varieties of hieroglyphics and also employed phonetic signs to indicate names of persons and places. The signs, unfortunately, were accommodated to a hieroglyphic system used in association with an oral tradition, long since forgotten; and so the whole arrangement is almost incomprehensible to the modern student of Aztec literature.[44] Despite the lack of an efficient alphabet the Aztecs had set up a compulsory educational system in which the study of astronomy and mathematics had reached a more advanced stage than in contemporary fifteenth-century Europe.[45]

Unhappily for the Indians, they were far behind the Europeans in the field of industrial arts; this was due in part to their failure to discover the wheel—so important for industrial progress. It was the Indian's lack of the wheel, and of adequate military equipment, that enabled the Europeans to bring to a standstill a cultural development that might have, given sufficient time, made a very significant contribution to a world civilization.[46]

RELIGIOUS CULTS AND SYMBOLS

That such a distinct contribution was in the making is the firm conviction of John Collier, who has spent much time among both primitive and advanced Indians in search of their spiritual inheritance. It is his conclusion that the Indians possessed a way of life that "is at once simple, since it is disciplined, and complex" because of its "institutionalized tradition and symbol-invested belief" — a credo in which man and nature co-operate intimately and are "mutually dependent" upon one another.[47] Coupled with this was a strong belief that the human spirit could influence the cosmos for good. Such a belief in the possibilities of a disciplined human nature, says our authority, created a resourceful personality of great hardihood. Another student of pre-Columbian culture in America, Professor W. G. Moreno, also emphasizes the importance the Indian placed upon the preservation of the cosmic order through the exercise of his will. The Indian he says "feels the necessity of constantly propping up the cosmic order which is always in danger of being disturbed by evil deities."[48]

Indubitably this cosmic consciousness was better articulated among the more advanced religious cults of the Mayas, Incas and Aztecs than it was by the animistic cults of Canada; yet there is a great similarity of religious ideas throughout America, indicating an original source of inspiration. For example, the air god Quetzlcoatl of the Aztecs bears a distinct likeness to the sun or sky god of the Micmacs or to the chief deity of the Plains Indians; they imposed the same kind of ethical practices upon their devotees. Another quite universal practice of the Amerindians was a search through prayers and visions for guardian spirits, producing a religious experience that designated certain tokens and amulets to ward off evil spirits. A rather unique system of burying the dead, prevalent from Canada to Patagonia, is perhaps the strongest testimony we have of "some previous communication between widely scattered tribes."[49]

It is possible that this communication may have occurred before the Indians arrived in the New World, as has been suggested by observers impressed by the resemblance of some Indian cult practices and myths to Old World rites and myths. Marc Lescarbot, Canada's first historian, who spent the year 1606-07 in Acadia, believed "that the voice of the apostles may have reached so far,"[50] because he had heard from the Micmacs a story of a great flood that bore a striking resemblance to the biblical flood. Spanish friars were astounded to find that Mayans went to confession, and also practised a form of baptism. The many similarities they found between Christianity and the Mayan religion led them to the conclusion that St. Thomas must have been there some fifteen hundred years earlier.[51] Early missionaries to Mexico were amazed to find crosses raised in various shrines as objects of worship; their amazement grew when they were informed of the traditions associated with the goddess Cioacoatl which reminded them of the Syrian Eve. Even more amazing was the story of a Messiah, who had come from the East on the great Atlantic Ocean and who, before he disappeared, promised to return again to renew the golden age of Anahuac.[52] Most striking of all was the similarity of the cults of Indian goddesses to the cult of the Virgin Mary in medieval Europe, particularly the accompanying mother-child relationship which bore a resemblance to the Christian symbolism of the Virgin and child. These affinities do suggest an Old World connection, but most students of the subject think this highly unlikely since they are convinced of the indigenous nature of Indian culture, in which religion is the formative element. Such a hypothesis is quite unnecessary at the present time since we are now well aware that the "collective unconscious as the common psychic foundation of mankind"[53] has produced similar religious symbols in every part of the world.

Like the religious symbols of all religions the Indian symbols were intended to make a man feel at home both in the world here and in the hereafter; but their deeper significance is often obscured for us by the close association with the animistic cults, particularly among the tribes of Canada. Here animism prevailed mightily, and the spirits inhabiting cataracts, stones, buffaloes et cetera, were vague nameless creatures whose actual functions are difficult to comprehend. But above these *genii locarum* there were higher levels of deities like the thunder god of the Plains Indians, the sea goddess Sedna of the Eskimos and the sun god of the Micmacs, who were imposing a fairly rigid moral code upon their worshippers; and even beyond this polytheistic stage some of the Canadian Indians were reaching out to the conceptions of one Great Spirit, the Creator of the Universe.[54]

It is extremely difficult to work out a system of theology in relation to the sky-gods, but the mysterious forces which emanated from them are to be recognized in the mana and taboos which shaped the behaviour patterns and the value judgments of Indian communal life. Unfortunately, the first visitors to this continent, particulary the traders and the missionaries, never took the time to estimate the disciplinary qualities of these taboos, which did create, as has been observed, very resourceful personalities who could endure great hardships with remarkable serenity. Europeans took considerable pride in demonstrating to the Indians that they could defy venerated taboos with impunity; the effect was to undermine the fundamental basis of Indian morality with dire consequences to his cultural and social life. The taboos of the Aztec religion, for example, were responsible for imposing a very high standard of ethical conduct, but once the Aztecs abandoned them in the process of becoming Christians there was a notable decline in morals.[55] Similar results were common phenomena across Canada in the wake of the traders and missionaries scornful of the aborigines' taboos.[56]

MISSIONARY TECHNIQUES

The evil effect of undermining the established mores of the Indian was not entirely disregarded by all the missionaries to America, and a few of them advocated that their converts should be permitted to retain some of the Indian cult practices even while they accepted Christianity. But the older orders such as the Dominicans and Franciscans were utterly opposed to any such syncretism and felt that the only way to make the Indian a good Christian was to attempt to erase from his mind all remembrances of his heathen way of life. The Jesuits, on the other hand, already had been experimenting with a different form of missionary technique in the Orient, where they had made concessions to pagan religions, particularly in what they considered the externals of religion, if these did not conflict with fundamental Christian doctrine.[57]

Father Matteo Ricci, the founder of the Catholic missions in China, in furtherance of this objective adopted the costume of the educated Chinese and used ancient Chinese books to find proof for the existence of God. Similarly in India Father Robert de Nobili declared himself a Brahmin and allowed his converts to remain in their caste system and to retain their ancient religious practices.[58] Ultimately they were condemned by the papacy (1774) for tolerating a dangerous form of syncretism; but before the blow fell the Jesuits in America were following fairly closely the pattern set by their colleagues in the Orient, not without strenuous opposition from the Franciscans. It was around the devotions paid to the Virgin of Guadalupe in Mexico that the fiercest controversy raged. The eminent Franciscan, Barnardino de Sahagun, strongly opposed any encouragement of this cult, as the Virgin had the unmistakable features of an Indian goddess. Despite de Sahagun's objections the Jesuits continued to tolerate the cult and according to one authority on pre-Hispanic culture in Mexico this victory for syncretism helped to save the Indian's self-respect in face of the encompassing Spanish civilization.[59]

The controversy that began in Mexico around the middle of the sixteenth century was to be continued in Canada in the opening years of the seventeenth. Father Joseph Lafitu, a Jesuit missionary in Canada, repudiated strongly the idea that the savages in America were little better than beasts and sought eagerly in "legends and customs for intimations"[60] of the Indian's apprehensions of God, as a means whereby he might lead them gently into the Christian fold. The Franciscans, who were the first missionaries in the St. Lawrence Valley, were inclined to the view that the Indians were "incapable of Christianity" until they were first civilized through contact with Europeans. Before the entrance of the Franciscans into Canada, however, the Jesuits were permitted for a few years to follow their own unique method, undisturbed by controversy, along the coasts of the Bay of Fundy. To this Acadian adventure, which was to serve as a prelude to a much more ambitious project in Huronia, we now turn.

NOTES TO CHAPTER FOUR

1. *Vide* J. Mooney, *The Aborigine Population of America North of Mexico* ("Smithsonian Miscellaneous Collection" [Washington, 1928]), LXXX, No. 7, p. 33, for population at time of white settlement. *Canada Year Book 1963-64* (Ottawa: The Queen's Printer, 1964), p. 185, gives the Indian population in 1961 at 191,799 and points out that "the rapid growth of that population in recent years is indicated by the fact that in 1959 more than 56 per cent of the Indians were under twenty-one years compared with the 42 per cent of the population of Canada as a whole."

2. Prospect for their future is discussed in *The Canadian Indian* (Ottawa: Department of Citizenship and Immigration, 1932), *passim*; also *Human Relations* (Toronto: The Human Rights Commission, December, 1964), Vol. V, No. 10, p. 1 *et seq.*, makes a passionate plea for social justice for Canada's Indians.

3. D. Jenness, *Indians of Canada* (Bulletin 65; Ottawa: Department of Mines, 1932), p. 249.

4. F. Parkman, *Pioneers of France in the New World* (5th ed.; Boston: Little, Brown, 1867), p. 418 says, "The story of these missions, marvellous as a tale of chivalry or legends of the lives of the saints...."

5. *Vide* F.-X. de Charlevoix, *History and Description of New France*, trans. J. G. Shea (New York: Harper, 1900), Vol. I, p. 106.

6. Quoted by J. H. Kennedy, *Jesuit and Savage in New France* (New Haven: Yale University Press, 1950), p. 14.

7. *Vide* F. Parkman, *op. cit.*, p. 182.

8. *Ibid.*; also J. H. Kennedy, *op. cit.*, p. 15.

9. *Ibid.*, p. 16.

10. Samuel de Champlain, *Works* (translated and edited under general editorship of H. P. Biggar; Toronto: Champlain Society, 1922-36), Vol. III, p. 18.

11. J. H. Kennedy, *op. cit.*, p. 16.

12. *Vide* R. G. Thwaites, ed., *The Jesuit Relations and Allied Documents* (Cleveland: Burrows, 1896-1901), Vol. I, p. 161.

13. F. Parkman, *op. cit.*, p. 417.

14. *Vide* Thwaites, *op. cit.*, Vol. I, p. 161.

15. Quoted by J. H. Kennedy, *op. cit.*, from "Jesuits in North America in the Seventeenth Century," p. 131.

16. Louis A. Brennan, *No Stone Unturned; An Almanac of North America Prehistory* (New York: Random House, 1959), pp. 16-23, suggests on the basis of carbon 14 dating that human beings inhabited the Americas 30,000 years ago. J. Hawkes and L. Woolcy, *Prehistory and the Beginnings of Civilization,* Vol. I of *History of Mankind: Cultural and Scientific Development* (New York: Harper 1962), p. 54, do not think man has been on this continent much more than 10,000 years.

17. *Vide* Louis A. Brennan, *op. cit.*, pp. 97-99.

18. Hawkes and Wooley *op. cit.*, p. 91.

19. *Encyclopedia Canadiana* (Ottawa: The Canadiana Company, 1957-58), Vol. V, p. 254.

20. *Vide* W. H. Prescott, *History of the Conquest of Mexico and History of the Conquest of Peru* (New York: Modern Library, 1936), p. 691.

21. Waldo Frank, *The Rediscovery of Man* (New York: Braziller, 1958), p. 199.

22. *Vide* L. A. Brennan, *op. cit.*, p. 25.

23. D. Jenness, *op. cit.*, p. 8.

24. The method followed by T. F. McIlwraith in the *Encyclopedia Canadiana, op. cit.*, p. 257 *et seq.*

25. A good anthology of the *Jesuit Relations* has been made by Edna Kenton, *Black Gown and Redskins* (London, New York and Toronto: Longmans, 1956).

26. *Vide* D. Jenness, *op. cit.*, pp. 411-415.

27. *Ibid.*, pp. 327-76.

28. J. Collier, *Indians of the Americas* (Abridged ed.; New York: New American Library, 1953), p. 102.

29. D. Jenness, *op. cit.*, p. 261; F. E. LaViolette, *The Struggle for Survival* (Toronto: University of Toronto Press, 1961), pp. 161-3 sees in the establishment of the *Native Voice*, an Indian newspaper, an indication of a more assertive Indian in the future.

30. *Vide* J. Collier, *op. cit.*, p. 99.

31. F. Johnson, *Man in Northeastern North America* (Andover, Mass.: Phillips Academy, 1946), Vol III, p. 199.

32. *Ibid.*, p. 201.

33. *Ibid.*, p. 207.

34. *Vide* Chrestien Le Clercq, *First Establishment of the Faith in New France* (trans. J. G. Shea; New York: Shea, 1881), Vol. I, pp. 110-11.

35. D. Jenness, *op. cit.*, p. 259.

36. *Ibid.*, p. 260.

37. F. E. LaViolette, *op. cit.*, pp. 18-43; an account of cultural dismemberment and reconstruction on the northwest coast of Canada.

38. On the revindication of the Mexican Indian *vide* W. J. Moreno, "The Indians of America and Christianity" in *History of Religion in the New World* (Washington, D.C.: Conference on the History of Religions in the New World during Colonial times, 1958), p. 91, *et seq.*

39. *Vide* J. Collier, *op. cit.*, p. 19.

40. On the food resources of the Canadian Indian *vide* D. Jenness, *op. cit.*, p. 40 *et seq.*; also J. E. S. Thompson, *The Civilization of the Mayas* (6th ed.; Chicago: Natural History Museum, 1958), p. 9.

41. J. Collier, *op. cit.*, p. 11.

42. *Vide* Alberto Ruz, *Uxmal: Official Guide* (Mexico: Instituto Nacional de Antropologia e Historia, 1963), p. 4.

43. *Vide* J. E. S. Thompson, *op. cit.*, p. 26.

44. *Vide* W. H. Prescott, *op. cit.*, pp. 54-7.

45. *Ibid.*, p. 72.

46. *Vide* J. Collier, *op. cit.*, p. 11; also H. Herring, *A History of Latin America* (2d revised ed.; New York: Knopf, 1961), p. 44 *et seq.*

47. *Vide* J. Collier, *op. cit.*, p. 11.

48. *Vide* W. J. Moreno, *op. cit.*, p. 78.

49. W. H. Prescott, *op. cit.*, p. 699.

50. *Vide* Marc Lescarbot, *Nova Francia, A Description of Acadia* (trans. P. Erondelle 1609; republished, London: Routledge, 1928), p. 171.

51. J. E. S. Thompson, *op. cit.*, p. 65.

52. *Vide* W. H. Prescott, *op. cit.*, p. 695.

53. Erich Neumann, *The Great Mother, An Analysis of the Archetype*, (trans. Ralph Manheim; London: Routledge and Kegan Paul, 1955), p. 90.

54. *Vide* D. Jenness, *op. cit.*, p. 171.

55. *Vide* J. E. S. Thompson, *Mexico before Cortez* (New York and London: Scribner, 1933), p. 40.

56. *Vide* D. Jenness, *op. cit.*, p. 181.

57. *Vide* W. J. Moreno, *op. cit.*, p. 88.

58. *Vide* The *Catholic Encyclopedia*, "Development of the Missions" (New York: The Encyclopedia Press, 1907-22), Vol. XIII, p. 36 *et seq.*

59. *Vide* W. J. Moreno, *op. cit.*, p. 88. Vincent Cronin in *A Pearl to India: The Life of Roberto de Nobili* (London: Dutton, 1959), p. 9, writes, "Because each missionary strove to identify himself with his chosen country Nobili's life is as different from Ricci's as India is from China." *Vide* also David Jenks, *Six Great Missionaries* (Oxford: Mowbray, 1930), pp. 80-134.

60. *Vide* C. Le Clercq, *op. cit.*, Vol. I, pp. 255-56.

FIVE

The Acadian Adventure

From its inception the Acadian adventure was fraught with peril. It originated from a charter[1] designed to combine missionary work with trade and commerce. The French government under the sway of the Duc de Sully was little inclined to give financial aid to colonization[2] and so it was hoped that by linking monopoly with trade a colony would pay its own way and also provide funds for missionary work among the aborigines. But this combination of a trading post with a missionary project early precipitated a tension within the colony that contributed much to a colonial disaster in an ill-defined piece of territory, first called Acadia but shortly thereafter to be designated Nova Scotia. An even more serious menace to the future well-being of the proposed colony was the fact that it had been set down in one of the most competitive areas of commercial rivalry in the New World. All of which brought about what one of its historians has called the *drame acadien*.[3]

EARLY HUGUENOT SETTLEMENTS

The Acadian drama arose out of a long series of tragic failures by the French colonies in the New World. After the rather half-hearted attempt at colonization in the St. Lawrence area by Roberval and Cartier with the ostensible purpose of converting the Indians, the French government next turned its attention to finding a haven of refuge for persecuted Huguenots. The idea first took form when Nicolas Durand de Villegaignon,[4] a knight of Malta turned Protestant, suggested to Admiral Coligny, the powerful leader of the Huguenots, that it might be possible to find an asylum for his co-religionists in Florida. Florida at the time was an inclusive term for a land of promise whose boundaries were far in excess of the state which now bears that name.[5] For Villegaignon it included Brazil and in 1558, with a company of French Protestants, to whom John Calvin had given a blessing, he set sail for the land of promise. He then organized a settlement called Coligny on a tiny island near present-day Rio de Janeiro, which was soon reinforced by additional settlers from Switzerland and France.

There was much talk among these arrivals of building a new Geneva in America, and the religious arguments that arose out of this attempt to transfer a Genevan polity to the New World soon marred the peace of the colony. Villegaignon was not really a Calvinist and soon declared Calvin a heretic; when he finally abandoned the project and returned to France he was so convinced of the heresy of his former friends that he enrolled to fight on the side of the Catholics in the wars of religion in France. Without strong leadership the colony rapidly deteriorated in morale and was ultimately dispersed by the Portuguese, who claimed the land as part of their share of the papal division of the New World.[6]

With the failure of this first settlement Coligny turned his attention to another area which appeared to be more properly called Florida. This time he secured the services of a good sailor, Jean Ribault, who was also a convinced Protestant. In 1562 Ribault set forth with a company of Huguenots to found an overseas Port-Royal; whether the name was chosen in honour of the famous Abbey of *Port-Royal-des-Champs* which was soon to embark upon a modified form of Calvinism, the records do not say;[7] but there is good evidence that the Huguenots who came out to America at this time were not greatly concerned about the religious aspect of their adventure. After they were established at Port-Royal, on St. John's River near the present day St. Helena in South Carolina, Ribault decided he must return to France for more settlers. During his absence morale deteriorated rapidly and some of the community became so homesick that they built themselves a rather crude boat and, inconceivably, some of them, after turning cannibal, managed to cross the Atlantic in their frail craft and get safely back to Europe.[8]

In the meantime Coligny had persuaded a French nobleman, René de Laudonnière, to take out reinforcements to Ribault's colony; they arrived in 1564 and proceeded to organize a second settlement north of St. John's River which they named Fort Caroline in honour of King Charles of France. The second colony was no more stable than Ribault's; the religious motive of the settlers for leaving France was soon replaced by an avid desire for fabulous riches which had long been associated with the land of Florida. Some of them even suggested that they should turn buccaneer and devote themselves to amassing wealth, clear evidence that they were not seriously interested in extending the faith of Protestantism to America. Laudonnière was about to abandon the whole project in disgust when Ribault returned with an additional three hundred settlers. The new arrivals contributed very little to the internal peace of Fort Caroline, but it might now have survived except that Spain included Florida in her share of the papal division of the New World. When Pedro Menéndez de Avilés, who had been entrusted by the King of Spain with the occupation of Florida, heard about Fort Caroline he immediately set out with an army and captured the fort. He then massacred all the prisoners, hanging over them the inscription: "I do this not as to Frenchmen but as to Lutherans."[9] This fearful massacre did not remain long unavenged; a friend of Ribault's, Dominique de Gorgues, organized a marauding band with the declared purpose of punishing the murderers. In 1568 he led a daring army to the fatal spot and succeeded in regaining the fort; he then, in turn, hanged on the spot some four hundred Spaniards over whom he placed the inscription: "I do not do this unto Spaniards, nor as unto Mariners, but as unto Traitors, Robbers and Murderers."[10]

All these massacres were part of the ruthlessness which had become characteristic of the religious wars of Europe. It was thought probable that the Catholic party in France had informed the Spanish authorities of the Huguenot settlement in Florida. Be that as it may, there can be little doubt that the continued frustration of Calvinist hopes of finding a place of refuge in America helped to contribute to an intensified religious animosity in France which finally culminated in the shocking massacre of St. Bartholomew (1572) — a massacre in which Coligny perished; and thus was brought to an end for the time being Huguenot colonization in America.[11]

Events, however, took a turn for the better with the accession of Henry IV to the throne of France in 1593; this former Protestant leader, before turning Roman Catholic, had given a guarantee to his former co-religionists that nothing would be done to prejudice Protestant interests. The wars of religion in France were now over and, with the pronouncement of the Edict of Nantes (1598) which proclaimed religious toleration, the way was now open for a cooperative effort on the part of both Protestant and Catholic to attempt to create a French colony in America.[12] It was during this period of toleration that Acadia emerged, but the antipathies aroused by the long series of religious wars and the frustration of earlier attempts at colonization were still very much to the fore in the Acadian drama and were the source of much bickering among the first settlers.[13]

OPPOSITION TO COLONIZATION

If, for the time being, the religious motive for colonization was being muted the new motive of trade and commerce was just as full of menace for the future well-being of the colonists as the religious had been. None of the fishing companies that had fished freely for many years in the North Atlantic and were now branching into the fur trade welcomed permanent settlements in this area,[14] particularly when they were being financed out of a monopoly of the fur trade. As events turned out the most serious menace to the new colony was the English who were also becoming decidedly interested in colonization and were beginning to draw up their own charters for settlements in the New World. The motive behind these charters at first seems to have been the need to find new outlets for land speculators. Land for speculation had become scarce in sixteenth-century England and consequently speculators were now looking beyond their native shores; Ireland first caught their attention and it was in Ireland that Sir Humphrey Gilbert, to whom Elizabeth I was to entrust the responsibility of colonization in America, first won his spurs as a colonizer.[15] To this trusty servant Elizabeth, at the urgings of the speculators, granted in 1578 "letters patent to inhabit and possess at his choice all remote heathen lands not in actual possession of any Christian prince."[16]

In pursuance of this object Sir Humphrey Gilbert arrived in 1583 at St. John's, Newfoundland, where he received according to an enthusiastic propagandist for English colonization, Richard Hakluyt, a warm welcome from the fishermen of various nations. It is difficult to believe that the French, Spanish and Portuguese who met Sir Humphrey "upon the side of a hill" were as happy about this proposed colony as Hakluyt would have us believe; but as the meeting took place "in view of all the fleet of Englishmen"[17] it may well be that they manifested some show of cordiality as the better part of valour; nevertheless, there must have been suppressed rejoicing when these fishermen were informed that Gilbert's ship had foundered on the way back to England and all on board had been lost. When in 1617 Lord Baltimore tried to found a colony as a place of refuge in Newfoundland for his Roman Catholic co-religionists, the true feelings of the fishermen were openly manifested; this time the West Country fishermen and merchants of

England took the lead in frustrating Baltimore's colony at Ferryland.[18]

One result of this aggressiveness on the part of the English fisheries was to push the French fishermen into the St. Lawrence area and the English colonizers farther south, where both French and English would soon be eyeing one another suspiciously over ill-defined borders. In moving into the St. Lawrence area, however, the French began to make contact with the Indians, with whom they began a fur trade, and they wanted no governmental interference with this lucrative business. But unwittingly they were preparing the way for the French government to become seriously interested in colonization.

It was quickly recognized by some economists in France that the fur trade was far more amenable to monopoly privileges than were the fisheries, and monopoly, as has been observed,[19] was regarded as an easy means of financing a colony. So it came about that Sieur de Monts was granted his monopoly of the fur trade in this area on the agreement that he would establish a French colony in the New World. The monopoly was granted, however, over the bitter protests of the free-enterprise fur traders who would long continue to do everything in their power to thwart de Monts' charter.[20]

PORT-ROYAL PRECARIOUSLY ESTABLISHED

Such were the menaces that faced the Huguenots and Catholics as they attempted to co-operate in building a new Port-Royal, far from the disasters of Florida, in what was considered a remote corner of the North Atlantic where a novel policy of religious toleration was to be allowed. Consequently, on board the two ships that sailed from Le Havre to Acadia in 1604, with 120 workmen as well as some men of noble birth, were a Protestant clergyman and two Roman Catholic priests. The harmony of the voyagers was greatly disturbed by theological arguments between the minister and the priests, nor did these cease after land had been reached. Sometimes the arguments led to blows and Champlain, who accompanied this party, remarked that he did not know which side gave the hardest blow but he was convinced that no blows would ever deter them from discussing the points in the controversy.[21] To make matters worse both settlers and Indians began to take sides in the argument and it required the best efforts of Champlain and du Pont-Gravé, the official in charge of the company, to keep the peace. These quarrels made such an impression upon the colonists, according to the Franciscan Sagard, that when a minister and priest died about the same time they were buried in one grave by the sailors who watched curiously to see if these protagonists of different faiths could now rest quietly together.[22] Such violent religious controversy did much to undermine the morale of this little outpost of French civilization so precariously established under the watchful eyes of resentful fur traders.

But what was a far more serious menace to morale in the early days of settlement was the dread disease of scurvy. The company was particularly unfortunate in its choice of a site on the Island of Sainte-Croix, situated on the river of the same name near the present boundary between Maine and New Brunswick. During the first winter on this bleak island thirty-five of the settlers succumbed to scurvy. Conditions improved somewhat when the settlers moved to a new habitation they named Port-Royal (now Lower Granville). Here they were joined in 1606 by Sieur de Poutrincourt who was replacing Sieur du Pont-Gravé as lieutenant in charge. The former had for some time been contemplating creating a seigneurie in the New World and had already fixed upon Port-Royal as a "fit place to retire himself into with his family, wife and children."[23] On this particular occasion Sieur de Monts, who was ready to make a grant of land to the prospective New World seigneurie, called upon Poutrincourt to help in the colonization of Acadia; he in turn asked a lawyer friend, Marc Lescarbot, to join him in the project. According to Lescarbot, before sailing they went to several churches looking for a priest "to relieve and ease him whom Monsieur de Monts had left there at his voyage (sic), whom we thought to be yet living".[24] They were unsuccessful in their search and finally sailed without a priest or minister but with a company of colonists so disorderly that they had to be kept under guard until the day of embarkation. When they arrived at Port-Royal they learned that both priest and minister were dead.

At this juncture it appeared that one of the professed purposes for founding the colony, the conversion of the Indians, was being badly served. As one historian of French missions in the New World sadly remarks: ". . . for the first time, in August 1605, a Christian nation had in these latitudes founded a village. But the church, where was she? The sacraments, where were they?"[25] Our commentator does grant, however, that the village was not completely devoid of all spiritual ministrations; in point of fact, religious instruction was now provided in a less polemical form than it had been or would be for a long time to come. The instructor was none other than Poutrincourt's legal adviser, Marc Lescarbot, a keen student of the scriptures who conducted the Sunday services. Although he used a Genevan translation of the Bible, which must have been pleasing to his Huguenot auditors, yet it is the opinion of Georges Goyau that "he firmly remained a good Catholic."[26] Whether a Catholic or not, and the evidence is strong in favour of his allegiance to the Catholic Church, he was no great admirer of the Jesuits and he used his literary talents, which were considerable, to discourage any thought of sending Jesuits to New France.

It was a memorable winter that Marc Lescarbot spent at Port-Royal where he co-operated with Champlain, who had founded *L'Ordre de bon temps*, in keeping the company "merry and cleanly concerning victuals."[27] But the good cheer was soon brought to an end when in the spring of 1607, a "young man of Saint-Malo, named Chevalier" brought the sad news to Port-Royal that the privilege which had been given to "de Monts for ten years was revoked."[28] And so the whole company had perforce to take ship for France, but Poutrincourt vowed he would return again with his wife and children to occupy the seigneurie of Port-Royal, whose possession had been confirmed to him by the king. He was also aware that the king and his confessor, Father Coton, wanted him to take out two Jesuits who were ready and anxious to begin a mission to the Indians. Poutrincourt like Lescarbot had little liking for Jesuits and so on his return to Port-Royal in 1610 he took instead of the Jesuits a secular priest from the diocese of Langres, Jessé Fléché. The latter's missionary activity, as has already been remarked,[29] was somewhat precipitate in that he baptized many aborigines without much instruction in the Christian faith; nevertheless Lescarbot, in his history of New France, lauds Fléché's missionary work and urges the French court to refrain from sending out to barbarous people learned men like the Jesuits who he felt could use their great talents to better effect in Europe.[30] His plea fell upon deaf ears, for the court under the guidance of Father Coton, a favourite of Henry IV, designated two Jesuit priests, Pierre Biard and Enemond Massé for missionary work in Acadia. Getting to Port-Royal was no easy matter for the two Jesuits, and here co-operation between Catholic and Protestant was again put under a serious strain. The Huguenot merchants were determined that Biard and Massé should not sail on their ships. At this juncture a very pious and wealthy lady, the Marquise de Guercheville, proclaimed herself "the patroness of American missions,"[31] bought up the dormant rights of Sieur de Monts in Acadia and with money she collected at the court, along with her own contribution, she was able to finance

Poutrincourt's voyage; the latter could do nothing less, though hardly with good grace, than provide passage for the two priests to Port-Royal.

MISSION TO THE MICMACS

Under such inauspicious circumstances began the Jesuit mission to New France, a mission that was to have a decisive influence upon the religious and social life of French Canada. The pioneers of this mission seem to have been carefully chosen for their task. To some extent they complemented each other: Father Biard was a savant; his colleague, Father Massé, was an ascetic.[32] The former, born at Grenoble, France (1567) had held the chair of scholastic theology and Hebrew at the College of Lyons before he was sent to Acadia. One is inclined to agree with Lescarbot that his education was far in excess of what was needed for missionary work in New France; on the other hand he originated a vogue that has provided the students of Canadian history with an invaluable source book, namely, the *Jesuit Relations*, written most vividly by intelligent and sensitive men "from the midst of a forest." Biard's letters, composed in the "grand style," were carefully preserved by the recipients and now grace the opening volume of Reuben Gold Thwaites' remarkable collection of all that transpired in the early days of the colonization of French Canada.[33]

This correspondence, which stirred up great interest and enthusiasm for missionary work among the aborigines in certain influential circles in France, may have been Biard's greatest contribution to the Jesuit cause in America. But it may well be that the less flamboyant Massé, also from Lyons, played a more significant role than Biard, for after the collapse of the Acadian mission he became a minister of the Collège at La Flèche, a house we are told, "dear to the heart of Henry IV,"[34] where he discoursed constantly on the challenge of the aborigines of the New World to the Catholic Church. A decade later when the Jesuits were enabled to return to Canada Massé was among those who landed at Quebec to begin a mission to the Hurons, and was to remain in the country of his adoption until his death in 1646.

The first concern of the two missionaries was the Indian church that Jessé Fléché had brought into being—a flock of which they had no high opinion. They appreciated Fléché's difficulties, for he had been under great pressure from the authorities at Port-Royal to produce results so that they could report home that they were fulfilling the missionary terms of their charter. Biard considered

Fléché a worthy enough man who had been held in high esteem by the Indians, since they had given him the honourable title of "Patriarch."[35] But he deplored the fact that so many of the aborigines had been baptized with little or no understanding of the Christian faith. Nevertheless both Biard and Massé were greatly impressed with Fléché's most notable convert, the Sagamore Membertou, chief of the Micmac groups from Gaspé to Cape Sable. Although he had formerly "had the name of being the worst and most traitorous man of his tribe," after his conversion he became an unusually pious Christian and it was Baird's opinion that "he greatly excelled all his countrymen in acuteness and good sense."[36] Membertou, however, was a very exceptional case; others did not make the same good impression, especially a convert who presented to the missionaries, with some pride, his seven wives.

Events such as these impressed upon Biard and Massé that they must inaugurate a more carefully thought-out plan than Fléché's for the evangelization of the aborigines. They soon recognized that their predecessor's greatest handicap had been his lack of knowledge of the Micmac language; so they attempted from the beginning to learn Micmac; at the same time they tried through interpreters to study the habits, beliefs and taboos of the Indians to discover, if they could, any aboriginal theological presuppositions upon which Christian teaching might be based.

TEACHING PROBLEMS

With this end in view Biard made a fairly close study of the Indian religion but failed to find much in it to serve his purpose. He found it full of strange incantations and sorcery dances; he was struck by the absence of temples, rites and ceremonies and by the lack of religious teaching and legal enactments. In place of these were certain customs and traditions in the custody of medicine men who threatened or prophesied dire events if these were not strictly observed. Biard did, however, detect among the Micmacs a faint notion of a supreme god, but it was so perverted by false ideas that he concludes that "they really worship the Devil."[37]

He also scrutinized carefully their social and cultural life in search of some possible affinities with Christian culture. Here he found even less to commend: "They are," he wrote, "wanderers, with nothing to attach them to a place, neither homes nor relationships, neither possessions nor love of country; as a people they have bad habits, are extremely lazy, gluttonous, profane, treacherous, cruel in their revenge, and given up to all kinds of lewdness, men and women alike, the men having several wives and abandoning them to others, and the women serving them as slaves, whom they strike and beat unmercifully, and who dare not complain; and after being half killed, if it so please the murderer, they must laugh and caress him."[38]

Biard's colleague, Massé, was not so harsh in his estimate of the communal life of the Indians. After a realistic description of their treatment of enemy prisoners, which was terrible beyond description, he remarks that in contrast to this ferocity "at home they cultivate peace and carefully avoid quarrels."

Both missionaries, however, could find very little in the Indian way of life that might serve as a bridge between Indian and Christian thought-forms and they must have been sorely tempted to advise the suppression of Indian culture as a preliminary to an Indian's entrance into the Christian family. But this was not the policy of the Jesuits, who believed that if they looked deeply enough they could find in Indian culture a basis upon which to establish a Christian superstructure. Before this could be accomplished they felt they must acquire a fluency in the Indian tongue.

As they became better acquainted with the language, however, they began to realize even more the immensity of the task before them. It was a great shock to find that there was nothing "abstract, internal, spiritual or distinct" in it; all the virtues, such as "wisdom, fidelity, justice, mercy, gratitude, piety and others" were missing. So the missionaries, perforce, had to make do with such words as "happy, tender love, good heart."[39] For some time they debated whether Micmac contained any word corresponding directly to the word "credo." "Judge for yourself," wrote Biard, to his provincial in Paris, "the difficulty surrounding the remainder of the symbols and fundamental truths of Christianity."[40]

While battling with this obstinate language the missionaries tried to impress upon the Indians the value of the Christian way of life, by symbols and by example. With the aid of pictures, crosses and other stimuli Biard felt that the Indians had "received the first faint ideas and germs of our holy faith, which will sometime take root and grow abundantly, please God, if it is followed by a longer and better cultivation."[41]

A YEAR OF TENSIONS

If symbols were showing some fruits, the same could not be said of example, particularly the example set by the Frenchmen at Port-Royal. It was naturally the desire of the missionaries to see the colonists behave like proper Christians before the Indians, who were always curiously watching every move and gesture of these strange intruders from another world. For this reason the Jesuits sought to enforce close supervision over the social life of the French colonies, first in Acadia and later at Quebec. This was resented by the secular authorities who regarded such activity as unjustifiable interference by the church in the affairs of state. The original settlers in Acadia were not particularly pious. Biard was greatly disturbed by the conduct of the sailors at Port-Royal. They had, he said, "no sign of religion except in their oaths, nor any knowledge of God beyond the simplest conception which they bring with them from France." As a result the first things the Indians learned of the European language were vile oaths and insulting words. "And you will often hear," he complained, "women (who otherwise are very timid and modest) hurl vulgar, vile and shameless epithets at our people in the French language."[42]

Since those in charge of the colony did little to curb the unseemly conduct of the colonists, the missionaries began to think of establishing somewhere in the area another colony that would not be subordinate to commercial interests. A small incident that helped to confirm the need for such a colony arose over a burial place for the aging Membertou. He himself expressed a wish to be buried among his own people; the missionaries were firmly of the opinion that a Christian must be buried in consecrated ground. Biencourt, the son of Poutrincourt, who was then in charge of the colony, was just as firmly of the opinion that Membertou should be allowed to make his own decision. The argument waxed long and furiously for a time, but in the end Membertou acceded to the priests' importunities. So victory in this affair lay with the representatives of the church.[43]

A more serious matter arose over the financial support of the mission. The Marquise de Guercheville, who now held a controlling share in the land grant of Acadia insisted that the civil government at Port-Royal should set apart a percentage of the commercial profits from the fisheries and fur trades for the upkeep of the mission to the Indians. Neither Poutrincourt nor his son took very kindly to a fixed levy upon the revenues of the colony. There were many in France who agreed that such a fixed drain upon the slender resources of a young and struggling colony might well imperil the whole project; among them was Lescarbot who argued that "if a contribution of a seigneurial nature were due to anyone, it was certainly due to Poutrincout and not the Jesuits, who could not exist without him."[44] Since the whole project was now being financed by the marquise, it was not too much to ask that a fixed income be put aside for missions.

Another cause of tension was a restriction that Biencourt imposed upon the freedom of movement of the missionaries. On one occasion Biard had mediated with some success in a quarrel that had arisen between Biencourt and the younger Pont-Gravé, the son of the original commander at Port-Royal. Both Biard and Biencourt had visited Pont-Gravé at a station somewhere along the St. John River, on the opposite side of the Bay of Fundy, for the purpose of effecting a reconciliation. During this trip Father Biard discovered that Pont-Gravé was quite fluent in the Indian tongue and was willing to teach the missionary Micmac, but when Biencourt was asked to provide passage for Father Biard's return to St. John he refused, or at least imposed conditions that were tantamount to a refusal.[45] In short the Jesuits were practically the prisoners of Biencourt "and all their apostolate was enshackled by the caprices of the latter."[46]

While these disagreeable controversies were raging the colony was becoming more and more destitute of the necessities of life; but once again Mme de Guercheville saved the situation by sending out a ship called the *Jonas*, laden with supplies. For a brief time there was great joy in Port-Royal but it was soon dampened down by a most violent quarrel between the Jesuits and Biencourt. On board the *Jonas* was a Jesuit lay brother, Gilbert du Thet, who was now representing Mme de Guercheville's interests in Acadia; he immediately reported to Biencourt that his father's agent, Simon d'Imbert, had been clandestinely selling some of the cargo; the latter, in order to cover up his dishonesty, accused the Jesuits of trying to take away from Poutrincourt the seigneurie of Port-Royal. Biencourt was inclined to accept the word of d'Imbert and made things so disagreeable for the Jesuits that they decided they would return on the *Jonas* to France; but the young lieutenant ordered them back to land and refused to allow them to communicate with the authorities in France. Biard now resorted to excommunicating Biencourt. This episode is passed over in silence in Biard's writings—a lacuna that Father Campeau in his article on the great crisis of 1612 at Port-Royal finds difficult to explain.[47] He concedes that the rupture between the missionaries and Biencourt was disastrous for all concerned, but it is his conclusion after careful research that the principal responsibility for the disaster that was soon to overtake the Acadian experiment must rest upon Poutrincourt and his son,[48] a view that stands in sharp contrast to the one held by Francis Parkman, who speaks of the help proffered by Mme de Guercheville and her Jesuit advisers to Poutrincourt in 1612 as "ill-omened succour" that "could not be refused."[49] Be that as it may, this year of tension started a train of events that led to the termination of the Jesuit mission in Acadia. When du Thet finally got back to France and reported on the state of affairs at Port-Royal, Mme de Guercheville decided to separate the mission from Poutrincourt's seigneurie and start a new colony dedicated primarily to missionary work.[50] So in the spring of 1613 the Jonas with a company of forty-eight prospective settlers, including Brother du Thet and another Jesuit priest, Father Quentin, under the command of Captain La Saussaye arrived at Port-Royal to pick up Fathers Massé and Biard. It then moved on to the Penobscot River, where the company selected a site to the east of Mount Desert Island, near present day Bar Harbor, for its permanent home to be known as the mission of Saint-Sauveur.

THE WRATH OF VIRGINIA

The selection of a site in the vicinity of Mount Desert Island was an unfortunate choice for the future of the new colony. By sailing so far south Saussaye's company was challenging a boundary line that had been recently proclaimed by highest authority in England. The English were now seriously embarked upon a scheme of colonization in North America. Sir Walter Raleigh, who had inherited Sir Humphrey Gilbert's charter[51] in 1584, had selected a site less bleak than Newfoundland, which he called Virginia. Its boundaries were finally spelled out in the first two charters issued by James I in 1606 and 1609; with Jamestown as a point of reference the area, according to the first charter, was to extend from the sea-shore one hundred miles inland; in the second it was extended from the Atlantic to the Pacific, and its depth from the 34th to 45th parallel, north latitude.[52] By 1612 the English at Jamestown were quite certain of the boundaries of their prospective colonial empire; according to Captain John Smith, one of the original settlers, Virginia was "a country in America, that lyeth [sic] between the degrees of 34th and 44th latitude. The bounds thereof on the East side are the great ocean. On the south lyeth Florida: on the north Nova Francia."[53] In this rather expansive definition of Virginia it is conceded that France's share of North America are those latitudes above the 44th or 45th degree of north latitude.

The founders of Saint-Sauveur had proceeded below this line and were bound to incur the wrath of the English if they were discovered. When Sir Thomas Dale, governor of Virginia, heard about this new French post he ordered Samuel Argall, later governor of Virginia, to seek out the French settlements and wipe them off the map. The latter arrived before the French colony was completely fortified, about the middle of July, 1613. With no hesitation he ordered a bombardment of the fort; one of the casualties of this brutal attack was Brother du Thet, who became the first of a long line of martyred Jesuits to lay down their lives in the service of the Indians. The inhabitants of Saint-Sauveur were taken so much by surprise that in a brief time they and the Jesuit fathers were all the prisoners of Captain Argall. They were then divided into two groups: one was put into a small ship and ordered to sail directly to France; the remainder, including Fathers Quentin and Biard, were put on the *Jonas,* which had been confiscated by the English, and were taken to Jamestown.

After their arrival at this English settlement they were in peril of their lives; for Sir Thomas Dale regarded the French as nothing less than pirates, since they had no letters of commission to show. At this point Captain Argall, who had stolen and hidden the letters patent that had been given to Captain Saussaye by the French court, relented and admitted his theft in order to save the lives of his prisoners; nevertheless it was necessary, according to Governor Dale, that he with Biard as guide should return to Acadia and demolish the French forts at Port-Royal and Sainte-Croix. There was little to destroy at Sainte-Croix, but at Port-Royal a pleasant little village was brought to an end by a brief bombardment followed by plundering, house burning and the killing of domestic animals.

Captain Argall seems to have created the impression in the minds of the Acadians that it was Biard who had urged the destruction of Port-Royal.[54] This improbable charge was indignantly denied by Biard; nevertheless the frustration of the latest attempt to create an overseas New France, due largely, as many thought, to the over-eagerness of the Jesuits in the prosecution of their missionary work, brought considerable obloquy upon their society. Surprisingly enough, however, they were back in New France almost within a decade to pursue an even more daring and tragic mission in Huronia far away from the troublesome fisheries and the controversial boundaries of the Atlantic seaboard.

In the meantime Acadia became the prey of rival trading companies and seigneurs who reproduced in the New World much of the senseless baronial warfare of the Middle Ages. But even during these rather pointless battles for forts, the evangelization of the Indians was never completely abandoned; this, however, is another chapter in the Acadian drama, which must be postponed until after our consideration of the Huronian experiment.

NOTES TO CHAPTER FIVE

1. *Vide supra*, p. 39. Several of the commissions issued by the king to Sieur de Monts are to be found in *Collections de Manuscrits . . . relatifs à la Nouvelle-France* (Quebec: Coté, 1883-85), Vol. I, pp. 40-51.

2. A. Bernard, *Le Drame Acadien Depuis 1604* (Montreal: Les Clercs de Saint Viateur, 1936), pp. 19-20.

3. *Ibid.*, *passim*.

4. *Vide* A.-E. Borély, *Histoire de la Ville du Havre et Son Ancién Gouvernement* (Le Havre: Lepelletier, 1880-81), Vol. I, p. 245; M. Borély points out that de Villegaignon received his first succour in money for his Brazil project in the port of Le Havre.

5. For a description of Florida at this time *vide* F. Parkman, *Pioneers of France in the New World* (5th ed.; Boston: Little, Brown, 1867), pp. 5-15.

6. *Ibid.*, pp. 16-27.

7. *Vide* A.-E. Borély, *op. cit.*, Vol. II, p. 249, *et seq.* For a brief account of the Abbey of Port-Royal and its popularity with "amiable recluses" at the time of Henry IV *vide* J. Stephen, *Essays in Ecclesiastical Biography* (4th ed.; London: Longmans, 1860), p. 280 *et seq.*

8. *Vide* F. Parkman, *op. cit.*, pp. 39-41.

9. F.-X. de Charlevoix, *History and General Description of New France* (trans. J. G. Shea; New York: Shea, 1866-1872), Vol. I, p. 234.

10. *Vide* A.-E. Borély, *op. cit.*, Vol. II, pp. 260-64.

11. For a discussion of the disastrous effect of the massacre of St. Bartholomew upon Calvinist scholarship in France *vide* A. A. Tilley, "French Humanism and Montaigne" in *The Cambridge Modern History* (Cambridge: Cambridge University Press, 1907-12), Vol. III, p. 59 *et seq.*; in the same volume A. J. Butler's chapter on "Wars of Religion in France", pp. 1-52, also deals with the evil effect upon Calvinism of the massacre of St. Bartholomew.

12. There was no intention on the part of the authorities to make Acadia a place of refuge for Huguenots as had been the case under Coligny; it was simply an attempt to establish a French colony as an outlet, as it were, for Calvinistic commercial activity. It is Lanctot's opinion that the phrase in de Monts' charter to "bring the natives to the Christian religion . . .' might designate the Calvinist quite as much as Catholic faith"; *vide* G. Lanctot, *A History of Canada* (trans. J. Hambleton; Toronto & Vancouver: Clarke, Irwin, 1963), Vol. I, p. 90.

13. Father Lucien Campeau in an article "La grande crise de 1612 à Port-Royal" in *Lettres du Bas-Canada* (Montreal: mars, 1961), XV, No. I, p. 8, sees at this time only a psychological conflict of personalities.

14. *Vide* H. A. Innis, *The Cod Fisheries, The History of an International Economy* (New Haven: Yale University Press, 1940), p. 93.

15. He was knighted for his services in Ireland; *vide The Voyages and Colonizing Enterprises of Sir Humphrey Gilbert* (London: Hakluyt Society, 1940, 2nd series), Vol. I, p. 17.

16. D. W. Prowse, *History of Newfoundland* (London: Macmillan, 1895), p. 7.

17. R. Hakluyt, *The Principal Navigations, Voyages and Discoveries of the English Nation* (London and New York: Dutton, 1907), p. 18.

18. *Vide* H. A. Innis, *op. cit.*, p. 64.

19. *Vide supra*, p. 53.

20. *Vide* Marc Lescarbot, *Nova Francia: a Description of Acadia 1606* (trans. P. Erondelle, 1609, introduction by H. P. Biggar; London: Routledge, 1928), pp. 125-27.

21. Quoted by G. Goyau, *Une Epopée Mystique: Les Origines Religieuses du Canada* (Paris: Grasset, 1924), p. 9; from Champlain, *Oeuvres*, Vol. V, p. 54.

22. G. Sagard-Théodat, *Histoire du Canada* (Paris: Librairie Tross, 1866), Vol. I, p. 26.

23. Lescarbot, *op. cit.*, p. 71.

24. *Ibid.*, p. 62.

25. G. Goyau, *op. cit.*, p. 10. M. Goyau is wrong in his dating; it was the winter of 1606-07 that Canada's first historian, Marc Lescarbot, spent at Port-Royal.

26. *Ibid.*, p. 11.

27. Lescarbot, *op. cit.*, p. 117.

28. *Ibid.*, pp. 126-127.

29. *Vide supra*, p. 39.

30. *Vide* R. G. Thwaites, ed., *The Jesuit Relations and Allied Documents* (Cleveland: Burrows, 1896-1901), Vol. I, p. 81.

31. *Vide* Charlevoix, *op. cit.*, Vol. I, p. 262.

32. For an interesting comparison of Massé and Biard *vide* C. de Rochemonteix, *Les Jésuites et la Nouvelle-France* (Paris: Letouzey et Ané, 1895), Vol. I, pp. 24-5.

33. The *Jesuit Relations* comprise reports from 1632-1673 sent back to France by the Jesuit missionaries in New France; they were published annually by Sébastien Cramoisy in Paris. In 1858 the Canadian government reissued the Cramoisy series; in 1896 Reuben Gold Thwaites, secretary of the State Historical Society of Wisconsin, became editor of a project to translate into English not only the *Relations*, but personal letters, memoirs, journals, state and church records. A page-for-page translation was made of the original French, Latin or Italian texts under the title *The Jesuit Relations and Allied Documents*. The project which extended to seventy-three volumes was completed in 1901 and is an invaluable source of information on the beginnings of Canada.

34. G. Goyau, *op. cit.*, p. 26.

35. Thwaites, *op. cit.*, Vol. I, p. 311.

36. *Ibid.*, Vol. II, p. 225.

37. *Ibid.*, Vol. II, p. 77.

38. *Ibid.*, Vol. I, p. 173.

39. *Ibid.*, Vol. II, p. 11.

40. *Ibid.*, Vol. II, p. 13.

41. *Ibid.*, Vol. II, p. 53.

42. *Ibid.*, Vol. II, p. 7.

43. *Ibid.*, Vol. II, p. 97.

44. Quoted by F.-X. Garneau, *History of Canada* (trans. A. Bell, 3rd revised ed.; Toronto and Sydney, N.S.: Belford, 1876), Vol. I, p. 52.

45. Thwaites, *op. cit.*, Vol. II, p. 233.

46. L. Campeau, *op. cit.*, p. 14.

47. *Ibid.*, p. 7.

48. *Ibid.*, p. 27.

49. F. Parkman, *op. cit.*, p. 270.

50. Thwaites, *op. cit.*, Vol. II, p. 233.

51. *Vide supra*, p. 56.

52. *Vide* M. N. Stanard, *The Story of Virginia's First Century* (Philadelphia and London: Lippincott, 1928), p. 26.

53. *Vide* L. G. Tyler, *Narratives of Early Virginia* (New York: Barnes and Noble, 1930), p. 80.

54. Thwaites, *op. cit.*, Vol. II, pp. 251-265.

SIX

The Huronian Experiment

Even before the destruction of Port-Royal French trading interests were concentrating in the St. Lawrence area. Sieur de Monts, who had been frustrated in his Acadian adventure by the cancellation of his charter, had again obtained from King Henry IV new letters patent which granted him a monopoly of the fur trade throughout the country for one year. Champlain then persuaded him to establish a post on the St. Lawrence rather than in Acadia as he thought it would be easier to exercise some restraint on the free traders along a river than to attempt to police the whole Atlantic seaboard; also there were more furs in this area and of a better quality. Consequently, the St. Lawrence Valley became the chief lure for official French efforts to exploit the riches of the New World, and a trading post at Quebec the chief centre for a most ambitious missionary project in the interior of the North American continent.[1]

THE FOUNDING OF QUEBEC

The real architect of the new project was Champlain. As a lieutenant of de Monts he proceeded up the St. Lawrence in 1608 and on July 3 he established a fur-trading post at Quebec. From now on Samuel de Champlain begins to loom large in Canadian history and rightly deserves the title "Father of Canada" since, as one enthusiastic biographer has expressed it, "he is the first Canadian to impose upon his fidelity to the homeland a greater fidelity to Canada."[2] Nor was this fidelity confined simply to a French colony for it included the aboriginal population as well. He had a vision of a Canadian empire made up of French colonists who would mingle and intermarry with civilized Indians and thus create a new people subject to the French king. He did not think that his dream could be made real before the Indians were Christianized. Therefore, a vigorous mission to the Indians was part of his vision.

It was a vision with many obstacles to surmount. The most serious of these was his dependance upon Huguenot merchants to supply the necessary capital for exploration, colonization and missions. These merchants for the most part were primarily interested in the fur trade, only lukewarm about colonization and downright antagonistic to Catholic missions. Champlain was well aware of this antagonism, but there seemed to be nowhere else to turn if his scheme was ever to get started. He was hopeful that he could persuade the Huguenot merchants to become more tolerant if they began to make a good profit out of the fur trade; nor does he seem to have had any antipathy towards their religion, for he was generally in the company of Calvinists while in France. It was from the Huguenot de Monts that he received his lieutenancy and it was from a Huguenot family that he took a wife. It was mostly Calvinist friends who were present at his wedding.[3] Huguenot companionship was apparently more congenial to him than any other, no doubt because of a mutual interest in overseas mercantile adventures. It is possible, as his Christian name Samuel hints, he was baptized a Protestant but there can be no question of the genuineness of his Catholicism in the later years of his life;[4] in point of fact he persuaded his wife to become a Roman Catholic, and after his death she became a nun. He would have preferred to have had Catholic patrons in the New World in order to have received more enthusiastic co-operation in his missionary projects. Bickerings between Calvinists and Catholics were a sore trial to him; and he was in agreement with the prohibition of the exercise of the Reformed religion within the territorial limits of New France, for the sake of internal peace. Huguenots, however, were not easily suppressed and "set the prohibition to naught, roaring their psalmody with such vigour from their ships that the unhallowed strains polluted the Indians on the shore."[5]

More serious for Champlain's project was the unwillingness of Calvinist traders to respect the trade monopolies, granted by the French king, which were intended to provide the necessary revenue for colonization.[6] The success of the projected colony at Quebec depended upon de Monts' making a good profit, but it soon became evident that it was just as difficult to prevent free trading in furs in the St. Lawrence Valley as it had been in the Bay of Fundy area. Consequently a great deal of Champlain's time was wasted travelling to and from France with the object of trying to work out an amicable agreement among the competing merchants. After a first miserable winter at Quebec, during which sixteen of his twenty-eight companions died of scurvy and dysentery,[7] Champlain returned to France to plead with Henry IV to renew de Monts' monopoly; but he pleaded in vain as the pressures against it by other merchants proved too strong for Henry to resist. This time, however, de Monts did not withdraw his support of Quebec as he had of Port-Royal and so Champlain returned to his newly founded post.[8]

Following the assassination of Henry IV in 1612, we find him back in Paris to plead with the regency to come to the aid of the hard-pressed de Monts, but with little better success than formerly. He now reached the conclusion that a French colony would never materialize without the patronage of some illustrious person. He sought out the Comte de Soissons and urged him to take Quebec under his patronage;[9] unfortunately, de Soissons died shortly after assuming the commission, and it was then transferred to Prince Henri de Condé. The latter was a rather unstable person who frequently got into trouble with the ruling authorities. No sooner had he assumed the title of Viceroy of New France than he was carried off to jail.[10]

At this juncture de Monts intervened and used his good offices to effect a compromise of Condé's monopoly with the merchants of Saint-Malo and Rouen in order to get some reality into the new arrangement, which had not been accomplishing anything substantial. Thus was brought into being a Company of Merchants (1614) which made a firm promise to assist in colonizing Quebec. Under this new management Champlain as the lieutenant of the viceroy was to be paid a salary, and one thousand pounds a year was given to Prince Henri to be used by the latter to settle six families a year in the vicinity of Quebec.[11]

RECOLLET MISSIONS

At long last Champlain felt he was in a position to civilize the Indians by bringing them "to the knowledge of God."[12] His next task was to find a suitable religious order to fulfil this laudable purpose. Father Pierre Coton, who was still advising the court on overseas missions, would have liked to have sent back the Jesuits, but this society was very unacceptable to the Company of Merchants who were providing the money for the mission. In his perplexity Champlain turned to Louis Houel, a secretary of the king, for advice; the latter suggested the Recollets as perhaps the most popular order with all classes of people.[13]

The Recollets were the spiritual descendants of the reforming or strict-adherence branch of the Franciscans, and laid great emphasis upon contemplation; but they seemed at the same time to have engaged in many activities. In essence they were a social service order and often associated with causes for the improvement of the working classes, which had made them very popular with the masses.[14] Champlain was aware of their general popularity, for he had known them during his youth in his home town of Brouage; at Houel's suggestion he sought out the Recollets at Brouage and asked if they could provide some missionaries for New France. Two monks volunteered at once for the hazardous mission but found it impossible to get the proper authorization from Rome before the ship to which they were assigned sailed for Quebec, and so they returned downcast to Brouage.[15]

Houel, however, was not easily discouraged: he got in touch with the regional superior of the Recollets, who in turn consulted the bishops of France who were then assembled in Paris to attend the Estates General. The bishops not only approved of the mission, but also gave it financial support. "This first gift for the Church in Canada," writes Abbé Gosselin, "came from the whole of France, represented by the Estates General of 1614, the last that would occur before the one immediately preceding the Revolution."[16] Through the intercession of the bishops a verbal permission for the Recollets to go to New France was secured from the Holy See in the autumn of 1614; the authoritative document did not arrive until March 20, 1618, the official date of the acknowledgment of the Church of Canada by the papacy.[17] Long before these official preliminaries were completed Champlain and four Recollets had reached Quebec (1615) and the mission was immediately under way. At its head was Denis Jamet with Jean Dolbeau as his chief assistant; the two other members were Joseph Le Caron and a lay brother, Pacifique Duplessis.

Father Jamet established his headquarters at Quebec and with the assistance of Brother Duplessis attempted to teach Christianity to the Algonquins in the immediate vicinity. Father Dolbeau was sent to Tadoussac to seek out the Montagnais who, along with the Naskapi, occupied most of the northern section of what is now the Province of Quebec. In a very short time the Recollets came to the same conclusion as had the Jesuits in Acadia:[18] that these migratory bands of Indians were quite unprepared to understand even the most elementary forms of Christianity. It was their opinion that the real cause of their difficulty was the migratory condition of the eastern

Indian; consequently they decided to seek out sedentary Indians in the hope of achieving better results. The obvious choice for such an experiment would have been the Iroquois who dwelt in fairly well organized settlements in the basins of the Genesee and Mohawk rivers. Such a mission was out of the question, however, because of a treaty of alliance against the Iroquois that Champlain had made with Algonquins, Montagnais and Hurons as early as 1603 and which these Indians insisted he should honour when he arrived at Quebec in 1608.[19] No doubt some such treaty was necessary if a colony was to be established in the midst of the Indians around Quebec, but in doing so Champlain had gained for the French settlers and missionaries the hostility of the Iroquois.

Since a mission to the Iroquois, for the time being, was out of the question the Recollets decided to establish one among the sedentary Hurons who dwelt in several large villages between Lake Simcoe and Georgian Bay, almost a thousand miles from Quebec. Father Joseph Le Caron volunteered to make the long and perilous journey to Huronia and thus gained the honour of being the founder of a mission that was to have very important consequences in the early history of French Canada.[20] In the summer of 1615 he arrived at the village of Carhagouha on the Penetanguishene Peninsula of the southern shore of Georgian Bay. Here with the help of the Indians he built a cabin apart from the village and raised an altar on which to offer the mass. With the arrival of Champlain that same year the adventurous father was able to celebrate the first mass in what is now the Province of Ontario. As Francis Parkman has so eloquently phrased it, "a true soldier of the church, had led her forlorn hope into the fastnesses of hell; and now with contented heart he might depart in peace, for he had said the first mass in the country of the Hurons."[21]

Le Caron did not immediately depart: while Champlain went off to his wars the missionary remained in Huronia through the winter and became convinced that the Hurons, with a culture superior to that of the Algonquins and Montagnais, might be more quickly won to Christianity.[22] He also foresaw a great opportunity for the Church of France to win in North America a new Catholic empire which might extend into a far west, the proportions of which he could only dimly surmise. In the spring of 1616 he hastened back to Quebec to urge upon Champlain and his colleagues that a delegation be sent to France to present the great challenge of the West to the proper authorities.

Following a reunion of the missionaries there was convoked what has been described as the first Assembly of Quebec; besides the Recollets there were present also Champlain and six members of the trading post.[23] Certain conclusions were set forth for future strategy: the missionaries, from their experience, actually suggested reversing Champlain's plan for creating a French-Indian empire; instead of Christianizing the Indians as a step in preparing them for assimilation into French culture they held that it would be necessary to make them Frenchmen first and then Christians, and this could be best achieved by mingling French and Indians together, even to the extent of intermarriage. There was, however, one serious drawback to this scheme, namely, the type of Frenchmen that manned the trading posts of New France—their example would do little to improve the morals of the Indians. It was suggested that in the future only people of good moral character should be allowed to come out to Canada. Colonies made up of exemplary people, so thought the Recollets, would attract the Indians away from their nomadic life; they would then settle down among the French, intermarriage would result and thus by degrees the whole Indian population would be led into the Catholic Church.[24]

It was an imaginative scheme with many obstacles in its way, not the least of these being the Company of Merchants. Prominent in the instructions given by the assembly to a committee returning to France was that it should bring to the attention of the court the need to exert great pressure upon the company to fulfil its charter obligations. The committee consisting of Champlain, Jamet and Le Caron returned to France in 1616, but accomplished very little in the way of disciplining the Company of Merchants. They received, however, some encouragement from private benefactors: Charles des Boves, Vicar General of Pontoise, added his name to M. Houel's as a patron of the Church in Canada and provided enough money to allow the Recollets to start to build (June 1620) the Convent of Notre-Dame-des-Anges on the bank of the St. Charles River, not far from Quebec. There they opened up a seminary and a novitiate under the direction of Father Guillaume Galleran.[25]

Interest was again turned to the Huronian mission with the arrival in 1623 of Gabriel Sagard-Théodat who with Nicolas Viel and Le Caron made the long journey to the Huron country and wrote a book which has been valued by anthropologists as a mine of information on the state of Indian culture in the opening years of the seventeenth century.[26] Events, however, were not proceeding well for the Recollets. In 1621 the king had transformed the Company of Merchants into the Montmorency Company with the hope that this reorganization might stimulate more vigorous colonization and missionary activity. With the addition of the de Caëns, because of their great interest in exploration, the new company was now more militantly Protestant than the old one; furthermore, the aborigines for some obscure reason were becoming unusually hostile to the Recollets and had actually drowned one priest, Father Nicolas Viel, along with a young Huronian companion, Ahuntsic, at a place now known as Sault-au-Recollet.[27] Not the least of their problems was the implacable enmity of the Iroquois towards the French settlement at Quebec. The rather exposed Recollet convent was frequently in danger of capture, as were the missionaries themselves; in fact, one of them just escaped being burned alive by the Iroquois and was only saved by being exchanged for several Iroquois prisoners held by the French.

BRIEF RETURN OF THE JESUITS

Because of these unfavourable developments the Recollets came to the conclusion, reluctantly, that they ought to ask the powerful Jesuit society to share in what was now seen as a very difficult and perilous mission. When they consulted Champlain on the matter they found him "very equivocal"[28] and so they decided to do nothing until they had consulted with the Jesuits personally. A direct approach was facilitated by the resignation of the viceroy, Montmorency, to be succeeded by his nephew, Henri de Lévis, Duc de Ventadour, a well known friend of the Jesuits. Father Irénée Piat, who had become superior of the Recollets at Quebec, immediately asked the new viceroy if he might invite the Jesuits back to New France. The question had been put in the presence of de Ventadour's Jesuit confessor, Philibert Noyrot, a most enthusiastic supporter of the American mission. He in turn brought Father Coton, a long-time supporter of Jesuit missions in New France and now the king's confessor, into the discussion. A co-operative mission shared by Jesuit and Recollets was soon worked out and in a very brief time three Jesuit missionaries, Charles Lalemant, Jean de Brébeuf and Enemond Massé were on their way to Canada.[29]

A very disheartening welcome awaited them in Quebec. Their arrival had been preceded by the circulation of a pamphlet entitled *Anti-Coton* denouncing the Society of Jesus and all its works. It had been read with great anxiety by both Catholics and Protestants and there was almost unanimous agreement that the Jesuits could bring nothing but disaster to New France. They were seconded in this opinion by Emery de Caën who was now, during the temporary absence of Champlain, in charge at Quebec. When the Jesuits arrived not one inhabitant would give them a lodging place and they would have had to return to France if the superior of the Recollets had not intervened and offered to crowd them into the Recollet monastery.[30]

In asking the Jesuits to share in their mission the Recollets hoped that the former, through their powerful connections in France, would be able to bring out carefully selected workmen who would help in the work of constructing the necessary buildings for a successful mission. But perhaps even more necessary than construction was the need to make the colony self-sufficient through the cultivation of the soil. There was also the hope that if capable workmen were brought out they might in time be induced to turn to agricultural pursuits. In all this they were not disappointed. Father Noyrot, who seems to have been a very efficient organizer, soon had twenty workmen in Quebec who, in 1626, proceeded to build a Jesuit monastery; they were also persuaded to turn their hands to the cultivation of the soil, and with the arrival of plows and cattle in 1628 everything seemed to be working out as the Recollets had planned.[31]

Only one serious obstacle remained: the Company of Merchants were allergic to agricultural development in the New World and they probably would have brought misionary farming to an end if it had not been for the intervention of the all-powerful Cardinal Richelieu. His sudden interest in the colony was due to the persuasive eloquence of Father Noyrot who, until his untimely death by drowning during a fearful storm on the Cape Breton coast (1629),[32] was the mission's most enthusiastic supporter in every conceivable way. He was able to approach the cardinal personally and inform him of the opposition of the merchants to any serious attempt at colonization, and of their hostile attitude towards the mission. Richelieu thereupon decided to disannul the charter of the Company of Merchants and to found a new company which would be obliged to make colonization and missions a first charge upon its earnings.

There were a few adjustments to be made relating to former charters before the new company could be launched. First of all, it was necessary to compel de Ventadour to resign his viceregal office; then Father Noyrot was delegated to persuade the Marquise de Guercheville to surrender her rights in Acadia in favour of the contemplated company of which Cardinal Richelieu would become the first shareholder. Thus came into being the Company of One Hundred Associates, whose first objective was not commercial, but who actually set forth the conversion of the aborigines as primary. For this reason the king made a munificent grant to the company of "full title in perpetuity to property, justice and *seigneurie* of the whole country of New France." The boundaries of this New France were as startling to New Englanders as those of Virginia had formerly been to the Acadians: "to wit Canada, along all the coasts from Florida to the Arctic."[33] Nor were the east-west boundaries any less surprising, for Canada, according to the new charter, was to extend from Newfoundland to Huronia. Into this vast territory the company promised to bring each year two to three hundred settlers, until they reached to at least four thousand persons.[34]

The very munificence of this charter was bound to create a fierce struggle in the New World, because at about the same time as the king of France was claiming most of North America for his Catholic subjects to roam about in, so King Charles I of England was granting similar grandiose documents to his Protestant subjects whom he would create baronets as soon as they acquired real estate in the New World. Already he had granted a concession of lands in Acadia, or Nova Scotia, as he called it, to Sir William Alexander. During a brief war with France he had issued letters of marque which allowed private persons to prey upon French shipping. A London merchant, Gervase Kirke by name, who long had been closely allied with Huguenot shipping interests at Dieppe, secured one of these letters and proceeded to make an agreement with Alexander to dislodge the French from both the St. Lawrence and the Bay of Fundy areas. They considered the time appropriate, as Kirke was well aware that Huguenot merchants were very bitter about the charter of One Hundred Associates. Through information received from a Huguenot sailor some English ships, under the command of Gervase Kirke's four sons, were able to capture the first ship sent out by the associates to fulfil the obligation of their charter. By this time the war between France and England had come to an end; but before the news reached the Kirke brothers they were laying siege to Quebec and compelled Champlain to surrender Fort Saint-Louis on July 19, 1629.[35]

RESTORATION OF QUEBEC

For three years the Kirkes occupied Quebec, though illegally,[36] for it was only a matter of time till it would be returned to French sovereignty. The terms of the restoration were worked out in the Treaty of Saint-Germain-en-Laye which was signed on March 29,

1632, by representatives of the English and French crowns.[37] During those years Champlain, the Recollets and the Jesuits all waited impatiently in France for the day of restoration when they would be able to fulfil the high hopes that had been quickened by the creation of the Company of One Hundred Associates.

But when the day of return arrived the Recollets were among the missing. Apparently all was not harmonious within the Franciscan family, for Father Joseph Tremblay, a Capuchin monk and administrator of foreign missions, when consulted on the matter advised Richelieu not to send them back to New France; he then suggested that his own order, the Capuchins, should go in their stead. Whether he was animated by some bitter dislike of the Recollets or whether he thought that they had not the resources or influence for prosecuting a successful mission in the New World, the records do not say.[38]

Whatever the reason, it seems clear that the Capuchins themselves did not think that they had the resources for an inland mission and asked to be allowed to confine their activities to Acadia. Richelieu then decided that the Jesuits should be allowed to return to Canada free from any entanglement with any other order as it was his opinion that pioneer communities should have only one religious order in their midst.[39] The intendant of the Company of One Hundred Associates, Jean de Lauson, seems to have had a real animus against the Recollets, for he heartily concurred in Cardinal Richelieu's decision and made it his especial task, in spite of the papal support of the Recollets' demand to return, to keep them out of Canada. It was a cruel blow to the Recollets; their bitter resentment has been recorded by their historian, Le Clercq, who berates the Jesuits for their ingratitude for the kindness that had been shown them by the Recollets when no one in Quebec would provide them with shelter; he even contends that Father Joseph Le Caron, the pioneer missionary to Huronia, died of chagrin when he realized that "he and his brethren" had been "interdicted by a secret conduct."[40]

When the Jesuits got the word to return to New France they did not stop to ask questions but proceeded at once to secure passage to Quebec, and even got there before Champlain. This time their reception was far more pleasant than on their previous arrival. The French who had remained throughout the English occupation had been much troubled by the absence of the sacraments and they rejoiced to hear mass said once again in the house of Mme Hébert, widow of Canada's premier colonist.[41]

With the arrival of Champlain in 1633, accompanied by Fathers Massé and de Brébeuf, it was not long before Quebec began to take on a peculiarly devotional character not usually associated with pioneer colonies. Champlain himself took the lead in developing the ecclesiastical life of New France. One of his first acts on his return to Quebec was to proceed with the erection of a large chapel to be called Notre-Dame-de-la-Recouvrance, in thanksgiving for the restoration of New France to French rule; near it was built a small presbytery where Father Charles Lalemant took up his residence as the parish priest. Under Champlain's direction the whole colony became a school of religion.[42] At Fort Saint-Louis life was lived very much as in a monastery; there was reading during the meals, history in the morning and the lives of the saints at supper. Champlain introduced the old French custom of ringing the church bells three times a day during the recitation of the Angelus. At night every one was invited to the governor's room for prayers said by Champlain himself.

For only a brief period after the restoration was the founder of Quebec spared to enjoy this idyllic sort of life. In October 1635 he was struck by paralysis and died on the following Christmas. Before his death he had been greatly cheered by hearing of the renewal of the mission to Huronia, and of the good prospect for the spread of French civilization to the Far West of Canada. The leading spirit in this new attack upon heathen darkness was Jean de Brébeuf, one of the most daring and saintly characters in the annals of Christian missions.[43]

MISSION TO THE HURONS

Prior to the English occupation of Quebec de Brébeuf had spent three years in Huronia in a little cabin at Toanché and had endeared himself to the Hurons. On his return to Quebec in 1633 he was most anxious to go back to Toanché, but access to Huronia was no longer a simple matter of making a long journey. French fur traders during the British occupation had created a series of incidents that made the Hurons very wary of allowing Frenchmen to settle amongst them. A famous interpreter, Etienne Brûlé, who had been a thorn in de Brébeuf's side during the latter's earlier stay in Huronia, had so provoked the Indians that they had murdered him. Ill-feeling stirred up by this act of lawlessness compelled the abandonment of Toanché as a trading post and the aftermath of this unfortunate event caused a delay of a year before de Brébeuf and his companions could return to Huronia.[44]

The saga of this saint among the Hurons has intrigued a host of researchers, because of the great variety of interests de Brébeuf sustained while, to all intents and purposes, he was cut off from the world. A very close student of his works affirms that his contributions in "the triple domain of history, ethnology and mysticism"[45] are of real merit and account for the large library that has collected around the name of Saint Jean de Brébeuf. His martyrdom also has caught the imagination of poets and novelists and has been hallowed in "a compassionate novel in verse"[46] by Canada's best known English-speaking poet, E. J. Pratt.

From the point of view of *belles lettres* the fifteen years of de Brébeuf and his brethren in Huronia may have been a very productive era, but from the point of view of extending French influence and culture in America these years are the most frustrating and tragic in the annals of French colonization. They began in great anticipation for the future of New France, when de Brébeuf and two fellow missionaries, Antoine Daniel and Ambroise Davost, with the aid of four French workmen set up their headquarters at Ihonatiria, on the southwest corner of Georgian Bay.[47] In 1635 five additional missionaries arrived with the sad news of the death of Champlain; but also with the good news that the new governor was Charles Huault de Montmagny, a strong supporter of Jesuit missions and also well known for his piety. Among the new arrivals was Isaac Jogues, whom de Brébeuf had known in France when he was a young teacher at Rouen. His adventurous and tragic career in Canada became almost as striking as de Brébeuf's. Like de Brébeuf, as a young idealist he had been caught up in the religious enthusiasm of seventeenth-century France, an enthusiasm that never deserted either of these men in New France.[48]

There was need of much religious enthusiasm and also great courage in Huronia, for the Hurons from the first were deeply suspicious of the intentions of the white men in their midst. The persistence of plagues and the outbreak of new diseases brought from Europe often deepened their suspicions to the point of exasperation and murderous intent. It was during those critical moments, when the Indians felt they must slaughter the whites, that de Brébeuf displayed his courage and also his skill in allaying the unreasoning anger of the Indians; because of his ability to dispel Indian suspicions, his brethren were thrown into consternation when they heard that he was to be replaced as leader of the mission by Jérôme Lalemant; the news of the change had been conveyed by Lalemant himself who arrived at Ihonatiria in 1638. It is reported that only de Brébeuf rejoiced over this surprising intelligence which the rest of the company regarded as an unjustified humiliation. The deposed superior did not so regard it for, as he explained, "when any humiliation befell him, he blessed God for it and felt from it an inward joy."[49] Such are the ways of a saint!

After they had recovered from the shock of the sudden change of leadership the missionaries soon recognized that Lalemant was a man worthy of the honour that had been conferred upon him. He was chosen by the authorities in the Jesuit Society because of his proven ability as an administrator with a creative imagination. Huronia was now regarded as one of the most strategic posts in the far flung Jesuit missions in the New World. One of his first imaginative acts was to found a class of lay auxiliaries to help in the work of construction in this distant land where it was so difficult to find suitable workmen and also to secure the proper building materials. These auxiliaries were called *donnés* and they were recruited from among those who wished to serve God in some capacity but hesitated to take irrevocable religious vows. They were bound to the society by a civil contract to work without remuneration; they gave up all their possessions and promised to remain chaste and to obligate themselves to the work in hand by a private vow. The mission agreed, also in a civil contract, to look after their material needs. A good many of the volunteers for this service were craftsmen of considerable skill; but for the most part they were unskilled labourers, not devoid, however, of high idealism. By thus enrolling men dedicated to a religious ideal, it was possible to get rid of the vicious and licentious workmen who by their examples were a continual embarrassment to the missionaries.[50]

Being a systematic administrator the new superior immediately proceeded to compile some statistics about his mission. These turned out to be quite discouraging; a census of the Huron settlements revealed that out of a population of some twenty thousand Hurons there were only fifty Christians! What was even more discouraging was to learn that there had been a rapid decline in population from the estimates given by Champlain and Le Caron when they first visited the area. The diseases brought by the white men, along with the wars so closely associated with the white man's fur trade, were taking a heavy toll of the Huron nation. Strangely, Lalemant did not seem to see it as a man-made disaster; it was his rather harsh judgment that "the climax of their sins is approaching which moves divine justice to exterminate them, as well as several other nations whose remnants have come to take refuge among them."[51] Father Lalemant's theological conclusion would be difficult either to prove or disprove, but he probably believed that the tardiness of the

Hurons in accepting the gospel message was one of the sins that called for the exercise of divine justice; so believing, the superior was determined to save as many of them from the wrath to come as possible by a more vigorous missionary programme.

To speed up the spread of the good tidings he decided to build a central house from which the missionaries could spread out in all directions, but to which they would return from time to time for renewed spiritual strength and for further directions. This strict oversight of the missions from a central house was a reversal of de Brébeuf's policy, which had been to establish a separate house in each village, as opportunity permitted, where a missionary would settle down and become identified with the community in which he served. These two methods were later to become a serious matter of dispute between the first and second bishops of Quebec, the former favouring a centralized direction while the latter preferred that priests should become identified with their parishes.[52]

Sainte-Marie-des-Hurons, as the central house became known, was erected in 1639 on the southern shore of Georgian Bay not far from the present town of Midland. Recent excavations at the site are making it possible for anthropologists to piece together more detailed information about how seventeenth-century Europeans coped with the forces of nature in the midst of a stone-age people. It is estimated that there were sixty or more Frenchmen at Sainte-Marie who had learned to combine their superior technical knowledge with the primitive skills of the Hurons.[53] Thus the Jesuits were bringing about in the heart of the North American continent a synthesis of European and Indian cultures which, if it had not been suddenly and brutally brought to an end, might have given the "Great West" a very different cultural complex from that which prevails today.[54]

At first the new central house was a real stimulus to missionary expansion. From Sainte-Marie the Jesuits moved out among Indian bands who lived south of Lake Simcoe and along the shores of Lake Erie; some of them even reached the Saulteaux, a band spread out along the rapids leading from Lake Huron to Lake Superior; also they made contact with the Potawatomis, who told them about the Sioux, a nation constantly at war with the Crees to the north and the Illinois to the south.[55]

A letter from de Brébeuf to the general of the society (June 1648) reflects the challenge and hope stirred up by these new contacts with the West. The many and varied opportunities for promulgating the gospel in America is the theme of his letter and he assures his general "that the Faith would make great progress in a short time if the extreme dearth of labourers did not hinder our desires and efforts and opportunities."[56] If Sainte-Marie had been allowed to continue, there is little doubt that seventeenth-century France would have provided religious enthusiasts in sufficient number to meet the challenge of the West. But Sainte-Marie did not long survive and this letter to the general was the last optimistic one from de Brébeuf or any of his brethren in Huronia.

TRAGEDY IN HURONIA

The remainder of the story of the Huronian experiment can be told briefly: shortly after de Brébeuf sent off his letter from Sainte-Marie, he was informed that the mission of Saint-Joseph at Teanaostaiaë had been wiped out, its inhabitants slaughtered and among the dead was Father Antoine Daniel. From now on a fatalistic mood prevailed in Huronia; as one student of the experiment has expressed it, "The violent death of Daniel and even the ever recurrent and increasing danger from the Iroquois undoubtedly affected the spiritual life of Jean de Brébeuf and the other missionaries. They felt certain that many of them or all of them would fall victim to these enemies."[57] Accompanying this mood was an anxiety to suffer martyrdom: after hearing that Father Daniel was dead de Brébeuf went into the chapel and "prayed to Antoine rather than for him, and begged God to grant him the same token of love."[58] Similar intercessions were offered up by other missionaries.

Their prayers were only too well answered: de Brébeuf, along with a young colleague, Gabriel Lalemant, fresh from Paris, returned to their missions of Saint-Louis and Saint-Ignace as soon as they heard of the fall of Teanaostaiaë. Both these missions met the same fate as St. Joseph's but the two priests, instead of being immediately killed like Father Daniel, were carried away for prolonged torture. The story of their long agony has been told in awful detail by Father Ragueneau: of how de Brébeuf was compelled to look on while Gabriel Lalemant, the young Parisian, was literally roasted alive, and to listen to his unavailing shrieks to Heaven; de Brébeuf, himself, with a collar of red-hot hatchets around his neck and boiling water poured over his head in mocking baptism, never flinched nor uttered a word. And yet the robust de Brébeuf only survived his torture for four hours, whereas the frail Lalemant endured it for almost seventeen![59]

For a time Sainte-Marie became a haven for Hurons fleeing from the wrath of the Iroquois. Forty Frenchmen who were able to handle muskets drove back the enemy and were able to secure the remains of de Brébeuf and Lalemant, which are still preserved at Quebec as precious relics of two notable Canadian saints. It soon became evident, however, that Sainte-Marie was too exposed to the enemy for a long siege and so the Jesuits decided to build a new Sainte-Marie on the Island of Ahoendoe (Christian Island), or St. Joseph's as the missionaries called it. Even here there was no real security as the Iroquois were now determined to exterminate all the Indians in the area. To add to the general despair came the news that Father Charles Garnier, who had remained south of Lake Huron, had been murdered by an apostate Huron. On Christian Island so many Hurons were dying of starvation and exposure that all hope of survival in this remote retreat was abandoned. Father Ragueneau, now in charge of the mission, had to make the hard decision to abandon the whole Huronian experiment and attempt to return to Quebec. "It was not without tears," he writes, "that we left the country which possessed our hearts and engaged our hopes; and which even now, reddened with the glorious blood of our brethren, promised us a like happiness and opened to us the way to Heaven and the gate of Paradise."[60]

With sixty canoes, the fathers made the long trek back to Quebec with a party of three hundred Hurons and fifty Frenchmen. When they reached the Ottawa they made the alarming discovery that the Algonquins were also being decimated by the Iroquois. This intelligence gave Ragueneau much to think about. He writes: "When I ascended the great River, only thirteen years ago, I had seen it bordered with large numbers of people of the Algonquin tongue. These in the midst of their unbelief, looked upon themselves as the Gods of the earth for the reason that nothing was lacking to them in the richness of their fisheries, their hunting grounds and the traffic they carried on with allied nations. . . . But since they embraced the Faith and adopted the cross of Christ, He has given them a heavy share in this cross and made them a prey to misery, torture and cruel death. In a word they are a people wiped off from the face of the earth."[61] Ragueneau was indeed finding it difficult to justify the ways of God to man.

FRUSTRATION OF "THE GREAT DESIGN"

To the historian unfettered with providential apologetics there is an obvious explanation for the frustration and spoliation of the Jesuit missions. The Hurons and their Algonquin allies were competing with the Iroquois as carriers of furs from the West. The former were the middlemen for the French, whereas the latter were the carriers for Dutch, and later English, merchants. The latter armed their agents better than did the French, and this made it possible for the Iroquois to overpower all their rivals. There are some, however, who have seen a providential purpose in the Iroquois victory. "Liberty," writes Parkman, "may thank the Iroquois that by their insensate fury, the plans of her adversary were brought to nought, and a peril and a woe averted from her future." Parkman had a high opinion of the admirable traits of the Jesuits and their virtues, "which shine amidst the rubbish of error, like diamonds of gold in the gravel of the torrent";[62] what he feared, and thanked the Iroquois for preventing, was that if the Jesuits had succeeded in creating an Indian Catholic state in the western plains, such as they created in Paraguay, absolutism would have prevailed in North America as it has to some extent in South America.

From the point of view of the aborigines this might have been preferable to the way the West was won for liberty, which was usually at the cost not only of the red man's liberty, but of his life.[63] In the Jesuit scheme of things the Indian heritage was to be securely guarded and the Iroquois, if they had co-operated, might well have played an honourable role in the great design of the Regnum Dei that was always part of the goal of these seventeenth-century missionaries. All the available evidence points to the conclusion that the Jesuits wanted to create in Huronia an ideal state, similar to Paraguay. Commercial rivalry between the English and French frustrated their plans at every turn, a rivalry that would ultimately bring French rule to an end in Canada. Before this heavy blow fell, however, they had succeeded in laying the foundation of their concept of the Regnum Dei, not on an aboriginal basis as they had hoped but in a neglected colony of their own compatriots, always pitiably small in number and often forgotten by the Fatherland. They did this so well that French Canada has been able to maintain a way of life considerably different from that of the rest of North America and this, as one of its own apologists has said, "in spite of the fact that we are a small group in continual contact with the most powerful forces of assimilation in modern history."[64] All the credit for this achievement cannot go to the Jesuits; they were compelled to share their work of supervising the spiritual life of Canada (though somewhat reluctantly) with another order, the Sulpicians. This Sulpician intrusion will be the theme of the following chapter.

NOTES TO CHAPTER SIX

1. *Vide* G. Lanctot, *A History of Canada*, Vol. I: *From Its Origins to the Royal Regime, 1663* (trans. J. Hambleton; Toronto and Vancouver: Clarke, Irwin, 1963), pp. 102-14, for an interesting account of the founding of Quebec.
2. M. Bishop, *White Men Came to the St. Lawrence* (Montreal: McGill University Press, 1961), p. 79.
3. *Vide* Samuel de Champlain, *Works* (translated and edited under general editorship of H. P. Biggar, Champlain Society: Toronto, 1922-36), Vol. II. Included in this volume are "Six Contemporary Documents relating to Champlain 1610-1618"; among them (pp. 315-25) is the record of Champlain's wedding, extracted from the *Archives Nationale*, Paris.
4. For a discussion of the possibility of Champlain's being baptized a Protestant *vide* M. Bishop, *Champlain* (New York: Knopf, 1948), pp. 5 and 6.
5. Champlain, *Works, op. cit.*, Vol. V., p. 207.
6. *Vide* E.-M. Faillon, *Histoire de la Colonie française en Canada* (Villemarie: Bibliothèque Paroissiale, 1865-66), Vol. I, p. 121, for an indignant account of the obstacles raised by the merchants to prevent colonization.
7. Champlain, *op. cit.*, Vol. II, p. 59; the ever curious Champlain writes: "I had some of them opened to see if they were affected like those I had seen in the other settlements. The same conditions were found."
8. *Ibid.*, pp. 111-2.
9. Faillon, *op. cit.*, Vol. I, p. 132.
10. Champlain, *op. cit.*, Vol. II, pp. 245-7.
11. Faillon, *op. cit.*, Vol. I, p. 135.
12. Champlain, *op. cit.*, Vol. III, p. 13.
13. Louis Houel assured Champlain "there would be no lack of worthy people who would give them (the Recollets) what they needed." Champlain, *op. cit.*, Vol. III, pp. 17-18.
14. *Vide* Les Franciscans, *Les Frères Mineurs*, (Montreal: Revue du Tiers-Ordre et de la Terre-Sainte, 1915), p. 33.
15. *Vide* Chrestien Le Clercq, *The First Establishment of the Faith in New France* (trans. J. G. Shea; New York: Shea, 1881), Vol. I, p. 71.
16. A.-H. Gosselin, *La Mission du Canada* (Evreux: Imprimerie de l'Eure, 1909), p. 9.
17. *Vide* Le Clercq, *op. cit.*, Vol. I, pp. 74-7, for the Brief of Paul VI.
18. *Ibid.*, Vol. I, pp. 110-2, a detailed description by Le Clercq of the findings of the Jesuits in Acadia, as supporting the Récollet policy.
19. Champlain, *op. cit.*, Vol. II, p. 69 *et seq.*
20. *Vide* Le Clercq, *op. cit.*, Vol. I, pp. 94-7.
21. Francis Parkman, *Pioneers of France in the New World* (5th ed.; Boston: Little, Brown, 1867), p. 369.
22. *Vide* Le Clercq, Vol. I, pp. 105-7.
23. *Vide* A.-H. Gosselin, *op. cit.*, p. 25.
24. *Vide* Le Clercq, *op. cit.*, Vol. I, pp. 109-12.
25. *Ibid.*, Vol. I, p. 145 and p. 175 *et seq.*
26. Gabriel Sagard-Théodat, *The Long Journey to the Country of the Hurons* (trans. H. H. Langton; Toronto: Champlain Society, 1939); G. M. Wrong in an introductory note says, "When the *Grand Voyage* appeared in 1632, it must have been widely read, for a new edition was soon required; this came out in 1636, and for some reason Sagard changed the title to that of *Histoire du Canada*," p. xvii.
27. *Vide* Le Clercq, *op. cit.*, Vol. I, pp. 225-6.
28. *Ibid.*, Vol. I, p. 226.
29. *Ibid.*, Vol. I, p. 229 *et seq.*

30. *Ibid.*, Vol. I, pp. 237-99; *vide* also letter of Father Lalemant to Champlain in R. G. Thwaites, ed., *The Jesuit Relations and Allied Documents* (Cleveland: Burrows, 1896-1901), Vol. IV, p. 171.

31. *Ibid.*, Vol. IV, p. 219 *et seq.*

32. *Vide infra*, p. 111.

33. *Collection de Manuscrits . . . relatifs à la Nouvelle-France* (Quebec: Coté, 1883-85), Vol. I, p. 65.

34. Faillon, *op. cit.*, Vol. I, p. 226 *et seq.*

35. *Ibid.*, Vol. I, p. 244; *vide* also Le Clercq, *op. cit.*, Vol. I, p. 303.

36. As this occupation is closely asociated with a mercantile and religious contest between New France and New England which embraced not only the St. Lawrence Valley but also Acadia, Newfoundland and the New England colonies, it can be better understood within the context of this larger struggle; *vide infra*, Chap. VIII.

37. Treaty of Saint-Germain-en-Laye is included in *Collection de Manuscrits, op. cit.*, Vol. I, pp. 86-92.

38. *Vide* Le Clercq, *op. cit.*, Vol. I, p. 310 *et seq.* for an account of the "unavailing efforts of the Recollets to restore their former mission." Also *vide infra*, pp. 115-17.

39. *Vide* Faillon, *op. cit.*, Vol. I, p. 279.

40. Le Clercq, *op. cit.*, Vol. I, p. 324.

41. The excitement and enthusiasm of this return is well set forth in Le Jeune's famous *Relation* of 1632, the first of the Cramoisy series; Thwaites, *op. cit.*, Vol. V, p. 11 *et seq.*

42. *Ibid.*, Vol. VI, p. 103.

43. *Vide* F.-X. Talbot, S.J., *Saint Among the Hurons* (New York: Doubleday, 1949), *passim*; on p. 149 is recorded the arrival in Huronia of the sad news of Champlain's death.

44. *Ibid.*, pp. 103 *et seq.*

45. René Latourelle, S.J., *Etude sur les écrits de Saint Jean de Brébeuf* (Montreal: L'Immaculée Conception, 1952), Vol. I, p. 7.

46. A. J. M. Smith, ed., *The Oxford Book of Canadian Verse* (Toronto: Oxford University Press, 1960), p. xliii; the poem is printed in part, beginning at p. 142.

47. Thwaites, *op. cit.*, Vol. VI, p. 69.

48. *Vide infra*, p. 94.

49. F.-X. Talbot, *op. cit.*, p. 192.

50. *Ibid.*, p. 193.

51. Thwaites, *op. cit.*, Vol. XIX, p. 127.

52. *Vide infra*, pp. 137 and 161-2.

53. *Vide* Wilfrid and Elsie McLeod Jury, *Sainte-Marie-among-the-Hurons* (Toronto: Oxford University Press, 1954), *passim*.

54. What that cultural complex might have become is set forth by Mason Wade "The Culture of French Canada" in the *Culture of Contemporary Canada*, ed. Julian Park (Toronto: Ryerson Press, 1957), pp. 367-95.

55. *Vide* Thwaites, *op. cit.*, Vol. XX, p. 93 *et seq.*

56. *Ibid.*, Vol. XXXII, p. 59 *et seq.*

57. Quoted by F.-X. Talbot, *op. cit.*, pp. 287-8.

58. *Ibid.*, p. 282.

59. *Vide* Thwaites, *op. cit.*, Vol. XXXIV, *passim*.

60. *Ibid.*, Vol. XXXV, p. 197.

61. *Ibid.*, p. 265.

62. F. Parkman, *The Jesuits in North America* (11th ed.; Boston: Little, Brown, 1878), pp. 446-9.

63. *Vide supra*, Ch. IV, *passim*.

64. Quoted from a *Brief* submitted by the *Federation des Collèges Classiques* to the Royal Commission of Inquiry in Education (Quebec: The Queen's Printer, 1963).

SEVEN

The Sulpician Intrusion

A very different Quebec from that which they had left in 1633 greeted the Huronian missionaries on their return in 1651. True the colony had not made any startling progress in the material realm but in what may roughly be designated the spiritual it had made unusual strides forward, exceeding even the expectations of the Jesuits themselves. What was hardly more, to outward appearance, than a poorly fortified trading centre was indeed pulsating with charitable and religious activities. In the words of Parkman, "Quebec . . . had a seminary, a hospital, and a convent before it had a population."[1] Also it was blessed with an unusually pious governor who by rigid disciplinary methods had made his tiny palatinate a model of sanctity and decorum.

Enthusiasm for this novel experiment in building the kingdom of God here on earth had been communicated to France by the admirably written Jesuit *Relations* with the theme that "the road to Heaven seems shorter and sure from our great forests than from your larger cities."[2] One result of such glowing reports which were widely read in France was to stimulate the desire among the members of several religious orders to be off to New France to share in the creation of the *Regnum Dei*. The most significant achievement of the *Relations* at this time, however, was the emergence in France of a new kind of charitable organization, the Associates of Notre-Dame which ultimately established the Sulpician Order in Montreal, an order that very early challenged the spiritual hegemony of the Jesuits in New France.

ECCLESIASTICAL STRUCTURES

Many of the Huronian refugees who arrived in Quebec in 1651 were nursed back to health in the Hôtel-Dieu which had been erected in 1644. This was just one of the many ecclesiastical structures that

had arisen in Quebec during the Huronian experiment and which
have given New France its proud place as a pioneer in the field of
social welfare.[3] Some of the credit for this early development, in a
field notoriously neglected in the English colonies to the south, must
go to several men of substance who accompanied Governor de Montmagny to New France in 1636. Concerning the governor himself Le
Jeune wrote, "Truly God has favoured us with a man after his own
heart";[4] in an earlier letter he had pointed out that "all the principal
persons of our colony honour Religion; I say with joy and God's
blessing, that those whom his goodness has given command over us
and those also who are coming to establish themselves in these
countries enjoy, cherish and wish to follow the most sincere maxims
of true Christianity."[5]

Such propaganda as this from the facile pen of Le Jeune and
widely disseminated throughout France by the Cramoisy press had
brought large donations of money to New France for the purpose of
erecting schools, hospitals and churches. The Marquis de Gamache
gave sixteen thousand crowns to found a college at Quebec which
was opened for students in 1635, a year before, as Parkman observes,
the building of Harvard College in New England.[6] With a further gift
from an anonymous donor the Jesuits also erected a small seminary
at Notre-Dame-des-Anges for Indian boys. Another generous patron,
Noël Brulart de Sillery, contributed thirty thousand livres towards
providing a special mission to the Montagnais Indians: thus emerged,
about six miles from Quebec, the Sillery settlement (1638), with a
chapel, hospital and fort. Still another anonymous donor made it
possible to build a mission house at Trois-Rivières (1640), where
Algonquin converts were particularly welcomed. From the same
source came enough money to build a similar house at Tadoussac
where Father Vimont organized a mission in 1641.[7]

The most exciting of all these building projects was the erection of
the Hôtel-Dieu at Quebec, which came about through the initiative
of the Duchesse d'Aiguillon, the niece of Cardinal Richelieu. The
duchess had been reading Le Jeune's Relation of 1635 in which he
had made a passionate plea for financial assistance for some brave
"Amazons" who had indicated their willingness to go to New France
to care for the sick. With the collaboration of her spiritual adviser,
who was none other than Vincent de Paul, she undertook to see that
these women[8] (whom Le Jeune had endowed with the courage of the
female warriors of ancient Scythia but who were in fact Sisters of
Mercy at Dieppe) were provided with suitable accommodations at
Quebec. A contract for the establishment of the hospital was signed

by the duchess in Paris (1637) and the sisters, who were also known as the Augustine Hospitalières, were represented at the signing by Sébastien Cramoisy, the famous printer of the Jesuit *Relations*. A capital of 22,400 *livres* was set aside for the hospital and in due course (1644) the sisters were able to move into the Hôtel-Dieu erected on the site which it has occupied down to the present day.[9] Scarcely less exciting than the establishment of the Hôtel-Dieu was the erection of the first Ursuline convent in Quebec (1642). This was made possible by another wealthy widow, Madame de La Peltrie, who also had been reading the Jesuit *Relations* and had also come under the spiritual direction of Vincent de Paul.[10]

URSULINES AND AUGUSTINES

Long before these physical structures were completed nurses and teachers had been braving the perils of the turbulent Atlantic to begin their civilizing work in the New World. These early female arrivals added much to the colour of Quebec's social and religious life and provided it with a new spiritual dimension. The most colourful of these pioneer women was Marie Guyart, *dite* de l'Incarnation, whom the Abbé de Salèsmes has boldly proclaimed as "one of the most engaging and noble figures of the seventeenth century."[11] Father de Charlevoix is equally emphatic, ranking her as the most spiritual woman of his century.[12] Her ecstatic experiences have long fascinated students of mysticism.[13] The Abbé Casgrain credits her with a hidden source of illumination that gave her a unique knowledge of Scriptures, which he describes as a celestial nourishment that "kept her joyful even to her death."[14]

Combined with her mysticism was a very practical good sense that served her well in the business world before she became a religious. Upon the insistence of her parents she had married at an early age but soon found herself a widow with an infant son to provide for. As Mme Martin (her widowed name) she became a shrewd merchant, but her mercantile success was not enough to still the call to the religious life. We are told by those who knew her intimately that she had a strong maternal instinct; but even this was not strong enough to blunt her religious vocation and so at last she resolved to entrust her son to the care of a monastery while she herself took vows at the Ursuline convent at Tours, a city famous for its saints and its religious.[15]

The Ursuline order was an inevitable choice for Mme Martin. Founded by the high-spirited Angela Merici, the order had been constantly pioneering in new fields of religious endeavour. Its adventurous history had long appealed to Mme Martin whose sense of vocation was coupled with a desire to do something new and unusual for God.[16]

A chance meeting with Mme de La Peltrie opened the way to an unusual adventure. For some years Mme de La Peltrie had longed to devote herself entirely to some great religious project, but had been frustrated by her parents. Like Marie de l'Incarnation she had been compelled by her father to marry. The marriage seems to have been a happy one, and for a time she was prominent in social life. After five years of marriage, however, her husband died and the old desire to serve God in a distinct way returned. She was now an heiress of considerable wealth and began to plan how she could use her inheritance for some noble cause. She did not as some of her biographers have implied wish to become a nun, for as has been pointed out in a penetrating study of Marie de l'Incarnation Mme de La Peltrie "coveted independence" whereas Marie de l'Incarnation "coveted subjection."[17] Le Jeune who greatly admired the latter's stability found Mme de La Peltrie's zeal a little impetuous. These contrasts of temperament do not seem to have been any bar to a remarkable and enduring friendship, although Marie de l'Incarnation's loyalty to the foundress of her convent was severely tested at times.

As has already been observed Mme de La Peltrie's interest in Quebec had been aroused by reading Le Jeune's *Relation* of 1635 with its plea "for some brave Lady . . . who will give a Passport to these Amazons of the great God . . . and endow them with a house in which to praise and serve his divine Majesty."[18] After consultation with Vincent de Paul she resolved to help the Ursulines to build a convent in Quebec. There were, however, some serious obstacles to be hurdled before she could make her dream come true; the most serious of these was her father's insistence that she remarry before being entrusted with the responsibility of administering her inheritance. She did not wish to remarry but succeeded in overcoming her father's scruple by going through a mock marriage with an unusually accommodating M. de Bernières, or as one kindly commentator has said she "took refuge in the age-old sanctuary of bullied women, deceit."[19] Her inheritance now at her own disposal, she proceeded to Tours where it was agreed that Marie de l'Incarnation should become the mother superior of the contemplated convent in Quebec, with Cécile de Sainte-Croix and Marie de Saint-Joseph as her assistants.

In May 1639 Mme de La Peltrie and the three Ursulines embarked from Dieppe for New France; accompanying them was Father

Barthélemy Vimont, who was being sent out by the Jesuits to replace Le Jeune as superior at Quebec. On the same ship were the Augustine Hospitalières from Dieppe, who were sailing to Quebec to take charge of the hospital that was being built through the generosity of the Duchesse d'Aiguillon. They proudly proclaimed themselves Le Jeune's "Amazons," and they were in their own particular sphere just as noteworthy pioneers in Canada as the Ursulines.[20] The mother superior, Marie Guenet, *dite* de Saint-Ignace, and her two companions, Anne Le Cointre, *dite* de Saint-Bernard, and Marie Forestier, *dite* de Saint-Bonaventure, have rightly won a niche in the temple of fame for establishing a French-Canadian nursing tradition that gave French Canada a unique reputation for humane treatment of the sick and infirm. A foretaste of the dimension that was to be added to the religious and social life of Quebec became evident on the ship that bore these women to New France. During the crossing the sisters observed the rules of their respective orders as far as circumstance permitted and recited their offices as in a choir, "the Augustines on one side, the Ursulines on the other."[21]

When they reached Quebec they were greeted with a cannon salute; and on debarkation they were cordially welcomed by the very pious governor. After hearing mass they were conducted by the Jesuits to the new settlement of Sillery where accommodations for women were far better than at Quebec; here they stayed until their respective buildings were completed.

Building operations were now in full swing and this had brought out many workmen from France and slowly the mission-fort on the heights of Quebec began to look like a capital city of a thriving community; at last it appeared that Champlain's dream of a new nation consisting of French and Indians intermingling and intermarrying freely was to become a reality. A spirit of optimism was taking hold of all concerned. It had been greatly increased with the arrival of the nursing and teaching sisters and was indeed manifest in the rapturous joy with which the colony greeted the birth of the king's son in 1639. This consisted of a general celebration with cannon booming and fireworks shooting "up towards heaven"; particularly were the settlers charmed "to hear two Choirs of Virgins praising the Greatness of God in this new world."[22]

Unfortunately, the mood of optimism was short-lived, to be replaced at times by a mood bordering on despair. There were good and sufficient reasons for despair: the loss of Huronia, the increasing menace of the Iroquois and the establishment in 1642 of what was to become a competitive colony at Montreal brought consternation to

Quebec and turned it into a small world of fears and tensions. Much of this was due to bad political management both in old France and new, all of which is reflected in the innumerable letters written by the politically alert Marie de l'Incarnation, who frankly admits she is puzzled at the strange ways of God with New France, but keeps on hoping that "the arrival of the vessels will give to us a new instruction and perhaps a new courage to work harder than ever in the serving of our master."[23]

DIRECTION OF POLICY

Constitutional development in New France is not the most happy aspect of its history. From the death of Champlain until the establishment of royal government in 1663 political experiments were under the close supervision of the Jesuits, in whom Governor de Montmagny had complete confidence. The ultimate source of authority, however, lay with the One Hundred Associates.[24] Unfortunately this chartered company was dominated by a very devious and covetous intendant, Jean de Lauson, who strangely enough was greatly admired by the Jesuits. Because of the failure of the company to follow any consistent line of policy, some of the leading colonists decided to take upon themselves the task of governing the colony. Thus came into being in 1645 the community of Habitants who assumed the trading monopoly of the One Hundred Associates. The governor now became responsible to an appointed council consisting of three Quebec merchants; three years later the council was reorganized to include the governor, an ex-governor, the superior of the Jesuits, two inhabitants of Quebec and three syndics.[25]

In this reorganization the Jesuits were again exercising considerable direction of policy, but at the same time they were coming in for some pretty harsh criticism. This was due to the fact that they were loath to support aggressive military action against the Iroquois, who were making it almost impossible for the community of Habitants to collect furs from friendly Indian traders—and furs were the very lifeblood of the colony.

For a brief moment it had seemed that the Iroquois menace had been contained when the Duchesse d'Aiguillon persuaded her uncle, Cardinal Richelieu, to send out forty soldiers for the defence of New France. The soldiers had constructed a fort named Richelieu about halfway between Quebec and the new colony on the Island of Montreal, but such a sparsely manned fort did little to bring to an end the

Iroquois raids. The Jesuits then advised the governor to try to negotiate a firm peace with the enemy and suggested that Father Isaac Jogues try his hand in arranging the terms of peace.[26] This dedicated priest, who had formerly been fearfully tortured by the Iroquois and whose life had only been saved by the friendly aid of a Dutch trader at Orange (now Albany), was sent again into Iroquois territory on a most perilous journey. For a time it appeared as if his mission would succeed and that the Mohawk valley would compensate for the loss of Huronia; but all these high hopes were shattered when Father Jogues was suddenly struck down by an unfriendly Mohawk in the cabin of a chieftain, bringing to an untimely end as Parkman says, "one of the purest examples of Roman Catholic virtue which this western continent has seen."[27]

It also meant a discrediting of Montmagny's peace policy and so undermined his prestige that he felt compelled to resign as governor. He returned to France in 1648 and was replaced by one of the recent settlers on the Island of Montreal, Louis d'Ailleboust. This seems to have been an unusual appointment but d'Ailleboust had brought out his wife from France with the intention of making Canada his permanent home and he was determined at all costs to make New France a viable state, as were the Jesuits who now gave the new governor very loyal support and even encouraged him in firm action against the Iroquois. So dedicated were they to the new policy that they eagerly acquiesced in an attempt to form an alliance with the heretical New England colonies.[28]

The initiative for such an alliance came from the New Englanders themselves, which seems very surprising in view of their distaste for the Roman Catholic Church. But very early in their history the Puritan colonists became devoted to trade and commerce and they were unwilling to allow any ideological differences to come between them and a profitable bargain. Once again a Jesuit priest, Gabriel Druillettes, was chosen by the council of Quebec to conduct the delicate negotiations with the heretics. As a missionary to the Abenaki Druillettes had already met some of the leading New England colonists and had established friendly relations with them; nevertheless, the choice of a Jesuit seemed a bit injudicious, for the Massachusetts legislature had decreed that any Jesuit who ventured into the colony should be hanged. Father Druillettes, however, received a very cordial welcome or, as Parkman so picturesquely expresses it, "Massachusetts, in the person of her magistrate became the gracious host of one of those whom next to the Devil and an Anglican bishop she most abhorred."[29]

An interesting interlude in these negotiations was a visit by Druillettes to the home of the famous New England missionary to the
Indians, John Eliot. At Roxbury, Massachusetts, the two missionaries discussed a common problem—how to convert the Indians to
Christianity. Despite the courtesy and the good will shown by both
parties the negotiations broke down, for the New Englanders were
really only interested in a commercial treaty, whereas the French
were primarily concerned with a defensive alliance against the Iroquois, without which they would have little to trade.[30]

Shortly after the break-down of these negotiations d'Ailleboust's
three-year term as governor came to an end (1651) and he was
replaced by Jean de Lauson. For some inexplicable reason the Jesuits
remained blind to de Lauson's very evident deficiencies. Their joy at
his appointment was extravagantly expressed by Father Ragueneau
as follows: "But at last the fleet brought us Monsieur de Lauson, our
new governor, and in his person the desires, the hopes and the joy
of New France; in an instant the whole country assumed a new
aspect. . . ."[31] Joy was to be short-lived, for the new governor's first
concern was to enrich both himself and his relatives at the expense
of the settlers; and this at a time when the colony was becoming
more and more the hapless prey of marauding Iroquois.

A series of disasters were creating an atmosphere of panic in New
France. A very depressing event was the murder of a long-time
missionary among the Algonquins, Father Buteux, along with two
companions while they were travelling along the Saint-Maurice. This
was followed by a brutal massacre (1652) of settlers at Trois-
Rivières. Many of the colonists fled to Gaspé in the hope of finding a
fishing vessel that would take them to France, or at least carry them
beyond the reach of the pitiless Iroquois.[32]

In the midst of this deepening gloom the Iroquois of the Genesee
Valley made an offer of peace and the Jesuits immediately reverted
to their earlier policy of winning over the Iroquois to permanent
peace with the French; at once they began to plan a bold missionary
endeavour in the Genesee Valley, still hoping to redeem the Huronian
disaster. A new "grand design," as Marie de l'Incarnation called it,
took shape: Father Simon Le Moyne was sent into the heart of the
Iroquois country; and arrangements were made to establish a French
colony near Lake Gannentahwa on the Oswego River, under the
military leadership of Sieur Dupuy. Again the treachery of the
Iroquois brought this latest grand design to an ignominious end. The
only consolation in the whole affair was the escape of the colonists
from a trap that had been set for them by the Iroquois through the

skilful leadership of Dupuy; his retreat at the head of fifty-three Frenchmen along an almost frozen river has been compared by one enthusiastic historian to the "retreat of the ten thousand."[33]

The policy of appeasement had now become most unpopular with the settlers at Quebec and they succeeded at last in conveying to the king's council in France their lack of confidence in Governor de Lauson and his Jesuit advisers. As a result of these complaints de Lauson was asked to resign, and in 1657 a general reorganization of the council was carried out which has been described as a landmark in the history of New France. It came close to establishing a form of popular representation, for the council now included four councillors elected for two years by free suffrage: two councillors from Quebec and one each from Montreal and Trois-Rivières. The Jesuits at their own request were exempted from attending the newly organized council, for they realized that Ragueneau had seriously compromised the good name of his order by his too intimate association with the discredited de Lauson, and had as superior "immersed himself too much in civil and administrative affairs."[34]

Such a withdrawal from the administrative life of the colony no doubt was made reluctantly, for the *Regnum Dei* which they had planned with such high hopes was now being taken over by the seigneurs of Quebec whose missionary zeal was subordinate to their interest in profits from the fur trade. At this low point in their fortunes they found their spiritual hegemony being challenged by the Sulpicians of Montreal, an upstart order which the Jesuits to some extent helped to foster and establish in the New World.

ASSOCIATES OF NOTRE-DAME

Montreal, or Ville-Marie as the new colony was first called, arose out of the same kind of religious ferment as had shaped the ecclesiastical life of Quebec, but with a difference, due to what has been designated "Berullian piety."[35] The two men most responsible for the colonization of Montreal with a definite religious purpose were Jean-Jacques Olier and Jérôme de La Dauversière; neither of them ever saw this colony which arose out of their mystic impulse, and it is difficult to say which of them played the more significant role in the pioneer days of Canada's premier city. Prior honour should perhaps be given to Olier, who is most responsible for the extension to Montreal of the Berullian piety which gave to the new colony a more relaxed way of life than the vigorously disciplined sort of behaviour that the Jesuits enforced upon Quebec. La Dauversière's contribution was more in the field of organization. Both men, however, and the associates they gathered around them were "fond of ceremonies and images mystic even to the vision,"[36] and these cannot be eliminated from any history of Montreal.

It was in the midst of founding a seminary for training priests as Pierre de Bérulle would have trained them that Father Olier received a summons by way of a vision to assist in the establishment of a colony on the Island of Montreal.[37] Shortly afterwards La Dauversière came to Paris to confirm the summons and from then on the two men became inseparably associated with the Montreal project. La Dauversière had already begun to plan for the welfare of the projected colony by founding in his native city, La Flèche (1636), the institute of the Sisters of St. Joseph, which he hoped would one day extend its work to Montreal. According to his biographer it was La Dauversière who formed the original design for Ville-Marie, "marked out the plan and took all steps for its erection" and "followed all its activities during the first ten years."[38] He began by persuading several people of wealth and distinction to join with him in forming a company to be known as the Associates of Notre-Dame; the objective of the company was to found a colony in North America whose chief purpose would be the conversion of the aborigines to Christianity.

One of his early companions in this adventure was Baron de Fancamp, a wealthy nobleman who accompanied him on a momentous trip to Paris to consult with Father Olier to win his support for the plan they had in mind. When the latter first set eyes on La Dauversière at the home of a mutual friend he is reported to have said, without any formal introduction, "I know what you want and I am going to pray to God for it at the holy altar." After saying mass Father Olier gave the surprised La Dauversière one hundred *pistoles* saying, "Take this to begin the work of God."[39] In so doing Father Olier became the first contributor to the Associates of Notre-Dame.

During the preliminary stages of the founding of the new colony the Jesuits were most helpful; it was they who secured the Island of Montreal for the associates from the greedy de Lauson. Charles Lalemant who conducted this delicate transaction also secured a military governor for the projected colony and made a most wise choice in the person of Paul de Chomedey, Sieur de Maisonneuve, who had been engaged in warfare from the age of thirteen. Maisonneuve was not the usual type of military man one might have expected from his long apprenticeship in warfare, for he had been able to retain "a strong and ardent faith and an innocence of the licence of the camp."[40] What was perhaps even more gratifying to the associates was that he had kept his Catholicism intact in the midst of a Calvinist environment.

It was still necessary to secure other key personnel if the various activities that the associates contemplated at Ville-Marie were to be properly carried out. These had been set forth in a famous document that had been drawn up before any of the settlers had left for New France: a seminary for training boys and preparing priests for missionary work, a convent for teaching Indian girls and a Hôtel-Dieu for the sick and infirm.[41] It was agreed that the seminary would have to be deferred until Father Olier had trained some priests at Saint-Sulpice for seminary work; in the meantime the Jesuits would look after the spiritual needs of the colonists.

There was no immediate possibility of securing an acceptable leader to found a school for girls, but among the externals of the Sisters of Notre-Dame at Troyes was a young lady by the name of Marguerite Bourgeoys who was anxious to undertake such a project but who had had difficulty in getting admitted to any religious order. For some reason, never disclosed, the superior of the Carmelites had turned her down as had also the Poor Clares, so she had to be content with presiding over the eastern congregation of the Sisters of Notre-Dame at Troyes, a position she assumed in 1640. Here she had the good fortune to come under the instruction of Sister Superior Louise de Maisonneuve, a sister of the future governor of Montreal, and it was this happy combination of circumstances that finally made it possible for her to reach Ville-Marie in 1653.[42]

Although the school for girls could, like the seminary, be deferred for awhile, it was not so feasible to leave the colony without any health service. The Sisters of St. Joseph at La Flèche were not yet sufficiently trained for their designated role, so the associates began to look around for "a girl or woman of character sufficiently heroic and of determination sufficiently masculine"[43] to accompany the first contingent to Canada to look after the sick and, as they fully expected, the wounded. Almost miraculously such a lady appeared in the person of Jeanne Mance, a native of the ancient and picturesque city of Langres who had reached the mature age of thirty-five. From childhood she had longed for an opportunity to consecrate her life to God through service to the sick and infirm; latterly, she had heard mystic voices urging her to go to New France and volunteer her services there. Through the good offices of Charles Lalement she was introduced to La Dauversière who immediately recognized that she was the woman that the associates had been praying for; his judgment did not fail him for the "Angel of the Colony,"[44] as she has been called, was second to none in the field of nursing and social work.

With the arrival of a nurse it was now possible for Governor Maisonneuve with a party of about twenty-five men in one ship and Mlle Mance with twelve men in another to proceed to the Island of Montreal. Meanwhile the associates, who numbered about forty-five members, assembled in the church of Notre-Dame in Paris and solemnly dedicated their prospective seigneurie to the Holy Family; more specifically: the seminary to Christ, the Hôtel-Dieu to St. Joseph and the school to the Virgin Mary.[45]

THE FOUNDING OF MONTREAL

All did not proceed as planned for the pioneers of this dedicated colony; for many years it was questionable whether they could survive the vicissitudes of the New World. They were not received with any enthusiasm in Quebec; apart from Mme de La Peltrie, who immediately "fell in love with the young lady from France [Jeanne Mance] and became a partisan of the Montreal contingent,"[46] there was a distinct coolness towards what was quickly dubbed "The Foolish Enterprise."[47] Governor Montmagny tried hard to persuade the party not to go to Montreal which, as he pointed out, was dangerously exposed to attacks by the Iroquois; in place of the Island of Montreal he offered Maisonneuve the Island of Orleans as a much more secure place for settlement. To this suggestion Maisonneuve gave a ringing reply: "Sir, what you tell me would be excellent if I had been sent to look about and select a place. But as it has been decided by the Company who sent me that I should go to Montreal, my honour obliges me to go there and found a colony, were every tree on the island changed into an Iroquois, and you will, I am sure approve my decision."[48] Montmagny was so impressed with this spirited reply that he at once volunteered to make a preliminary survey of the Island that very autumn, in preparation for permanent settlement the following spring. To this Maisonneuve agreed and so the party spent its first winter at Quebec.

With the arrival of spring (1642) Montmagny guided the colonists up the St. Lawrence to the longed-for island. Accompanying the party was Mme de La Peltrie who was deserting Quebec for this new adventure in colonization, much to the chagrin of Marie de l'Incarnation. The latter wrote a crisp letter to a friend in France complaining that "our good foundress who had with heroic gener-osity brought us to Canada" has now joined "the persons who came here last year to establish a colony in Montreal."[49] What was par-ticularly annoying was the fact that the fickle foundress had taken with her many things that she had formerly given to the church in Quebec. Ultimately, Mme de La Peltrie returned to Quebec and she and Marie de l'Incarnation became reconciled and remained firm friends to the end of their lives. Father Vimont also accompanied the party and won the honour of saying the first mass and preaching the first sermon in Montreal. He then assigned two Jesuits to remain with the settlers until Father Olier should have trained some priests to replace them.[50]

It was soon realized by all concerned that the Iroquois menace was real enough; hardly had the settlers got to their destination than two workmen who wandered from the stockade were immediately slaughtered. With the Iroquois forever lurking outside the crowded fort that had been hurriedly constructed there was little that could be done towards erecting the buildings that were necessary if Ville-Marie was to become the great missionary outpost that had been visualized for it by its founders. Impatience on the part of the settlers at last compelled Maisonneuve, against his better judgment, to lead a small force of thirty men against some two hundred Iro-quois. The battle did not go well for the French who soon ran out of ammunition and had to retreat with some losses from an area which has since been known as Place d'Armes.[51]

Considerable relief was afforded the beleaguered colony when Sieur de La Barre arrived in 1643 with additional settlers and a large sum of money from a so-called anonymous donor, Mme de Bullion, to be used to build a hospital. With this assistance a hospital was finally erected as a first step in carrying out the objectives of the associates. Ironically enough it was kept full to capacity by the cruel depredations of the Iroquois, who at the same time prevented any further large-scale construction.

Along with this frustration came news from France that the Asso-ciates of Notre-Dame were disintegrating. At this juncture the indom-itable Jeanne Mance returned to France (1648) and took part in a general reorganization of the company which saved it from breaking up; she also persuaded her patroness, Mme de Bullion, to put at the disposal of Governor Maisonneuve some twenty thousand *livres* that the former had donated for the upkeep of the hospital, to be used to raise an adequate army to beat back the Iroquois from Montreal.[52] On her return Jeanne Mance before handing over the money to Maisonneuve secured from him a hundred *arpents* of land which provided a future revenue for the hospital. The governor then proceeded to France where he recruited an army of one hundred men and brought them to Montreal in 1653. Along with the army the governor also brought out Marguerite Bourgeoys, whom he described as "a person of good sense . . . who will be a powerful aid to Montreal."[53] The young lady fully vindicated Maisonneuve's high opinion of her, for immediately upon her arrival she embarked upon her great educational adventure in a dilapidated house that had been abandoned by one of the settlers. Thus she inaugurated the justly renowned Congregation of the Sisters of Notre-Dame in Montreal which along with many other deeds of charity on the part of its founder won for Marguerite Bourgeoys the honour of beatitude.[54]

All that was now needed to fulfil the triune dedication to the Holy Family was the Seminary of Saint-Sulpice. In 1657 Maisonneuve and Jeanne Mance decided that the time had come to remind Father Olier rather forcibly of his promise to set up in Montreal a branch of the Sulpician Order. There was need for haste, for Father Olier was "all weighed down and close to death . . . through his mortifyings of the flesh and his vigorous austerities."[55] The reminder was conveyed to him just in time, for it was shortly before his death that he despatched to Montreal three priests: Gabriel de Queylus, whom he named superior, Gabriel Souart, Dominique Galinier, and a deacon, Antoine d'Allet.

It seemed as if Montreal was now ready to enter upon its assigned tasks, nevertheless, there were still many obstacles to be overcome before it would become a smoothly functioning missionary outpost in the New World. As we shall see, the seminary was to have very rough sailing for a time; the school was seriously understaffed, and the hospital was on the verge of collapse because Jeanne Mance had broken her arm and for some unknown reason the break refused to mend properly. Finally she decided she must return to France to seek better medical treatment and also to bring out some nursing sisters from La Flèche to help her in the always over-crowded hospital. Leaving the hospital in the temporary care of two nursing sisters from Quebec she and Marguerite Bourgeoys sailed for France in 1657. Shortly after her arrival there she went to view the remains of Father Olier and while praying at his bier her arm was suddenly healed.[56] She then proceeded to La Flèche where she enrolled three sisters for her hospital. Meanwhile, Marguerite Bourgeoys had not been idle for she had persuaded thirty-two young women to volunteer to come to New France, some of them to help her in her school and others to add to the distaff side of the colony, which had a surplus of males.[57]

They all arrived in Montreal in 1659, only to find that despite Maisonneuve's army the colony was still in mortal danger from Iroquois attacks. This danger, however, was greatly lessened when Dollard des Ormeaux and a few followers made a daring stand at Long Sault (1660) at the cost of their lives. It was indeed a heroic exploit, but many of the details as recorded by Abbé Faillon have been called in question. There seems little doubt that Dollard and his companions did not deliberately resolve to make a supreme sacrifice of themselvs but, as a recent historian of French Canada has observed, "All contemporaries are agreed that the defence put up there [Long Sault] had saved the colony from the most dangerous invasion that had yet threatened it."[58]

CONTROVERSY: SULPICIANS AND JESUITS

During these perilous days an acrimonious controversy suddenly erupted between the Sulpicians and the Jesuits. It is difficult to assess the blame for this unseemly quarrel: its origin precedes the arrival of the Sulpicians in New France and was closely associated with a most sensitive issue in French national life, namely Gallicanism. For some time the Jesuits had grown cool towards the Associates of Notre-Dame, suspecting that the latter wished to introduce Gallican privileges into New France. The suspicion arose because the associates as early as 1646 had been agitating for the appointment of a bishop at Quebec, and this the Jesuits believed entailed the importation into the colony of the same kind of subordination of the church to the state as prevailed in France. If such were the case then there would be little hope of creating a church-dominated society in New France such as the Jesuits had achieved in Paraguay. In their opposition to a bishop they had the firm support of Marie de l'Incarnation who was of the opinion "that God does not wish a bishop in this country which is not yet well enough established."[59] This observation on the part of the Mother Superior of the Ursulines indicates that the subject of a bishop was becoming a topic of heated debate in the Quebec community.

In spite of these doubts and hesitations among the religious, the Associates of Montreal kept urging the authorities in France to establish an episcopate at Quebec and they succeeded in getting the French clergy who were meeting in Paris in 1657 to support their plea, even to the extent of recommending the superior designate of the Montreal Sulpicians for the office.[60] To the Jesuits this was a shocking suggestion, but by this time they realized that an episcopal appointment was inevitable and that they must now move quickly to find a candidate more in sympathy with their ultramontane views than was de Queylus.

It was not only the importunities of the Montreal Associates but also the serious jurisdictional problems that had arisen in New France that had brought the Jesuits around to the acceptance of a bishop. When they had first gone to New France they assumed that they had adequate authority to perform sacramental acts of a civil nature through the authorization of the general of their order. Priests, however, coming to Canada, belonging to no order, could not make any such assumption; consequently, they sought for authorization to perform sacraments from the Archbishop of Rouen just before sailing for New France. This practice led the archbishop, Mgr de Harlay de Champvallon, to claim complete jurisdiction over the colony until such time as it acquired a bishop, a claim that the Jesuits were very loath to concede, as the archbishop was strong for Gallican rights.[61] Rather than leave any doubts in the mind of the community concerning the validity of their sacramental acts they decided to ask the archbishop to make the Jesuit superior at Quebec his grand vicar, a request which was granted in 1649.[62]

This amicable arrangement had prevailed until 1657 when Abbé de Queylus on his way to his new post at Montreal called on Mgr de Harlay and asked for jurisdictional authority over Ville-Marie; he not only received it but he also was made a grand vicar of New France. On his arrival at Quebec de Queylus compared his jurisdictional authority with the Jesuit superior and it appeared that they had equal authority; but as the Sulpician superior held the more recent letter, the Jesuit superior, de Quen, agreed that de Queylus should be regarded as the ecclesiastical head of New France. If the latter had shown a little tact as this time all might have been well, but tact was not de Queylus' strong point and he immediately began to act as if he was the bishop of New France with little regard for the feelings of de Quen.[63]

His first administrative act was to confirm Father Poncet in his office as curé of Quebec, and when he arrived in Montreal he made Abbé Souart the curé of the parish of Ville-Marie, replacing the Jesuit Father Pijart.[64] The Jesuit superior appears to have taken this exercise of power on the part of a rival grand vicar good naturedly, expecting to be reconfirmed as the ecclesiastical head of the colony when new letters arrived from France; but he finally exploded when

Father Poncet without consulting him published a bull of indulgence on the occasion of the papal jubilee of 1657. When de Quen protested Father Poncet replied that he had been authorized to do so by Abbé de Queylus before the latter had left for Montreal. The upshot of this defiance of his father superior was that Poncet was relieved of his duties as curé and banished to a western mission. On his way to his mission, however, Poncet stopped in Montreal to inform de Queylus of his abrupt dismissal from his parish; the latter regarded de Quen's action as a personal affront and hurriedly returned to Quebec and warned the Jesuits that they must cease interfering with parochial matters, which were strictly his responsibility as ecclesiastical head of New France.

As in all small pioneer communities a feud of this nature created great excitement and everyone in Quebec became anxious to play some role in the drama; Mme d'Ailleboust, the wife of the acting governor, apparently got caught up in the excitement and added fuel to the fire by passing on to de Queylus some bits of gossip she heard about the Jesuits who, so the story goes, were saying unkind things about the Sulpician superior. The alleged remarks so infuriated the abbé that he proceeded to denounce the Jesuits from the pulpit as Pharisees.[65] When the report of this unseemly quarrel finally reached the Archbishop of Rouen he moved to bring it to an end by reaffirming both de Queylus and de Quen as grand vicars but stipulating that the former must confine his jurisdiction to Montreal. Thus prevailed an uneasy peace between Montreal and Quebec until the arrival in 1659 of Abbé François de Laval de Montigny, as the bishop of New France, when the whole quarrel was renewed with additional animosity.

A VICAR APOSTOLIC FOR NEW FRANCE

Laval's appointment as bishop, or more correctly as vicar apostolic had been a great disappointment to the Associates of Montreal who had been supporting the candidacy of de Queylus. It had come about because the Jesuits were much admired by the queen mother who at this time was exercising a great influence in the political affairs of France. As soon as the Jesuits realized that an appointment of a bishop to New France was inevitable they interceded with the queen mother to select a candidate who would be favourable to their policy; she immediately suggested Paul Le Jeune, but a rule of his society made it impossible for him to accept the office. The selection of a candidate, however, was now to all intents and purposes Le

Jeune's responsibility and after consulting with the Lalemants and Father Annat, the king's confessor, they agreed that Laval would make a very satisfactory bishop. There was little difficulty in getting royal approval, as Cardinal Mazarin was now in control of the affairs of France and he was quite willing to humour the queen mother in the rather minor concern of a bishop for Quebec.[66] There remained, however, a very serious obstacle to be hurdled before Laval could proceed to his diocese and this was to secure papal confirmation; for the pope relied upon the advice of the Congregation for the Propagation of the Faith when appointing overseas bishops, and this organization, in the words of Father Rochemonteix, "little liked the Jesuits and still less liked their nominees to the mission field";[67] indeed they were able to block papal approval for fifteen months. They had as allies in their opposition the *parlements* of Rouen and Paris and the Archbishop of Rouen himself, who refused to give Laval his letters of appointment.

The opposition within France was based upon the fear that Laval was not a good Gallican, a justified fear; but in the long run it played into the hands of the Ultramontanes, for it forced Laval to resort to some unusual procedures before he was consecrated and helped him to avoid making any strong commitment in favour of Gallican rights. The Bishop of Bayeux, whom Laval had sought as his chief consecrator, refused to act and so Laval had to turn to the apostolic nuncio who, with the co-operation of two French bishops, consecrated the bishop-elect in a church exempt from French episcopal jurisdiction; thus it was unnecessary for Laval to take the usual pledge to uphold Gallican rights. To make doubly sure that no such oath would be required, the Jesuits suggested that it might be discreet for Laval to become simply a vicar apostolic in the New World, which explains why the first bishop of Quebec arrived in New France with the title, Bishop of *Petraea in partibus infidelium*.[68]

There were, however, some serious disadvantages in being a mere vicar apostolic, of which Laval was soon to become aware; the office was a device worked out for missionary areas where the ordinary hierarchy of the church had not yet been established, and where it fell under the immediate jurisdiction of the pope;[69] although the pontifical brief whereby Laval got his appointment had given him all the powers of a bishop they were delegated powers, so that he could have no cathedral or chapter. This he soon found a very cramping restriction. But even more embarrassing was the resentment shown by the Archbishop of Rouen against the idea that the pope should intrude anybody with the powers of a bishop into New France which he considered part of the Archdiocese of Rouen. For a brief time after his arrival in Quebec Laval was without any status whatever, for the letters patent, signed by the king, which had created the Diocese of Quebec also acknowledged the jurisdiction of the Archbishop of Rouen over the same area. The queen mother, however, had anticipated such a complication and had written the governor to ignore any communications that might come from Rouen. It was a difficult assignment for the governor, Viscount d'Argenson, who had just entered upon his duties. To complicate matters even more, the king had sent a letter confirming de Queylus as the ecclesiastical head of New France; and the latter was quite ready to exercise this authority over the newly arrived Bishop of *Petraea*.[70]

These contradictory communications from France were the reflection of a most confusing civil war known as the *Fronde* in which the age-long controversy over Gallican rights played a prominent role; the young King Louis XIV could not at this time make up his mind whether he was a Gallican or an Ultramontane; at a later day he was to become the Gallican *par excellence,* but at this juncture he finally yielded to his mother's importunities and sent to Quebec two further letters: one to the governor, disallowing the Archbishop of Rouen's jurisdiction in New France; the other to Laval, confirming his episcopal jurisdiction.[71] De Queylus was now ready to accept Laval's authority and to go back to the Montreal seminary which had hardly yet been established; but the Bishop of *Petraea* was by this time unwilling to endure the Sulpician within his diocese; so he asked the governor to send a squad of soldiers to see that de Queylus was firmly placed on the next ship sailing to France.

Such high-handed action stirred the Associates of Notre-Dame to make a still further effort to retain a certain independence of action for the Montreal seminary; they sent de Queylus to Rome to secure a rescript from the papal chancery making the superior of Saint-Sulpice a coseigneur of Montreal. De Queylus secured the rescript and returned to New France, confident that he was now safe from any harassment from the bishop, but no sooner had he arrived at Quebec than he was informed that he could not proceed to Montreal; nevertheless, with the connivance of the governor he slipped away quietly to his Montreal seminary. His stay, however, was very brief, for a new governor, Davaugour, appeared upon the scene with a letter from the king ordering de Queylus back to France.[72]

For the time being the Sulpician threat to the spiritual hegemony of the Jesuits had been thwarted; de Queylus remained in France with little hope of returning to his badly frustrated seminary. But seven years after his expulsion from Canada, Laval on a visit to France became reconciled to his erstwhile foe and permitted him to return to Montreal to carve out a distinguished career for himself as the delayed founder of the Sulpician Order in Montreal.[73] As Laval himself had adopted some of the policies that had been initiated by de Queylus during his brief tenure as grand vicar, particularly in relation to the liquor trade, harmony prevailed among the Sulpicians, Jesuits and the bishop while de Queylus was superior at Montreal. Disharmony, however, was still the order of the day at Quebec, but it was of a different nature to that of the rivalry between two religious orders.

With the appointment of a bishop who felt himself no longer bound by Gallican privileges there arose a rivalry between church and state very similar to the age-long contest that provides much of the drama of medieval history. In the revival of this medieval drama, so conspicuous in the era of Laval, Jesuit and Sulpician stood shoulder to shoulder in the defence of the church's claim to dictate to the state in matters belonging to God. This, however, is an aspect of our study to be deferred until after we have considered a more serious intrusion into the affairs of New France, a New England incursion that would ultimately bring to an end the whole project of a French-Catholic empire in the New World.

NOTES TO CHAPTER SEVEN

1. F. Parkman, *The Jesuits in North America* (11th ed.; Boston: Little, Brown, 1878), p. 167.

2. R. G. Thwaites, ed., *The Jesuit Relations and Allied Documents* (Cleveland: Burrows, 1896-1901), Vol. XVIII, p. 85.

3. *Vide* John Murray Gibbon in collaboration with Mary S. Matthewson, *Three Centuries of Canadian Nursing* (Toronto: Macmillan, 1947); chapters one and two are very informed accounts of the work of the pioneer nursing sisterhoods in dealing with recurring epidemics among the aborigines.

4. Thwaites, *op. cit.,* Vol. XVIII, p. 127.

5. *Ibid.,* Vol. XI, p. 75.

6. Parkman, *op. cit.,* p. 168.

7. Thwaites, *op. cit.,* Vol. XIV, p. 125 *et seq.,* contains Le Jeune's *Relation* of 1638; for mission at Tadoussac *vide* Vol. XXI, p. 81 *et seq.*

8. A. Floquet in *Anecdotes Normandes* (2nd ed.; Rouen: Cagniard, 1883), emphasizes the freedom of action of Norman women in seventeenth-century France. "Formerly in France the condition of the ladies was a great deal better than one sees in this century of iron," p. 266.

9. *Vide* Pierre-Georges Roy, *A Travers l'Histoire de l'Hôtel-Dieu de Québec* (Lévis: Le Soleil, 1939), an abridgment of a book by Mother Juchereau de Saint-Ignace, p. 34; also E.-M. Faillon, *Histoire de la Colonie française en Canada* (Villemarie: Bibliothèque Paroissiale, 1865), Vol. I, p. 311 *et seq.*

10. *Vide* H.-R. Casgrain, *Histoire de la Mère Marie de l'Incarnation* (Quebec: Desbarats, 1864), p. 223 *et seq.,* for a good summary of the life of Madame de La Peltrie.

11. Dom Claude Martin, *Marie de l'Incarnation, Ecrits Spirituels et Historiques* (Paris and Quebec: Desclée, 1929), Vol. I, p. 9.

12. *Ibid.*, Vol. I, p. 412.

13. Vide *The Life of the Venerable Mother Mary of the Incarnation by a Religious of the Ursuline Community* (Dublin and London: Duffy, 1880), in which the emphasis is upon the mystical.

14. H.R. Casgrain, *op. cit.*, p. 191.

15. In *Itinéraires de Touraine (Editions* Barcla), Tours is described as *métropole religieuse des Gaules*, p. 9.

16. For a lively description of the Ursuline Order vide Agnes Repplier, *Mère Marie of the Ursulines* (New York: Sheed & Ward, 1931), *passim*.

17. *Ibid.*, p. 38.

18. Thwaites, *op. cit.*, Vol. VII, p. 261.

19. A. Repplier, *op. cit.*, p. 41.

20. Vide P.-G. Roy, *op. cit.*, p. 6.

21. *The Life of the Venerable Mother Mary, op. cit.*, pp. 192-3.

22. Thwaites, Vol. XV, p. 229.

23. Abbé Richaudeau, *Lettres de la Révérende Mère Marie de l'Incarnation* (Tournai: Casterman, 1876), Vol. I, p. 159.

24. Vide *Collection de Manuscrits, Lettres, Mémoires et autres Documents Historiques relatifs à la Nouvelle-France* (Quebec: Coté, 1883), Vol. I, p. 62 *et seq.*, in which the motives for establishing the Company of One Hundred Associates are clearly set forth.

25. A brief outline of the government of Quebec from the death of Champlain to the establishment of the Superior Council is to be found in an article by G. Lanctot entitled "The Elective Council of Quebec, 1657" in *The Canadian Historical Review* (June, 1934), pp. 123-132.

26. Thwaites, *op. cit.*, Vol. XXXI, p. 111 *et seq.*

27. Parkman, *op. cit.*, p. 304.

28. Vide letter written by Gabriel Druillettes to John Winthrop; Thwaites, *op. cit.*, Vol. XXXVI, p. 75-81.

29. Parkman, *op. cit.*, p. 326.

30. Druillettes' narrative of his journey to New England is to be found in Thwaites, *op. cit.*, Vol. XXVI, p. 83 *et seq.*

31. Thwaites, *op. cit.*, Vol. XXXVI, pp. 161-3.

32. Vide E.-M. Faillon, *op. cit.*, Vol. II, p. 171.

33. A.-H. Gosselin, *La Mission du Canada* (Evreux: Imprimerie de l'Eure, 1909), p. 319.

34. C. de Rochemonteix, *Les Jésuites et la Nouvelle-France au XVIIᵉ Siècle* (Paris: Letouzey et Ané, 1896), Vol. II, p. 198.

35. Vide supra, p. 29.

36. H. Bremond, *Histoire Littéraire du Sentiment Religieux en France* (Paris: Bloud & Guy, 1923), Vol. III, p. 462.

37. E.-M. Faillon, *Vie de M. Olier* (4th ed.; Paris: Vattelier, 1873), Vol. III, p. 397 *et seq.*

38. C. Bertrand, *Monsieur de la Dauversière* (Montreal: Les Frères des Ecoles Chrétiennes, 1947), pp. 118-9; vide also René Buquin, *La Flèche, Histoire résumé des origines à nos jours* (La Flèche, 1952), pp. 64-9. La Dauversière's native city where his house still stands has played a prominent role in the life of Canada. A prominently placed plaque proclaims: "*En ce lieu Ancien Port du Pré Luneau se sont Embarqués En 1640-1653-1659 278 Hommes, 45 Femmes et Enfants Ainsi que 3 Religieuses Hospitalières Du Pays de La Flèche et des Provinces Voisines à l'instigation du Flèchois Jérôme le Royer de la Dauversière pour l'entreprise de la fondation de Montréal en Canada.*"

39. Quoted by Dollier de Casson, *A History of Montreal* (trans. and ed. R. Flenley; London and Toronto: Dent, 1929), p. 65.

40. P. Rousseau, *Histoire de la Vie de M. Paul de Chomedey, Sieur de Maisonneuve* (Montreal: Librairie St. Joseph, 1886), p. 28.

41. *Vide* De Casson, *op. cit.*, p. 65.

42. *Vide* Pierre Benoit, *Maisonneuve* (Tours-Paris: Mame, 1960); it consists of testimonies by the founders of Montreal: *Récit de Soeur Louise Sainte-Marie, née Louise de Chomedey, jadis supérieure du convent de Notre-Dame à Troyes,* pp. 13-26; *récit de Marguerite Bourgeoys, fondatrice de Congrégation de Notre-Dame du Canada,* pp. 91-106.

43. De Casson, *op. cit.*, p. 75; *vide* also P. Benoit, *op. cit.*, pp. 27-37 for *récit de Mlle Jeanne Mance, fondatrice de l'Hôtel-Dieu à Montréal.*

44. *Vide* J. K. Foran, *Jeanne Mance or The Angel of the Colony* (Montreal: Herald Press, 1931), *passim.*

45. E.-M. Faillon, *op. cit.*, Vol. IV, p. 403.

46. J. K. Foran, *op. cit.*, p. 43.

47. De Casson, *op. cit.*, p. 91.

48. *Ibid.*, pp. 91-93.

49. Quoted by J. K. Foran, *op. cit.*, p. 43.

50. *Vide* De Casson, *op. cit.*, p. 97 *et seq.*

51. *Ibid.*, note at foot of p. 119.

52. *Ibid.*, pp. 159-61.

53. P. Rousseau, *op. cit.*, p. 128.

54. A. Jamet, *Marguerite Bourgeoys* (Montreal: La Presse Catholique Panaméricaine, 1942), *passim.*

55. De Casson, *op. cit.*, p. 213.

56. *Ibid.*, p. 23 *et. seq.*

57. *Ibid.*, p. 243.

58. G. Lanctot, *A History of Canada*, Vol. I: *From its Origins to the Royal Regime, 1663* (trans. J. Hambleton; Toronto and Vancouver: Clarke, Irwin, 1963), p. 247; *vide* also E.-M. Faillon, *Histoire, op. cit.*, Vol. II, p. 389 *et seq.*

59. Abbé Richaudeau, *op. cit.*, Vol. I, p. 304.

60. E.-M. Faillon, *op. cit.*, Vol. II, p. 275 *et seq.*

61. Arcbhishops of Rouen, after the rehabilitation of Jeanne d'Arc were inclined to be very national; *vide* article by L'Abbé Lecompte on "Mgr François de Harlai de Champvallon, Archevêque de Rouen 1613-1653" in *Revue de la Normandie,* Tome Huitième, Année 1868 (Rouen, 1868).

62. Rochemonteix, *op. cit.*, Vol. II, p. 208 *et seq.*

63. *Ibid.*, p. 221.

64. *Vide* P. Benoit, *op. cit.*, p. 121 *et seq.* for *récit de M. Gabriel Souart, premier curé de Ville-Marie.*

65. Rochemonteix, *op. cit.*, Vol. II, p. 222.

66. *Vide* Laval's letter to the general of the Society of Jesus in Rome, which expresses his gratitude to the Jesuits for his appointment as the first diocesan of New France; Thwaites, *op. cit.*; Vol. XLV, pp. 221-5.

67. Rochemonteix, *op. cit.*, Vol. II, p. 282.

68. *Ibid.*, Vol. II, p. 283.

69. *Vide* article on "Vicar Apostolic" in *The Catholic Encyclopedia* (New York: The Encyclopedia Press, 1907-22), Vol. XV, p. 401.

70. Rochemonteix, *op. cit.*, Vol. II, p. 293.

71. *Vide* A.-H. Gosselin, *Le Vénérable François de Montmorency Laval* (Quebec: Dessault et Proulx, 1901), p. 104.

72. *Ibid.*, p. 105.

73. De Casson, *op. cit.*, p. 327.

EIGHT

The New England Incursion

While Jesuit and Sulpician were contending for the honour of organizing the parochial life of New France, a vast immigration of religious dissenters were establishing a new England on the eastern seaboard of North America. From this transplanted religious dissent emerged a new dynamic culture which was to prove inimical to the traditional patterns of life as represented by the established churches of both England and France. It is conceivable that if Anglicanism as formulated in the Elizabethan settlement had prevailed in New England there need not have occurred an ideological struggle that could only be resolved by an unconditional surrender by one side or the other. Admittedly, English explorers and trading companies, even before the great Puritan influx into North America, had been constantly harassing early French attempts at colonization; but this was a commercially motivated rivalry and religious reasons were only urged as an afterthought. Elizabethan buccaneers and their Stuart successors were little concerned about religion when they made their raids upon French settlements in the New World. Indeed, the first capture of Quebec by the Kirkes may well be regarded as the offshoot of a quarrel among rival Protestant trading companies rather than as an occupation by the English.[1] The arrival of the Jesuits at Port-Royal and Quebec had certainly heightened religious tensions in the French settlements, tensions which often played into the hands of their English rivals for trade; but in all this there was no evidence of a life-and-death struggle between two opposing ideologies. The conflict, however, took on an entirely different dimension with the new kind of immigrant who came out from England between 1618 and 1648.[2]

RENEWED MISSIONS IN ACADIA

It was in Acadia that the change of religious climate was first felt, and where occurred the most tragic consequences in the long-drawn-out struggle for a continent. Here the Jesuits had attempted to found a theocratic colony as the most effective way to evangelize the aborigines. After their expulsion by a Virginian captain[3] they planned to renew their mission to the Micmacs as soon as circumstances were propitious for their return.

In the interim the mission was entrusted to four Recollets from Aquitaine, who arrived in Acadia in 1619 under the sponsorship of a Bordeaux company of merchants. With the early dissolution of the Bordeaux Company and the intrusion of a Scottish company into Port-Royal, there was little alternative for them but to attempt to join their colleagues in Quebec, but not before one of their number, Father Sébastien, perished of hunger somewhere between St. John and Miscou.[4]

The formation of the Company of One Hundred Associates, which included Acadia in its territorial responsibilities, encouraged the Jesuits to attempt a renewal of their Acadian missions. In 1629 the Company sent out to New France four armed ships to bring relief to their beleaguered compatriots at Tadoussac and Quebec; the Jesuits were represented in this attempt by Father Barthélemy Vimont.[5] During a violent storm a ship under the command of Captain Charles Daniel, a brother of the Huronian martyr, was compelled to take shelter at Grand-Cibou on Cape Breton Island. Here the French learned to their surprise that a certain Lord Ochiltree had established a colony of some sixty Scots at Port-aux-Baleines, near present-day Louisbourg. On the presumption that this colony was a menace to French fishermen, and perhaps with Captain Argall's bad example in mind,[6] Captain Daniel immediately demolished the settlement and carried the colonists to Grand-Cibou where he put them to work building a fort and also a chapel for Father Vimont. Thus began the mission of St. Ann's which gave Father Vimont the distinction of initiating the first church work in the present diocese of Antigonish. Ultimately the prisoners who assisted in the building operations at St. Ann's were taken to France where they were given their freedom.[7]

Father Vimont was soon joined by another Jesuit priest who arrived in a ship that had been chartered by the Jesuits to bring supplies to the Canadian missions. It also got caught in a storm off the Cape Breton coast and foundered, with the loss of fourteen men including Father Philibert Noyrot, one of the most active supporters of the Jesuit missions in Canada.[8] Fortunately, Father Alexandre de Vieuxpont managed to survive the disaster and reached Grand-Cibou where he became Father Vimont's assistant. The mission was not a very tranquil one, as the aggressiveness of the Kirkes in league with Sir William Alexander made it impossible for the French to remain on Cape Breton Island.

After the restoration of peace between the English and French in 1632, the Jesuits were soon back at St. Ann's; two priests, Antoine Daniel and Ambroise Davost, arrived in 1634 for a brief stopover before they moved on to the more important mission among the Hurons.[9] They were replaced at St. Ann's by Julien Perrault and André Richard: the former remained only a short time, but Father Richard continued until 1641 when he was transferred to Miscou (situated at the northeast corner of what is now the province of New Brunswick). There he remained for twenty years and is the best remembered of all the early Jesuit missionaries in Acadia.

After Father Richard's withdrawal from St. Ann's, the mission remained vacant for almost a decade and was only renewed with the arrival of some Capuchin friars from St. Peter's, a mission that had been founded on the south side of Cape Breton in 1645 by three Capuchins from the province of Paris. The superior was Father Augustin de Pointoise who had served an apprenticeship in Syria; his assistants were Brothers Félix de Reims and Eléazer de Saint-Florentin. The latter had spent ten years among the Abenaki in Maine, and the knowledge gained there of Indian languages made him one of the most effective missionaries among the Micmacs of Cape Breton.[10]

The reason for the withdrawal of the Jesuits from Acadia and their replacement by Capuchins was due to Cardinal Richelieu's policy of permitting only one religious order in each of certain defined territorial areas.[11] Canada after the treaty of Saint-Germain-en-Laye had been assigned exclusively to the Jesuits, and Acadia to the Capuchins. There still remained, however, pockets of Jesuit missions in what was officially regarded as exclusively Capuchin territory. This was due to the fact that the Capuchins were experiencing considerable difficulty in getting their missions established because their financial patrons were engaged in what might be described as baronial warfare.

A NEW SCOTLAND

A contributing factor to this civil war in Acadia was a charter that had been granted by James I of England to a Scottish nobleman, Sir William Alexander, or, as he was later to become, the Earl of Stirling.

The latter had accompanied the king from Scotland to England as a tutor to Prince Henry, but he also served as the king's adviser on matters of conscience. A problem of conscience for the king had been raised by Sir Ferdinando Gorges, who in 1620 had received from James a charter for a New Plymouth Company; the company had been empowered to found a colony to be known as New England, embracing a piece of territory in North America "extending from the fortieth to the forty-eighth degree of north latitude and from the Atlantic to the Pacific." When Gorges discovered that there were some settlers to the north of his domain "who professed the Romish faith"[12] he urged the English government to expel them. James was not quite sure of the morality of expelling the French in time of peace and so he asked for the opinion of his philosophic friend Sir William Alexander. The latter came to the conclusion that the Roman Catholics could rightly be displaced from the territory concerned.

It was during a study of the maps relating to this issue that Sir William decided that there ought to be a New Scotland, as well as a New England, in the New World.[13] He broached the idea to the king who immediately made him a grant of land lying somewhere east of the Sainte-Croix River and south of the St. Lawrence, between the colonies of New England and Newfoundland; the last named was excluded from the grant because it had already been assigned, or at least part of it, to Sir William Vaughan.[14] Despite the vagueness of the boundaries it is obvious the territory intended was French Acadia without Newfoundland, which in the grant to the One Hundred Associates by the French king was considered an integral part of Acadia, and from which all Protestants, whether French or English, were to be removed by the Company.[15]

It does seem that, due to its proximity to Scotland, Newfoundland was early considered by the Scots the ideal place to create a New Scotland. Their interest had first been aroused by John Mason, one of the founders of New Hampshire, who had spent a year in Newfoundland (1615) and had written a little book extolling the wonderful possibilities for pioneer settlers in this fisherman's paradise. This panegyric had aroused a veritable "colonial fever"[16] among the Scots and helped to create the enthusiasm for adventuring into the New World that made it possible for Sir William Alexander to sell New Scotland, or Nova Scotia, baronetcies to eager buyers. These baronets would probably have preferred to have gone to Newfoundland since it was so much more accessible to Scotland, but from this they were blocked because it had been pre-empted by Sir William Vaughan who in 1617 was trying rather unsuccessfully to plant a colony of Welshmen at Trepassey Bay.[17] Nevertheless, the first company of Scotsmen destined for Nova Scotia, and consisting mostly of farm labourers accompanied by a minister, were driven by a storm into St. John's and spent the winter of 1622 there. At the end of the winter they returned to Scotland, apparently giving up the New World as a hopeless place to colonize.

While in Newfoundland they would have heard much to discourage them: they would have learned about Lord Baltimore's ill-fated colony of Catholics at Ferryland;[18] about an attempt by John Guy in 1610 to plant a colony of Anglicans at Port-de-Grace on Conception Bay, where Erasmus Stourton gained the distinction of being the first Church of England clergyman to serve a mission in Newfoundland, but whose "long preaching Anne Mason, the governor's wife, found rather dull"; and of a grant to Lord Falkland comprising part of Trinity Bay, called North Falkland and South Falkland; they would have learned that all the colonists on these grants had had a wretched time, even Sir William Vaughan's Welshmen at Trepassey Bay, due largely to the depredations of ship fishermen from Devonshire who apparently resented any restrictions upon the free and easy life they had been enjoying on the Newfoundland coasts.[20] These stories seemed to have convinced this first company of Scots that old Scotland was preferable to a new Scotland overseas.

Not all Scotsmen agreed, for there were still many adventurous spirits who wished to take advantage of the king's grant to Sir William Alexander. One of these was Sir Robert Gordon of Lochinvar who secured from Sir William the Barony of Galloway, as it was styled, which consisted of the Island of Cape Breton with some additional mainland territory. In 1629 he sent out his lieutenant, Lord Ochiltree, with a company of Scotsmen to take possession of the barony; the latter attempted to found a colony at Port-aux-Baleines, but was quickly frustrated, as we have seen, by Captain Daniel.[21] About the same time Sir William Alexander's son did succeed in settling about seventy Scots at Port-Royal, which was renamed Charlesport in honour of Charles I of England. The honour did not greatly impress the monarch; in 1632, in order to secure some money owing on his wife's dowry from Louis XIII, he agreed to return Acadia to French sovereignty.[22] Charlesport again became Port-Royal.

RIVALRY OF RECOLLETS AND CAPUCHINS

Although this first attempt to create a New Scotland was short-lived, it started a train of events that constantly tempted New Englanders or *bostonais,* as the Canadians irreverently called them, to interfere in Acadian affairs. One of these was the acceptance, during the Scottish interim, by Charles de La Tour of a baronetcy from Sir William Alexander.[23] The former, after the death of Biencourt, had attempted from Fort Lomeron, on the southern tip of Acadia, to keep the original colony of Port-Royal from disintegrating after its uprooting by Captain Argall. At Fort Lomeron, which he renamed Fort Saint-Louis, de La Tour maintained a precarious existence in the face of opposition from French traders and hostile Englishmen.

It is beyond the scope of this study to attempt to make any moral judgments on de La Tour's tortured relations with both the English and French authorities in Acadia. Within the Acadian community it is a very controversial subject with much to be said on the one side or the other.[24] Suffice it to say that when the Scots occupied Port-Royal, de La Tour, at the urging of his father, accepted a baronetcy from Sir William Alexander. But no sooner had he become a Scottish baronet than a certain Captain Marot, representing the One Hundred Associates, arrived at Fort Saint-Louis with two ships laden with supplies and bringing artisans to help strengthen the company's position in Acadia. On the same ship were three Recollet fathers: André Ronsaud, François du Long and Nicolas Bigot. They were extremely anxious to renew the rather promising mission to the Malecite Indians, so recently abandoned by members of their own order. At the urgings of both Captain Marot and the Recollets, de La Tour quickly returned to his French allegiance and undertook to establish a combined trading post and mission on the St. John River, which became known as Fort Sainte-Marie—a site now identified as Portland Point.[25]

The Recollets were under the impression that the way was clear at last for a vigorous mission to the Malecites under the strong protection of de La Tour, who had been accorded by King Louis XIII the rank of lieutenant-general in the country of Acadia. Much to their surprise, however, they discovered that another lieutenant-general for Acadia, Isaac de Razilly, outranked de La Tour and, what was even more startling, he had a royal command to carry the Recollets back to France and replace them with Capuchins.[26] According to Candide de Nant, who has written a very detailed account of the Capuchin missions in Acadia, it was the considered decision of the

Propaganda that brought the Capuchins to Acadia; it had learned in 1630 that four thousand English Puritans were about to embark for America and it was felt that the Capuchins were the best-trained order for dealing with the Protestant menace to the Catholic faith in America. Many of the French Capuchins had been trained for work in heretical countries;[27] some of them had accompanied Queen Henrietta, the wife of Charles I, to London, and had heard confessions in English at the court of Charles. There had been some thought of sending these Capuchins directly to New England, but it was considered the better part of valour to send them to Acadia whence they might in time find an opportunity to launch a mission in New England; even Virginia was included among the new fields that one day might be accessible to Roman Catholic missionaries trained for polemical warfare.[28]

Great reliance was placed on Isaac de Razilly, a cousin of Cardinal Richelieu, to prepare the way for such an ambitious project. In May 1632 he received a royal commission authorizing him to assume full responsibility for the government of Acadia, but also specifying that he was to remove the Recollet missionaries already there and to replace them with Capuchins.[29] In pursuit of this goal de Razilly, accompanied by a group of Capuchins and several prospective settlers, landed at La Hève (now La Have) on the south shore of Acadia. Here a new Acadian colony was inaugurated with a religious ceremony; this was conducted by a Capuchin preacher, Claude d'Abbeville, according to a Capuchin "ceremonial already consecrated by usage."[30]

Before settling down at La Hève, de Razilly had two chores to perform: first, to persuade Captain Andrew Forrester, Sir William Alexander's lieutenant at Port-Royal, to take his little Scottish colony back to Scotland; secondly, to send the Recollet missionaries back to France. He had little difficulty with the former as they felt compelled to obey the English king; however, about a half dozen Scots were permitted to remain at Port-Royal and were ultimately absorbed into the Acadian culture.[31] Matters did not proceed so amicably with the Recollets. Just what happened is not altogether clear from the available documents; according to Candide de Nant, a Capuchin partisan, the Recollets defied the orders from France and stayed on in the St. John area under the protection of de La Tour,[32] according to Abbé Couillard Després, whose sympathies are on the side of the Recollets, some members of the order did return to France to plead their right to remain in Acadia, and as a result of this plea their position was regularized by Ingoli, the secretary of the *Propaganda;* he also implies that there were more Recollets with de La Tour at St. John than the three whose names "are known to us."[33]

Be that as it may, the Recollets, despite de Razilly's orders to remove them, did stay on for some time in the St. John area, much to the chagrin of Father Joseph Tremblay, the French administrator of foreign missions, who had a grandiose plan for his Capuchins;[34] he was particularly anxious that they should establish themselves along the Penobscot River where they would be most likely to make contact with prospective English converts. It was felt that Pentagouet, where the English had built a trading post as early as 1626, would make an ideal place to set up a mission. Already de La Tour had come into collision with the English in this area (1633), while engaged in trade from his headquarters at St. John; during an argument over furs which were stolen from de La Tour, two Englishmen were killed in the vicinity of Machias.[35] De La Tour, however, left the English in possession of Pentagouet, but warned them not to trade beyond Pemaquid on the Kennebec River, thus attempting to establish a rough boundary line between New England and Acadia. This boundary did not appear satisfactory to de Razilly and so he sent his lieutenant, d'Aulnay, with firm orders to drive the English out of Pentagouet, which the latter did very effectively; and so the way was prepared to establish the hoped-for mission to New Englanders and perhaps Virginians![36]

MANORIAL SETTLEMENTS IN MAINE

Who were these settlers to the south whom the Capuchins hoped to win for the Catholic Church? A close inspection indicates that they were by no means a homogeneous group and that some of them might have been willing to give the Capuchins a hearing. The original settlers in the area that later became the province of Maine had been sent out by Sir Ferdinando Gorges in 1608, the same year that Champlain founded Quebec.[37] This first colony, under the direction of George Popham, the governor of the port of Plymouth, and situated at Sagadahoc on the Kennebec River, became known as the Popham Settlement. Like all pioneer colonies it was a very quarrelsome community and its Anglican minister, Richard Seymour, had great difficulty shepherding his flock. It has been suggested that the "colony was stocked 'out of all the gaols of England' "[38] which may explain Seymour's parochial difficulties. Relations with neighbouring Indians on the whole seem to have been quite amicable and some of these Indians learned English; two in particular, Samoset and Squanto, were able to surprise the Pilgrim Fathers when they landed at Plymouth Rock in 1620 by greeting them in good West Country dialect. Although the colony survived hardly a year, it was used as evidence that the English were in possession of the area around the Bay of Fundy before the French, and was the justification, in part, for Captain Argall's destruction of the first French settlements in Acadia.[39]

The root cause of the abandonment of the Popham colony was the lack of financial support from England. It had originated out of a benevolent desire to relieve pauperism and what was regarded as overpopulation in England. This did not prove to be a compelling enough motive for successful colonization and so Gorges, who had been the moving spirit behind the Popham settlement, decided to make the lure of profits the primary stimulus for his second attempt at the creation of an overseas New England. In association with John Mason, then governor of Newfoundland, he secured a patent from the crown allowing him to organize a Council of New England; the council's chief function was to raise funds for the establishment of plantations in certain designated areas in America; these plantations under the supervision of the council were to engage in fishing and trapping and thus provide a profit to their patrons.[40] In 1639 Gorges obtained an additional charter from the king, conferring upon him the title Lord Proprietor of the Province and County of Maine; he then proceeded to establish a half dozen settlements along the Kennebec River, consisting mostly of fishermen and hunters. Under patronal direction a manorial system of government, not unlike the baronial system of Acadia, began to take shape in Maine; it was expected that the Anglican Church through manorial patronage would provide for the religious needs of the settlers.

Relations between New England and New France would no doubt have been far more harmonious than they ultimately turned out to be if this form of manorial government, as designed by Gorges in Maine and John Mason in Newfoundland and New Hampshire, had become the prevailing New England pattern; neither Gorges nor Mason had any place for Puritanism—Mason's wife was an ardent high churchwoman. They were on the side of Charles I and Archbishop Laud during the Civil War in England, and perhaps like their masters were influenced by a form of pietism represented by Lancelot Andrewes whose prayers and meditations are not far separated in spirit from Saint François de Sales' *Introduction à la Vie Dévote*.[41] It is quite conceivable that Capuchin missionaries would have received a courteous welcome at either Gorges' or Mason's plantations.

It is also probable that they would have received at least a polite welcome from the Dutch who had been exploring along the Maine coast before moving into the Connecticut Valley, for these diligent traders never allowed their Calvinism to get in the way of trade and commerce. In point of fact Dutch immigration to America was never purely Dutch, for on the *New Netherlands* which arrived in Manhattan in 1624 there were thirty French-speaking colonists. And in the settlement when it finally took shape as New Amsterdam there were people of a great variety of religions, among them "papists" and "atheists."[42] Being in America primarily for trade and not for settlement, the Dutch traders always treated the French missionaries with kindness when their paths crossed. This same attitude was characteristic of the early English-speaking settlers both in Maine and Newfoundland. They seem to have lived on fairly friendly terms with their French neighbours, except during the period that Sir David Kirke was governor of Newfoundland. But Kirke's harshness was due to the fact that his "charter gave him authority to exact dues from foreigners,"[43] and so he was determined to wring as much from the French as possible. In this he was only half-heartedly supported by his Newfoundland subjects.

From the available evidence it seems probable that if a manorial type of government with its supporting Anglican parochial system had survived in New England, North American history would have developed along very different lines from the course it did follow. No doubt quarrels and acts of violence would have occurred between the French and English over fishing and hunting grounds until boundaries had been definitely delimited; yet it is not inconceivable that New England and New France could have developed side by side in friendly cultural rivalry with no public clamour for expulsion of one race or the other. It is even possible to imagine that a New Netherlands might have been permitted to share in the exploitation of North America; for there was an abundance of space for all, including the aborigines who were treated with the same regard by the first English explorers as by the French. All this, however, is vain speculation. Even before Gorges had got his plantations going he had delegated some of his colonizing privileges to subordinate companies, particularly to the Massachusetts Bay Company, made up mostly of Puritan gentlemen. This was to change the whole development of North American history.

PURITAN IMMIGRATION

The new phase began with what has been described as the "great immigration"[44] between the years 1618 to 1648, which brought to America men and women of strong religious convictions. They were, in the words of one of their admirers, "sober well-to-do men," who transferred "themselves, their families and their goods to new homes across the seas, there to found not a colony but a commonwealth."[45] Their transference across the seas began almost unnoticed in the midst of a political and religious unrest in England which was to eventuate in a civil war.

As in France, so in England the seventeenth century had been characterized by a great religious revival which had divided the country into two camps. On the one side were Charles I and his archbishop, William Laud, whose piety was similar to that of the mystics of France; on the other side were the Puritans who took for their master, in logic, one of the great martyrs of St. Bartholomew, Pierre de La Ramée.[46]

The difference between Puritanism and the mainstream of Anglicanism was not as great as that between Catholic and Huguenot in France; often it would seem they were divided by nothing more profound than the position of the altar or the kind of vestments to be worn in church; nevertheless, the contention of one notable Puritan, Lord Sage and Sele, "that every particular church and congregation might do as it pleased in the matters of order, of liturgy and worship"[47] did mean in fact a separation from the established church with very profound sociological consequences to the national life of England. Even before the great immigration the Puritans had begun to create a serious schism in English social life, and it was this same spirit of separatism and independence that peopled New England and ultimately led to the separation of the Thirteen Colonies from the mother country.[48]

Just as the Jesuits and other religious orders had come out to New France to create a new society based upon an ideal, so the Puritans came to New England to build a new Zion.[49] There was, however, considerable difference between the two visions: the former was based upon a philosophy of life that was explicit, complete and coherent; the latter was full of contradictory tendencies that were forever stirring up controversy on quite profound subjects in the infant colonies. Yet by the test of pragmatism the New Englanders were able to fit their contradictions into a social framework which gave an unusual dynamism to the New England way of life and which in time became an all-pervasive culture on the North American scene.

Among all the early Puritan settlers in America, regardless of their differences, there was an anxious search for an inner life of holiness; and when this ardour cooled in later generations it was constantly renewed by great waves of revivalism.[50] The search for purity was the chief concern of Puritan preachers, and the pulpit became an important element in fashioning public opinion on social and political affairs; it also helped in the creation of township government with its "body of liberties" by emphasizing the right to appeal for justice by any aggrieved person, either in public court or town meeting. Very early in their history the New Englanders became unduly sensitive about what they considered their God-given rights; they were encouraged by their preachers, and this assured them of the purity of their motives. Such self-righteousness hardly endeared them to the French Canadians who soon found them intolerable neighbours to live alongside. Their tendency to identify themselves with the chosen people of God, in literal Old Testament terms, proved fatal to the aborigines living in their vicinity and came close to being fatal for the Acadians to the north.

Because of their constantly increasing numbers through continuing waves of immigration, they early moved into an expansive mood and became greatly concerned over any foreseeable obstacles to expansion. Such apprehension is clearly set forth in a petition presented in 1635 to the Commissioners of Plantations in England by Edward Winslow on behalf of the plantations in New England, asserting "that the French and Dutch do endeavour to divide the land between them and in tender consideration hereof, your Petitioners humbly pray that your Lordships will either procure their peace in these foreign states, or else to give special warrant unto your Petitioners and the English Colonies the right to defend themselves against all foreign enemies."[51]

EMERGING ACADIAN CULTURE

Prominent among the foreign enemies disturbing the peace of mind of the New England petitioners was Charles de Menou d'Aulnay de Charnisay, who had become the chief ruler in Acadia. The New Englanders had received a sharp rebuff from d'Aulnay, when as a lieutenant of Isaac de Razilly, he had taken from them their trading post at Pentagouet and turned it into a French fort and a Capuchin mission.[52] D'Aulnay's increased authority had come to him through the sudden death in 1635 of de Razilly; one of his first acts on assuming his new role was to make Port-Royal the capital of Acadia, and there he removed most of the settlers at La Hève. The Capuchins also made Port-Royal their headquarters, whence they branched out to various parts of Acadia, including Pentagouet where they hoped to make contact with English settlers along the Kennebec.

During a brief tenure at Port-Royal d'Aulnay, in close co-operation with the Capuchins, laid the foundations of an Acadian culture which through many almost overwhelming disasters has persisted as a distinct entity down to the present time. Father Ignace de Paris, a practical man of affairs, became d'Aulnay's confessor and also his guide in the very delicate task of creating a viable communal life among the rather nondescript inhabitants of Acadia.[53] Both d'Aulnay and the Capuchins were keen to make the Micmacs full-fledged members of the Acadian community. There were at one time twelve Capuchins working in several scattered Indian villages; the governor himself often visited these missions to see how the work of conversion was progressing; he appears to have listened with interest to the sermons preached on such visitations. After he had dislodged his rival seigneur, Charles de La Tour, from St. John he built there a modest chapel to serve as a centre for a mission to the Malecites, who were always highly regarded by the French missionaries. At Pentagouet a church was raised in 1648 for the use of the Capuchins; and with the removal of the Recollets from the St. John area after the fall of de La Tour, the Capuchins administered to scattered Acadian families from Pentagouet as far north as Nipisiguit.[54]

A seminary for boys under the direction of Father Ignace was erected at Port-Royal, while Mme de Brice, *le bon ange de Port-Royal*, conducted nearby a school for girls. Subjects taught were of a very practical nature but all pupils were thoroughly drilled in the catechism. Capuchins, like Recollets, were opposed to the Jesuit system of isolating the aborigines from the Europeans; and so Indians and whites mingled freely at school and on all possible occasions. Such intermingling was encouraged by the missionaries as a method of bringing the Indians more quickly into civilized living; it was also done at the express wish of the authorities in France, who had written into the charter of the One Hundred Associates that when an Indian was baptized he was to be treated as a citizen of France.[55]

As will become evident there were some aspects of d'Aulnay's character that were far from admirable, but there is little doubt he had in him the instincts of a great statesman, and to him more than any other one man must go the credit for laying the foundations of an

Acadian culture. He was much concerned to have the Acadians become self-reliant in the matter of law and order. To this end he set up a Council of Acadians, which he consulted on matters of administration, and organized a judiciary under a Grand Provost with a notary, files clerk and other administrative officials. He also did his best to increase the population of the country by bringing out immigrants from France, knowing that this was most necessary if Acadia was to be able to protect herself from the New Englanders. Through his efforts the total population of Acadia was, by 1650, about 500 persons.[56]

It was still small in numbers compared to the fast growing New England colonies, but this number had only been achieved by the personal efforts of the governor himself; for France at the time was more interested in Quebec and Montreal and therefore disregarded the financial condition of Acadia. As a consequence d'Aulnay had to borrow heavily to finance his colonizing activities. Unfortunately, he borrowed from a wealthy but unscrupulous ship owner, Emmanuel Le Borgne, [57] who at a later date would make impossible demands upon an infant colony and add greatly to its woes in a very tragic era. Le Borgne, however, was not the real source of Acadia's troubles; the main cause was a local civil war which occurred at a most inopportune time in Acadian history. It is one of the ironies of the history of this much harassed colony that, just as Acadia was becoming a reality, there arose a bitter struggle between two Acadian seigneurs over territorial boundaries that inevitably invited the intervention of the New Englanders.

The opening phases of the drama of Acadia have already been touched upon,[58] but as the author of Le Drame Acadien has pointed out, the poignancy of this drama only becomes evident after 1642. Acadia before 1642 hardly existed; the few families that came out during the adventurous years that Champlain, de Monts and Poutrincourt stayed at Port-Royal did not really constitute a colony; the Huguenots who made up the greater number of these first adventurers were more interested in trade than settlement. Some of these first settlers did survive the English bombardments in the shelter of the forests where they intermarried with Indians and also with the Scots who were brought out by Sir William Alexander. Later they were to teach the new families who came out from France with de Razilly and d'Aulnay how to survive in a new land under the most adverse circumstances. Suddenly there emerged under the the leadership of d'Aulnay, and to some extent de La Tour and the firm tutelage of the

Capuchins, a novel and distinct race of people. Despite their unconventional existence in the forests, it is amazing how quickly the Acadians developed a strong family loyalty; and this, as Antoine Bernard puts it, "explains in part their profound attachment to their soil, their steeple and their priests." It is with bitterness that Bernard points out that the two seigneurs who had done so much to make Acadia a reality should have begun to engage in a struggle over territorial boundaries "and this to the great joy of the bostonais, very happy indeed to cool their heels while watching the detested French killing one another."[59]

BARONIAL WARFARE

Perhaps the real culprits were not the two seigneurs in Acadia, but the king and his advisers in France. In 1639 d'Aulnay was informed by the king that he was lieutenant-general along the north shore of the Bay of Fundy and governor of Pentagouet, and de La Tour that he was lieutenant-general along the coast of Acadia from the middle of French Bay. The similarity of titles and the indefiniteness of the boundaries were an open invitation to baronial warfare. One experiences considerable difficulty picking one's way through the tangled paths of two families who fought one another so bitterly and were finally merged by a bizarre marriage and whose descendents make up a fair proportion of the present day Acadian population, particularly as their stories have quite naturally been recorded in a rather partisan spirit.[60]

A most romantic heroine in this baronial feud was Françoise-Marie Jacqueline who in 1640 became the wife of Charles de La Tour. Very little is known of her early life in France or of her family's religion, but after her marriage she declared herself a Huguenot in the hope of winning New England's support for her husband in his war against d'Aulnay. De La Tour, himself, had already made overtures to New England through a certain Shurd, an influential settler at Pemaquid.[61] In 1641 he sent a messenger, described as a rochelois and a Protestant, to Boston with a letter of recommendation from Shurd to ask for free trade with Massachusetts and also for military aid against d'Aulnay. Rumours of these negotiations reached France, and as a consequence d'Aulnay received a decree from the king calling for the arrest of de La Tour as a traitor.

At this juncture Lady de La Tour began to play a leading role in the struggle between her husband and d'Aulnay; she sailed for France in 1641 to solicit aid from Huguenot merchants, and with considerable success. On her return to America she visited Boston twice with her husband. There they attended, with some fanfare, a Congregational church in the hope of softening the hearts of the *bostonais*. On a second visit to France she found her standing there had precipitately declined and so she had to find her way to America via England, on a boat that also carried Roger Williams, the founder of Rhode Island. She now persuaded her husband to cut all ties with France and resume his Nova Scotian title; she also persuaded him to ask that a Protestant minister be sent to St. John, much to the chagrin of the Recollets, who now decided to join d'Aulnay and the Capuchins at Port-Royal.

De La Tour's negotiations with the councillors of New England were never very successful, for despite his wife's best efforts to give a religious motive to the feud, the Puritans continued to regard the seigneur of St. John as an idolator.[62] The New Englanders began early in their history to practice *real-politik,* and if they had to make a distinction between two idolators, they preferred to be on the side of the stronger; they were well aware that d'Aulnay was the more powerful of the two contestants and that his legal position in Acadia was more firmly established. The latter had sent a Capuchin monk, Father Marie, disguised as a layman to Salem, Massachusetts, to negotiate a trade treaty with the New England Council. He seems to have been a very successful diplomat, for he succeeded in getting a treaty signed (1645) between d'Aulnay and representatives of the council, the first international agreement signed by two colonial powers without reference to the home authorities.[63]

With New England neutralized, d'Aulnay proceeded to push vigorously his war against de La Tour. While the latter was in Boston pleading in vain for help against his rivals on the strength of his Protestant reforms, his wife with a small garrison at St. John was putting up a remarkable resistance to the invaders. It was a hopeless struggle and St. John fell to d'Aulnay in 1645. The victor then selected those among the defenders whom he considered the most seditious and had them hanged by one of their own number, who thus saved his own life. Lady de La Tour with a rope around her neck was compelled to witness this gruesome scene. She was then treated with considerable respect by her captors. However she died three weeks later from "exhaustion and vexation" but not before she had "publicly abjured Protestantism."[64]

Acadia for a brief moment enjoyed a period of peace and relative prosperity; it was during this period that the Capuchins really had an opportunity to organize a parochial system for Acadia based upon their fairly liberal outlook, which never discriminated against the Indians. Then came a most unexpected setback when their strongest supporter, d'Aulnay, was accidentally drowned (May 24, 1650) when a canoe in which he was traveling overturned not far from his residence at Port-Royal. From now on the Capuchins became involved in Acadia's financial problems almost to the exclusion of every other concern. This came about when Emmanuel Le Borgne became alarmed over his loan and demanded that Mme d'Aulnay, who was acting as a regent for d'Aulnay's children, should make an immediate payment on the loan, and proceeded to collect interest forcibly by seizing her merchandise.

In the midst of this turmoil Charles de La Tour, who had been living at Quebec, returned to the Acadian scene. With the help of the One Hundred Associates he was again appointed a lieutenant-governor of Acadia and allowed to take up residence once more at St. John.[65] In the hope of bringing some order out of the confusion that had followed upon d'Aulnay's death, and in good baronial style, he proposed marriage to Mme d'Aulnay. The offer caused consternation in the ranks of the Capuchins, who were also having a difficult time defending their property from the depredations of Le Borgne's men. Mme d'Aulnay, however, despairing of being able to meet the demands of her creditors, accepted de La Tour's proposal, and the Capuchins helped to draw up the rather complicated property settlement that had to be worked out between the two contracting families.

The marriage did little to strengthen either Acadia's financial situation or her military security. Le Borgne continued to collect by force whatever merchandise became available at Port-Royal. It appeared that the authorities in France were abetting him in this unusual method of securing payments for a state loan; but this approval was no longer so evident when the king appointed the Duc de Vendôme coseigneur with d'Aulnay's children at Port-Royal.

During the complications that followed upon this appointment the Capuchins were mostly engaged in trying to formulate some kind of stable agreements among many conflicting interests, much to the neglect of their missions and with little thanks for their efforts. According to Candide de Nant, officers of Le Borgne chased three Capuchins from Port-Royal in 1652, and arrested Mme de Brice and sent her back to France along with two other missionaries.[66]

ENGLISH OCCUPATION

Behind this sad spectacle which was making *"pauvre Acadie"* a helpless prey to any adventurer that might come along—one was not far away—was a civil war in France during which Cardinal Mazarin followed a devious course to extricate himself from difficult situations. There was also a civil war in England, but this war was working out to the advantage of New England by creating something like religious unity among the colonists who previously had been torn apart by religious dissent. In 1648 a synod of churches held at Cambridge, Massachusetts, formulated a church discipline which became known as the Cambridge Platform.[67] This included an acceptance of the Westminster Confession of Faith that had been formulated in the midst of the civil war in England.

The Cambridge Platform proved to be a standard basis of reference for the religious and social development of New England and provided the rapidly growing colonies with a unity of outlook that boded ill for the as yet hardly formulated cultural life of Acadie. Even as the colonies formulated their religious consensus and created a league of amity for defence and "for propagating the truth and liberties of the Gospel" New England became more aggressive "in expanding its commerce with other American settlements" but ready to make these settlements, by force of arms if need be, conform to the New England way of life.[68]

With the triumph of Cromwell, New England's chauvinism became more pronounced and took on the form of a self-righteous imperialism, which was also characteristic of the Commonwealth regime in England. As part of this new imperialistic policy which became closely allied to the profit motive, Cromwell sent Major Robert Sedgwick to America with a fleet to seize the Dutch settlement on Manhattan Island. Just as Sedgwick was about to leave Boston Harbour for an attack upon New Amsterdam he received word from Cromwell that peace had been signed with Holland and the attack was cancelled.

The New Englanders who had been enthusiastic for the elimination of the Dutch colonies in America were disappointed; there were also the French, who they felt might some day interfere with their manifest destiny. They informed Sedgwick of the confused situation in Acadia and suggested that now was the time to strike down this potential enemy. The Major agreed and proceeded with his fleet to Pentagouet, which he seized in the name of the English Commonwealth; he continued on to St. John and compelled de La Tour to submit once more to English rule; the last stop was at Port-Royal where the representatives of Le Borgne also made their submission. Without a shot being fired Acadia in 1654 came under British rule. In the negotiations that followed upon this unexpected aggression, the settlers were allowed to remain on their farms or, if they preferred, they could return to France; the Capuchins were permitted to continue their missions. Religious tolerance, however, did not last long. The soldiers of occupation, mostly Puritan in outlook, could not abide what they considered Romish idolatry: they first burned the Roman Church at Pentagouet and then looted and burned the monastery at Port-Royal. The Capuchin superior, Father Léonard de Chartres, was killed while trying to put some restraint upon looting soldiers. It was a frustrating and tragic time for the missionaries who had come to Acadia with such high hopes of establishing a mission among Puritans and Virginians.[69]

They had to make a hard decision, but as the historian of their Acadian saga points out, with Le Borgne recognized as the governor of Port-Royal, de La Tour installed at St. John and with Nicolas Denys, never favourable to the Capuchins, "master around the Gulf" there was no alternative but to return to France.[70]

The first tentative arrangements for the government of Acadia, referred to by Candide de Nant, did not survive the withdrawal of the Capuchins; but the later arrangements would not have improved their situation. These first administrators were not able to meet the revenue demands that Cromwell and his merchant friends made upon them, and so were displaced by men of financial acumen. De La Tour was allowed to retain his title of Baronet of Nova Scotia, but the real administration of the country was in the hands of two of Cromwell's favourites who conducted a profitable fur trade in Acadia from their headquarters in Boston. De La Tour then retired to his old home at Fort Saint-Louis where he lived out his life in peace with his wife and five young children.[71]

France under Mazarin raised little objection to this most unprovoked occupation of her oldest colony. The Acadians deprived of all spiritual guidance endured an ambiguous existence for a decade, when suddenly another King Charles in England decided, for a subsidy from Louis XIV, to restore Acadia to France in 1669 as his father had done in 1632. The sadly neglected Acadian missions now became part of the new parochial system that was evolving in New France under the leadership of Bishop Laval.

NOTES TO CHAPTER EIGHT

1. *Vide supra*, p. 77.

2. *Vide* A. P. Newton, "The Great Immigration 1618-1648" in *The Cambridge History of the British Empire* (Cambridge: Cambridge University Press, 1929-36), Vol. I, Chap. V, pp. 136-81.

3. *Vide supra*, p. 66.

4. *Vide* A. Bernard, *Le Drame Acadien depuis 1604* (Montreal: Les Clercs de Saint-Viateur, 1936), p. 4; also Candide de Nant, *Pages Glorieuses de l'Epopée Canadienne* (Montreal: Le Devoir, 1927), p. 85.

5. A. A. Johnston, *A History of the Catholic Church in Eastern Nova Scotia* (Antigonish: St. Francis Xavier University, 1960), p. 3 *et seq.*

6. *Vide supra*, p. 66; for origin of Lord Ochiltree's colony *vide infra*, p. 114.

7. *Vide* A. Bernard, *op. cit.*, p. 50; also H. P. Biggar, *The Early Trading Companies of New France* (Toronto: University of Toronto Press, 1901), p. 147.

8. *Vide supra*, p. 76; the story of the "shipwreck near Canso" has been vividly related by A. A. Johnston, *op. cit.*, pp. 10-4.

9. *Vide supra*, p. 80.

10. *Vide* A. A. Johnston, *op. cit.*, pp. 19-20.

11. *Vide supra*, p. 78.

12. Charles Rogers, *Memorials of the Earl of Stirling and the House of Alexander* (Edinburgh: Wm. Patterson, 1877), Vol. I, p. 59; *vide* also A. L. Rowse, *The Elizabethans and America* (London: Macmillan, 1959), p. 105.

13. *Vide* Charles Rogers, *op. cit.*, Vol. I, p. 60-2 for copy of James I's communication to the Scottish Privy Council setting up New Scotland with a royal charter.

14. *Ibid*, Vol. I, p. 69.

15. *Vide supra*, p. 77.

16. Mason's "A Briefe Discourse of the New-found-land" etc. is printed in full by D. W. Prowse in *A History of Newfoundland* (London: Macmillan, 1895), pp. 105-8.

17. Sir William Vaughan seems to have run short of funds, for he sold a block of land in Newfoundland to Lord Falkland who "established at Trinity Bay and dispossessed of the remaining northern portion of his big territory to Lord Baltimore"; the latter brought about forty persons to Ferryland, along with some seminary priests, but after two seasons they returned to England. Prowse, *op. cit.*, pp. 110-3.

18. *Vide supra*, p. 56.

19. Concerning Stourton, Prowse says he "belonged to the ecclesiastical party in the English Church, which we now call Evangelical or Low Church," *op. cit.*, note 1, p. 101. Anne Mason on the other hand was "a High Church woman," p. 109.

20. Concerning the cause of the hostilities of the Devonshire fishermen against permanent settlers, Prowse, *op. cit.*, p. 99, writes, "No doubt the proclamation of laws made by the Alderman Governor on the 30th August aroused their indignation."

21. *Vide supra*, p. 111.

22. Charles Rogers, *op. cit.*, Vol. I, pp. 101-29.

23. A. Couillard Després, *Charles de Saint-Etienne de La Tour et son Temps 1593-1666* (Arthabaska: Imprimerie d'Arthabaska, incorporée, 1930), pp. 170-80, does not believe that Charles de La Tour accepted a baronetcy at this time. E. Lauvrière, *La Tragédie d'un Peuple* (Paris: Librairie Henry Goulet, 1924), Vol. I, p. 45 *et seq.*, says that the evidence makes clear he did; Candide de Nant agrees with Lauvrière.

24. Champlain, *Works* (H. P. Biggar, ed.; Toronto: Champlain Society, 1922-36), Vol. V, p. 173 says de La Tour had not allowed himself to yield to the persuasions of his father, who was with the English; for he would rather have died than consent to such baseness as to betray his King." Nicolas Denys, *The Description and Natural History of the Coasts of North America* (translated and edited by W. F. Ganong, Toronto: The Champlain Society, 1908), pp. 132-7, also says that de La Tour refused the baronetcy. Ganong in his introduction, p. 4, accepts Denys' version.

25. *Vide* H. P. Biggar, *op. cit.*, p. 152.

26. *Vide* Candide de Nant, *op. cit.*, pp. 109-10.

27. *Ibid.*, p. 101 *et seq.*

28. *Ibid.*, p. 98

29. The career of Isaac de Razilly has been set forth very briefly in Léon Deschamps' "Isaac de Razilly, Biographie-Mémoire Inédite" (An extract from *Revue de Géographie*, October 1886), p. 282 *et seq.*

30. Candide de Nant, *op. cit.*, p. 121.

31. *Vide* A. Bernard, *op. cit.*, p. 121.

32. *Vide* Candide de Nant, *op. cit.*, pp. 136-7.

33. A. Couillard Després, *op. cit.*, p. 228.

34. *Vide* Candide de Nant, *op. cit.*, pp. 147-51.

35. *Vide* A. Couillard Després, *op. cit.*, p. 202 *et seq.*

36. *Vide* Candide de Nant, *op. cit.*, pp. 127-128; the New England version of this incident is to be found in William Bradford's *Of Plymouth Plantation 1620-47* (A new edition with introduction by S. E. Morison; New York: Knopf, 1963), pp. 245 and 262-3.

37. *Vide* Edward Ballard, *Memorial Volume of the Popham Celebration* (Portland, Maine: Bailey and Noyes, 1863), p. 138 *et seq.*

38. R. P. T. Coffin, *Kennebec, Cradle of the Americas* (New York & Toronto: Farrar and Rinehart, 1937), p. 44. *Vide* also W. Bradford *op. cit.*, pp. 80-1.

39. *Vide* A. L. Rowse, *op. cit.*, p. 104.

40. *Vide* J. A. Doyle, *The English in America* (London: Longmans, Green, 1882), Vol. I, p. 276; also W. Bradford, *op. cit.*, p. 38.

41. *Vide* W. H. Hutton, *The English Church from the Accession of Charles I to the Death of Queen Anne* (London: Macmillan, 1913), p. 4 *et seq.*

42. *Vide* Ruth Putnam, "The Dutch Element in the United States", in the *Annual Report of the American Historical Association for the Year 1909* (Washington, 1911), p. 206; also in the same volume H. T. Colebrander, "The Dutch Element in American History," pp. 193-201.

43. D. W. Prowse, *op. cit.*, p. 148.

44. The Cambridge History of the British Empire, *op. cit.*, Vol. I, p. 136.

45. A. P. Newton, *The Colonizing Activities of the English Puritans* (New Haven: Yale University Press, 1914), p. 49; *vide* also T. J. Wertenbaker, *The Puritan Oligarchy, The Founding of American Civilization* (New York and London: Scribner, 1947); a chapter on "The Bible State," pp. 41-77, is particularly pertinent.

46. *Vide* P. Miller and J. H. Johnson, *The Puritans* (New York: American Book, 1938), the introductory chapter is a good summary of the likenesses and differences of Anglicans and Puritans; reference to Pierre de la Ramée begins on p. 28.

47. W. H. Hutton, *op. cit.*, p. 39.

48. *Vide* P. Miller, *The New England Mind from Colony to Province* (Cambridge, Mass.: Harvard University Press, 1953), *passim*, esp. pp. 119-29.

49. *Vide* John Robinson's farewell letters in W. Bradford, *op. cit.*, Appendix IV, pp. 367-71.

50. An interesting account on "Religion in the Colonies" with supporting documents is to be found in D. C. Douglas, ed., *English Historical Documents* (London: Eyre and Spottiswood, 1955-), Vol. IX, *American Colonial Documents to 1776*, p. 515 *et seq.*

51. Quoted in W. Bradford, *op. cit.,* pp. 272-3.

52. *Vide supra,* p. 116. *et seq.*

53. *Vide* Candide de Nant, *op. cit.,* p. 230 *et seq.*

54. *Ibid.,* p. 246 *et seq.*

55. *Ibid.,* pp. 233-5.

56. *Vide* G. Lanctot, *A History of Canada,* Vol. I: *From Its Origins to the Royal Regime 1663* (trans. J. Hambleton; Toronto and Vancouver: Clarke, Irwin, 1959), p. 291.

57. *Vide* Candide de Nant, *op. cit.,* p. 244.

58. *Vide supra,* Ch. V, p. 53 *et seq.*

59. A. Bernard, *op. cit.,* pp. 70-71.

60. *Vide* A. Couillard Després, *Charles de Sainte-Etienne de La Tour, Gouverneur en Acadie 1593-1666 au Tribunal de l'Histoire;* in this brief pamphlet the abbé reviews the evidence of Emile Lauvrière and others who have impugned the integrity of de La Tour and retains the high opinion in which he held the hero of his earlier work.

61. A. Couillard Després, *op. cit.,* p. 300 *et seq.*

62. *Vide* J. K. Hosmer, *Winthrop's Journal* (New York: Scribner, 1908), Vol. II, p. 110; Winthrop's Journal indicates a long-drawn-out argument, but those who held that "Papists are not to be trusted seeing that it is one of their tenets that they are not to keep promise with heretics," won the day; also J. A. Doyle, *op. cit.,* p. 333 *et seq.*

63. A copy of this treaty is included in the appendices of Candide de Nant, *op. cit.,* pp. 316-7.

64. A. Bernard, *op. cit.,* p. 72. A. Couillard Després, *Charles de Saint-Etienne de La Tour et son Temps, op. cit.,* pp. 376-7, doubts that Lady de La Tour abjured her Protestantism.

65. *Ibid.,* p. 399 *et seq.*

66. *Ibid.,* p. 422; also Candide de Nant, *op. cit.,* p. 275.

67. *Vide* R. G. Thwaites, *The Colonies 1492-1750* (New York: Longmans, 1920), pp. 162-3.

68. Louis B. Wright, *The American Frontier, Colonial American Civilization* (New York: Knopf, 1951), pp. 130-41; Wright says "The New England Puritans' code of ethics, with its everlasting insistence upon prudential virtues of sobriety, thrift and diligence provided an almost fool-proof guide to success."

69. J. G. Palfrey, *A Compendious History of New England* (Boston and New York: Houghton, Mifflin, 1883), p. 336, passes over "these transactions between New England and New France as of little interest." In contrast French historians regard them as of tragic importance; *vide* Emile Lauvrière, *op. cit.,* Vol. I, p. 84 *et seq.*

70. Candide de Nant, *op. cit.,* p. 296.

71. *Vide* A. Couillard Després, *op. cit.,* p. 441 *et seq.*

NINE

The Era of Laval

While Acadia was languishing under foreign rule, the settlers along the St. Lawrence River were laying the foundations for a unique way of life that has remained distinct from the North American complex to this day.[1] A suggested date for this transition from *françois* to *canadois* is the year which saw the end of the frustrating rule of the One Hundred Associates (1663) and the introduction into Canada of royal administration. This coincides rather closely with Bishop Laval's attempt to set up a new parochial system based upon a preconceived plan which had been impressed upon him by his Jesuit mentors.

The settlers themselves, however, brought about many adjustments and modifications to the original design; although they were few in number[2] they were in an enterprising and expansive mood and not much inclined to continue under the strict church discipline of an earlier epoch.[3] Both settlers and missionaries were curious to know what lay beyond the St. Lawrence Valley and they began to scatter far and wide over the great expanse of territory to the west: some of them reached the southwest shore of Lake Superior, crossed the Wisconsin and touched the northern boundary of what is now the state of Minnesota; others began to move up towards Hudson Bay; and, what was most exciting of all, others began to coast down the Mississippi to open up a route to the Gulf of Mexico.

Because of the ample space now available to roam through, and the consequent boundless opportunities to engage in free enterprise, the bishop was compelled to make many concessions to the spirit of democracy which seems to be the inevitable accompaniment of the open frontier. The result was the evolution of a parochial system quite original in western Christendom.[4]

CHURCH AND STATE CONTROVERSIES

Such adjustments as were necessary for the church in this new land must have been quite painful to the bishop at first as there was little of the spirit of compromise in Mgr François de Montmorency-Laval de Montigny. After his preliminary bout with the Sulpicians he immediately became involved in an acrimonious quarrel with Governor d'Argenson concerning ceremonial and protocol. It has been suggested by a very sympathetic biographer that an early stay at the Jesuit Collège at La Flèche, where the governor of the city was continually harassing the Jesuits, may have created in the young Laval a deep aversion to all gubernatorial pretensions; a more likely suggestion by the same biographer is that this younger scion of the family of Montmorency developed a strong dislike of the means employed by Richelieu for exalting the glory of France, which included the execution of the Duc de Montmorency, because the latter had opposed the "often arbitrary projects of the powerful minister."[5] Such a judicial murder of one of his own family no doubt encouraged Laval to agree with his Jesuit instructors at La Flèche on the necessity of ultramontanism as the best defense against Richelieu's chauvinism. This belief was further reinforced by Laval's instructors at the Collège of Clermont, where he continued his education, as well as at the Hermitage at Caen, where he stayed for four years (1654-58) preceding his sailing to Canada.

Here under the tutelage of Jean de Bernières, the founder of the Hermitage, he absorbed much of the mystical piety of the era; he was also alerted against what de Bernières considered the twin "pests" of Gallicanism and Jansenism. It was the opinion of Marie de l'Incarnation that Laval's stay at the Hermitage of Caen had had a decisive influence upon his policy during the early part of his episcopate.[6] Some of the tenets of de Bernières were being put into practice when Laval removed the governor's seat from the chancel and placed it outside the altar rail, and insisted that a thurifer and not a sub-deacon should salute the governor with incense. To many in Quebec, this appeared to be an unnecessary harassment of the governor, but it was pursued with such great vehemence on all ceremonial occasions that even the Jesuits were embarrassed and decided not to invite the two dignitaries to their refectory at the same time, since they were loath to take sides by giving one or the other the highest place of honour at their dining table.[7]

Governor d'Argenson soon became weary of quarreling with the young bishop and sought to be relieved of his post, particularly after he became involved in a controversy over the sale of intoxicating beverages to the aborigines. Laval had been greatly shocked when he saw the Indians, under the influence of alcohol, making beasts of themselves and endangering the lives of all who came in contact with them. In order to bring this scandal quickly to an end he pronounced a sentence of excommunication upon anyone selling alcoholic beverages to the Indians, and reserved to himself the right of absolution.[8] D'Argenson had been as shocked as Laval at the excesses of the Indians when intoxicated, but he believed that the regulation of the traffic in liquor was a civil reponsibility and that the use of excommunication to curb it was an intrusion of the church into the affairs of the state. He appealed to Paris for a definite ruling on this matter, but the decision was long deferred.

In the meantime, d'Argenson resigned his office (1661) and was replaced by Pierre Dubois, Baron Davaugour. Before the latter left France he had been strictly warned by the court not to allow the church to encroach on the prerogatives of the state. In order to avoid a repetition of d'Argenson's clash with the bishop over excommunication he immediately decreed very harsh penalties against anyone caught selling intoxicating liquor to the Indians; to emphasize his determination in this matter he had two men shot for violating his decree. Such harsh measures did not particularly endear him to the church which considered excommunication more humane and perhaps even more effective than the death penalty. When a little later a woman was imprisoned for selling brandy to an Indian, Father Lalemant, moved to pity by the entreaties of her relatives, went to the governor to plead for leniency and got an answer that he neither expected nor wanted; the indignant governor replied "that inasmuch as the liquor trade was not a fault punishable in that woman, it should not be in the future in anybody."[9]

Once again liquor was freely sold to all and sundry in Quebec, entailing so much debauchery and violence that Laval now began to despair of accomplishing anything worthwhile in New France. Controversies with the Sulpicians and with two governors, and even strained relations at times with the Jesuits, finally compelled him to return to France in order to carry his grievances directly to the king and to seek from Louis XIV greater authority for administering his diocese. Marie de l'Incarnation, writing to her son on the occasion of the bishop's departure for France said, "I believe that if he does not succeed in his purpose, he will not return, and that will be an irreparable loss to this new church and for all the poor French."[10]

Such fears, however, were groundless, for when Davaugour hastened back to France to place his side of the controversy before the king, it was the governor and not the bishop who remained in France.

A SOVEREIGN COUNCIL

It was with considerable pride that Laval returned to New France in 1663; he had succeeded in the purpose of his trip to Paris beyond his fondest hope. The king had been in a very accommodating mood: he promised to make it possible for Laval to exchange his title of Bishop of Petraea to that of Bishop of Quebec free from the inhibiting influence of the Archbishop of Rouen; he agreed to dismiss the Company of One Hundred Associates and establish a Sovereign Council for Quebec,[11] to which would be committed the task of regulating the liquor traffic; most surprising of all the king asked Laval to choose a new governor for Canada.

These overwhelming favours turned out to be more apparent than real, for Archbishop Harlay of Rouen continued to block the creation of an autonomous Diocese of Quebec; the new governor whom Laval had chosen proved to be as recalcitrant as former governors; and the Sovereign Council in time developed an independence that did not always please the bishop.

Laval proposed an old comrade at the Hermitage of Caen, the Chevalier de Mézy, for governor. As de Mézy had imbibed deeply of the mystical piety of de Bernières, Laval felt confident that under such a pious governor "all abuses which had brought him to France would disappear from Canada."[12] It was essential that he should find a kindred spirit for the office, for in setting up the Sovereign Council the king had stipulated that the governor and the bishop should act "conjointly in concert"[13] in its administration.

In thus attempting to bind church and state together in the government of New France, the king was, with the best will in the world, unwittingly creating a situation which would inevitably end in tragedy. Unavoidably the two men who were asked to act in concert represented conflicting interests, for the interests of church and state can never be identical. Although de Mézy's and Laval's piety sprang from the same source this did not necessarily mean harmony, for it was an uncompromising piety which compelled both men to be rigid in defending their own special interests or loyalties. It was in constituting the Sovereign Council that the diversity of interests and loyalties began to appear. In the council were to sit the governor and bishop as equals along with five other members to be named jointly by the two presiding officers. As Laval knew the citizens of Quebec far better than de Mézy did, he was able to select those who favoured the ecclesiastical point of view; this soon became evident to the governor, and in order to bring about a better balance in the council he dismissed three members and called upon the citizens of Quebec to elect suitable men to replace them. Quebec was now in a state of turmoil with the bishop rebuking the governor from the pulpit and the latter placarding the town, to the accompaniment of a drum, with his version of the quarrel.[14]

At the height of the dispute the governor fell seriously ill and the citizens of Quebec who had a short time before been terrified by an earthquake, which had generally been interpreted as a divine warning[15] against an erring people, were now convinced that God was again intervening directly in the affairs of New France. The illness proved fatal for de Mézy who died on May 5, 1665, but not before, as reported in a Jesuit *Relation*, he confessed, received communion and was fully reconciled to the church.[16]

Although it now appeared that Laval had been dramatically vindicated in his controversy with the governor, the sequel did not prove to be as favourable to the bishop's cause as might have been expected. The council met shortly after the governor's death and conferred on one of its own members "all the functions that had formerly belonged to the late Governor de Mézy."[17] There followed a general reorganization of the council, including the addition of the Intendant Talon, who immediately took over all the functions that had been previously exercised by the bishop. From now on Laval attended the council's meetings very infrequently and began to devote himself more assiduously to matters purely ecclesiastical.

A NEW RELIGIOUS ESTABLISHMENT

From the moment of his consecration Laval had it in mind to create in the New World a religious establishment which would be a model of efficiency and piety. He soon discovered, however, that he could not start afresh in working out his design. Before his arrival in Quebec the outlines of a parochial system were already emerging within the framework of a seigneurial system. The church in New France, like any individual, received seigneurial land grants. This custom began in 1624 when the "Reverend Fathers of the Society of Jesus" were granted "the seigniory of Notre-Dame-des-Anges, lying along the river St. Charles, near Quebec."[18] In time seigneurie and parish boundaries were almost conterminous, the church and the manor house became the foci of the religious as well as the social life of the community: "the curé and seigneur . . . walked side by side."[19]

A representative element in the parochial life of New France had also emerged before the bishop's arrival. In 1645 the parishoners of Notre-Dame at Quebec had elected three church wardens, who became the people's representatives on the church council, or *fabrique*; this council united both the civil and religious concerns of the community. Thus very early in the life of New France the parish corporation came to be administered by a committee composed of the parish priest as president and the duly elected church wardens.[20] Bishop Laval wisely decided to continue what appeared to be a very democratic form of church government at the local level but at the same time to combine it with the principle of centralized authority, which would be in accord with the royal absolutism as set forth in the constitution of the Sovereign Council. Although the bishop was to be the ultimate source of authority, Laval planned to share a great deal of administrative work with a grand seminary that he planned to set up which might serve as a national *curia* for New France.[21]

A seminary began to take form in 1663, the year of the foundation of the *Séminaire des Missions-étrangères* in Paris, to which Laval affiliated his own institution, since it was his hope that this New World seminary would become a great educational centre for training missionary priests. To it he attached a *petit séminaire* for teaching boys, from which he expected to discover young men with vocations to the priesthood.[22]

The *Grand Séminaire*, however, was to be far more than a teaching centre: it was also to be a home, not only for the bishop but for all parochial priests. Curés were encouraged to look upon it as their true home where they were to stay when visiting Quebec and to which they would turn in sickness and old age. In thus weaning curés away from any permanent attachment to their parishes Laval was subtly trying to undermine Gallicanism which laid great stress upon the independence guaranteed to parish priests by permanent curacies, free from any arbitrary recall by their bishop. It was Laval's intention that in consultation with the seminary authorities he should locate priests in their parishes and that he would be able to recall or transfer them to other parishes as he thought desirable; priests under these circumstances would not, as was usual in France, receive their stipends from tithes—the seminary itself would become their paymaster.[23]

Consequently, it was imperative that the seminary should be well endowed. As a start Laval donated to it his own income; he also persuaded the king to give to it the income from three abbeys in France. One further source of revenue which he attempted to secure was destined to create among the habitants a great deal of hostility both to himself and to the seminary. Since the seminary was going to pay the stipends of the parish priests, the bishop thought it should receive the tithes that were normally levied for this purpose. The citizens of New France under the generous shepherding of the Jesuits had not been accustomed to contributing to the upkeep of the church and were in no mood to assume this financial burden. At first Laval asked the Sovereign Council to make a levy of one-thirteenth of the produce of farms but this demand stirred up such resistance among the habitants that the bishop finally agreed to a levy of one-twenty-sixth.[24].

Once the seminary was securely established Laval began to share with its officers a large part of the administration of his diocese. At the head of the seminary he placed Henri de Bernières, the curé of Quebec, and thus the new institution was closely associated with the Parish of Quebec. Along with de Bernierès were five other directors who acted as an advisory body to the bishop in his episcopal administration and served him with a fidelity and loyalty which continued on into the administration of Laval's successor, much to the chagrin of the latter.[25] Classical instruction such as the seminaries provided was not the only form of education that Laval bequeathed to French Canada; he was also concerned with practical education for the sons of craftsmen and farmers, and for this purpose he founded at Saint-Joachim a justly famous school of arts and crafts and associated with it an experimental farm and normal school.[26]

Very little in the way of religious devotion missed the sharp eye of Bishop Laval who was keenly interested in the proper performance of all liturgical acts. In a letter to the Holy See (1664) he describes with pride the offices conducted in the recently erected stone basilica at Quebec. "The divine office," he writes, "is celebrated here according to the ceremonial of the bishops; our priests and seminarists along with ten or twelve choir boys are regularly present. During the major festivals, the mass, vespers and the evening salutation are sung with orchestra and organ accompaniment."[27] It would seem that Quebec in 1664 was as well equipped as any European city for any ceremonial occasion.

Several confraternities, such as the Rosary and Scapular, had been established in the infant colony before the bishop's arrival; these he examined closely and took great care to regularize their performance;

he also had the honour of establishing in his diocese the feast of the Holy Family, which the pope later extended to the whole church.[28] Early in his episcopate he secured a piece of land at Petit-Cap (1660), and had built there a very simple chapel for the Confraternity of Sainte-Anne. Marie de l'Incarnation in one of her letters calls attention to this little chapel "in which," she says, "our Lord does great marvels."[29] As a consequence of remarkable cures associated with the cult of Sainte-Anne, the primitive wooden chapel at Petit-Cap was replaced in 1675 with a stone church and it in turn, even during Laval's time, was replaced by an immense basilica.

ECONOMIC DEVELOPMENT

While Bishop Laval was busily engaged in shaping the devotional life of Canada, the intendant, Jean Talon, was just as industriously engaged in shaping its economic life. This latter task had long been neglected by the French court, but in 1665 there entered into the service of the French government a figure of the first rank in finance, marine and industry, namely, Jean-Baptiste Colbert, who immediately turned his attention to the economic future of Canada.[30] From now on much less is heard about the building of the Kingdom of God in New France and much more about the building of a great commercial empire for old France.[31] The man chosen by Colbert for this task in Canada was Jean Talon.

But before the latter could embark upon a contemplated scheme of industrialization something drastic had to be done about the Iroquois menace. So, along with Talon, the French government sent out to the New World Seigneur de Tracy as lieutenant-general over all French possessions in America, and Daniel de Courcelles as Governor of Canada. Accompanying them was the famous Carignan-Salières Regiment, despatched for the purpose of compelling the Iroquois to desist from troubling New France. The exuberant joy with which the inhabitants greeted this regiment was well expressed by the Jesuit superior, François Le Mercier, who wrote, "Never will New France cease to bless our great Monarch for undertaking to restore her to life and rescue her from the fires of the Iroquois."[32]

By 1666 de Tracy and his regiment had compelled the Iroquois to sue for peace; after the signing of what was considered a firm peace treaty, de Tracy returned to France and the way was now clear for Talon to embark upon an ambitious plan to make New France a viable colony dependent upon its own natural resources.[33] Although the intendant had left France with some reluctance, no sooner did he view the St. Lawrence Valley with its picturesque scenery and its rich farm lands than he fell in love with the place and turned to his assigned task with an enthusiasm that became infectious throughout the colony.[34]

Unfortunately, he had to work within the framework of a company ownership; for despite the failure of the Company of One Hundred Associates to take their colonization responsibilities seriously, Colbert was of the opinion that only trading companies could successfully create an overseas empire; consequently, in 1664 he set up the Company of the West Indies as the grand Seigneur of Acadia, Newfoundland and Canada. Talon early recognized that this company might become a serious obstacle to immigration, but he discovered that effective power was in the hands of the king who appointed the governor, the intendant and the members of the council.[35] By working closely with Colbert and the king he was able to circumvent the company's monopoly.

The great failure of company ownership had been its persistent neglect to bring out colonists to the New World. It was Talon's first task to overcome this neglect and he proceeded immediately to find inhabitants for the vacant farmlands along the St. Lawrence. Fortunately, there were at hand some prospective settlers, namely, the officers and soldiers of the Carignan Company, which was being disbanded. The court agreed that they might remain in Canada; and thus was provided for Talon a wonderful opportunity to give some reality to a seigneurial system which up to this time existed more in name than in fact.[36]

It had been difficult to get seigneurs to reside in their seigneuries without tenants; or to place tenants without a seigneur. The Carignan Company was an ideal source from which to secure settlers, for the officers became seigneurs and the soldiers tenants. It was soon observed that these new settlers altered the earlier pietistic outlook of New France, but there is little question that they gave greater variety and depth to the cultural life of their adopted country.

With this good start Talon then persuaded the French court to send out additional settlers at the expense of the royal treasury. Between 1665 and 1668 almost a thousand people were transferred from France to Canada, including prospective brides, picturesquely called "the King's daughters." To increase the population even more rapidly the intendant made grants to fathers of large families and encouraged early marriages by helping young people to set up housekeeping; at the same time he used every device possible to provide employment for the fast growing colony.[37]

It is beyond the scope of this study to detail the many local industries that Talon initiated in his endeavour to provide jobs for all, or to comment on his search for natural resources; suffice it to say that there was great stir and excitement in Quebec which created a new spirit of emulation and a striving after mundane rewards that had received little emphasis under the pious leadership of an earlier day.[38]

There is considerable evidence that both the bishop and the Jesuits were greatly alarmed at this extravagant search for material comforts, and the obvious desire of the settlers to throw off many of the puritanical inhibitions that their spiritual leaders had imposed upon earlier colonists. Talon, himself, was little inclined to be admonished by the Jesuits, as he had been warned by Colbert before he left France that this society had been usurping the authority of the state and that he was to keep them in proper subjection to the temporal authority.[39] If Talon had been more submissive to ecclesiastical advice it would still have been difficult for either the bishop or the Jesuits to impose their puritanical discipline upon a people enjoying, for the first time in the history of the colony, a far better prospect of entering upon a more opulent way of life than had ever been remotely possible in France. Many of the religious, among them Marie de l'Incarnation, were caught up in the excitement of the times. The mother superior of the Ursulines did indeed resent Talon's suspicious attitude towards the Jesuits but she could not forbear to pay her tribute to him for the many good things that the dynamic intendant had done for her beloved *canadois*.[40]

There was one issue, however, upon which the bishop would never compromise or yield—the sale of alcohol to the Indians; on this matter he caused the intendant considerable embarrassment by the use of excommunication. When Talon discovered that it was impossible to prevent the *coureurs de bois* going far from the French settlements and exchanging brandy for furs, he reverted to the policy of earlier governors and permitted the sale of liquor within the settlements as the only way to compete with the free traders. The opposition from the clergy to this move was so bitter that Talon returned to France to resign his office. At the urgent request of the king he agreed to return to Canada, but on the condition that the Recollets might occupy once more their old home on the St. Charles River.[41] As might have been expected neither the bishop nor the Jesuits were favourably impressed with the six Recollets who came out with their superior, Allard; it is Rochemonteix's opinion that they arrived in a belligerent frame of mind and were quite surprised with the kind reception they received from the bishop. There was really little friction at first, as the Recollets gave most of their attenion to organizing daring missions in the mysterious West.[42]

MISSIONS IN THE WEST

The supervising of these missions in the west, where three orders were competing for glory and honour, was to become a serious problem for Laval who still bore the dubious title of Bishop of Petraea. It was, however, the Sulpicians and not the Recollets who gave him most concern, for his relations with them were coloured by a constitutional issue which involved the Sovereign Council. Montreal continued to be jealous of its independent foundation and resisted strongly any directions coming from Quebec. When the Society of Notre-Dame disbanded in 1663 and handed over its seigneurial privileges to the Gentlemen of Saint-Sulpice, Governor de Mézy thought that he ought in the name of the Sovereign Council confirm Maisonneuve in his office of governor. The latter would not submit to any such procedure and asserted strongly that confirmation or appointment of a governor lay in the hands of the Sulpicians upon whom had devolved the seigneurial rights of the Society of Notre-Dame.[43]

Maisonneuve successfully resisted the pressures of de Mézy, but he was not so successful in a confrontation with Laval. The latter had asserted his right to scrutinize the records of the religious institutions of Montreal. In running over the financial accounts of the Hôtel-Dieu he noticed the transfer of 20,000 *livres* of hospital endowment to Maisonneuve; as was well known this had been given to the governor by Jeanne Mance for the purpose of bringing out soldiers from France for the protection of Montreal against the Iroquois raids. Although the hospital had been generously compensated by a land grant, nevertheless Laval insisted that Maisonneuve should return the money to the hospital. On his refusal the governor-general intervened and ordered Maisonneuve to return to France to explain his conduct.[44] In Paris the seminary cleared the venerable Governor of Montreal of any charges of wrongdoing and allowed him to retain his title for some years, but he was never allowed to return to his beloved Ville-Marie. He died in Paris in 1676 still protesting the unjustifiable claim against the Sulpicians—hardly a fitting end to the courageous founder of Montreal. An ironic footnote was added to the affair by the appointment as his successor of François-Marie Perrot, a thoroughly commercially minded man who showed little loyalty to Montreal in that he ran a rival fur-trade mart on an island that now bears his name, and managed to impoverish the city whose interests he had sworn to uphold.[45]

This humiliation of Montreal hardly reflects any credit upon Bishop Laval, but he persisted in urging the unjustified claim upon Saint-Sulpice for twenty years, and it was only dropped by Laval's successor in 1695. In other ways, however, Laval began to make some gestures of friendliness to the Sulpicians: at long last he gave permission to Abbé de Queylus to assume his post as Superior of the Seminary of Saint-Sulpice. Accompanying the superior to Montreal were three additional priests, including René de Brehant de Galinée who was to become famous as a recorder of explorations. Now that their seminary was firmly established the Sulpicians were anxious to begin western missions; they had in mind particularly a mission to some Iroquois who had actually invited them to settle down in a community on the north shore of Lake Ontario, now known as the Bay of Quinte area.[46] De Queylus was very careful not to give any further offence to Laval, so he consulted the bishop about such a project, which he feared the Jesuits might resent. This time he found his former critic in a very accommodating frame of mind. Laval gave his consent readily, but for some inexplicable reason he made Abbé Trouvé the chief of the mission rather than Abbé Fénelon, who had been the real organizer of the project.[47] Another member of the party was Dollier de Casson, the author of a very famous history of Montreal, who was soon to succeed de Queylus as superior of the seminary.

During the winter of 1668 the little company began their mission on the north shore of Lake Ontario, where they learned from the Nipissings of a great river to the southwest that might lead to either a southern or a western ocean. Such information was carried back to Montreal and was heard with great interest by a newly installed seigneur in the vicinity of Ville-Marie, Sieur Cavelier de La Salle. He was so intrigued by what he heard that he accompanied the Sulpicians on a second trip westward that carried them as far as Georgian Bay, where the famous explorer first resolved that he would find his way to China along an as yet undiscovered river that led to the ocean. Thus the Bay of Quinte mission became the forerunner of the exploration of the Great West and the Mississippi Valley; it also opened up to the Sulpicians a new career of adventure and exploration hardly contemplated by the founders of Ville-Marie.[48]

In a very short time the Jesuits and Recollets were caught up in the same questing mood and were off in various directions looking for new lands to enlarge the king's domain and new nations to convert to Christianity. As these orders were attracting more and more adventurous souls who were rivals in trying to get to far away places first, so the bishop, endeavouring to keep some semblance of order in his fast expanding diocese, became seriously alarmed about the ambiguity of his title. Finally he decided that he himself must return to France to plead with the king personally to impress upon the *curia* of Rome that he must become a bishop in his own right, free from the inhibiting influence of the Archbishop of Rouen. But the archbishop was not easily persuaded to yield any of his powers in the New World and so the Bishop of Petraea was to spend four long and critical years in France waiting for the coveted title of Bishop of Quebec.[49]

THE ARRIVAL OF FRONTENAC

Consequently, Bishop Laval was absent from his diocese in 1672 when Louis de Buade, Comte de Frontenac, was installed as Governor of Quebec and Lieutenant-General of Canada. The new governor was one of the most self-willed and glamorous rulers yet to come to the New World.[50] Upon his arrival he proceeded to establish his authority with as much éclat as possible. To the surprise of everyone, including the King of France, he convoked an estates general and harangued the assembly on the duty of absolute obedience to the crown. Ignoring the Sovereign Council, he attempted to work out a new body of regulations for the government of Quebec which he said was to become the "capital of a great empire."[51]

Shortly after his arrival he was rebuking the Jesuits because of a sermon preached by one of the fathers denouncing the sale of liquor to the Indians, a very familiar theme by this time in Quebec pulpits. Such a matter, Frontenac said, was purely the concern of the secular authorities and should not be touched upon from the pulpit; he urged his point of view so vehemently that Abbé de Bernières, whom Laval had placed in charge of the diocese, felt compelled to disavow the sermon.[52] But Frontenac was not yet satisfied and he continued to denounce the Jesuits: for spying upon the community, for abusing the confessional and setting husbands against wives and parents against children. As a further humiliation for the Society of Jesus, he began to show obvious favoritism towards the Recollets. Under constant attack from the governor, the Jesuits saw their dream of a theocracy for New France fast fading from view. With the departure of a disgusted Talon to France there seemed no one left in Canada who had the courage to stand up to the imperious governor.

Surprisingly enough, the first sign of defiance came not from Quebec and the Jesuits, but from Montreal and the Sulpicians, or perhaps one Sulpician, François de Salignac de La Mothe-Fénelon, a half brother of the famous Archbishop of Cambrai.[53] Unfortunately, it was a commercially based defiance rather than the defence of spiritual freedom; nevertheless, it did reveal to the authorities in France that they had sent out to Canada an unusually arbitrary governor. Montreal, being closer than Quebec to the source of supply for the fur trade, had become under Sulpician ownership the very noisy auction centre of Canada: here *coureurs de bois*, Indians, traders, clerks and seamen bought and sold their wares. It was indeed a strange scene for a religious order to preside over; one observer with little tolerance for "the yells, the hubbub, the fights, the disputes accompanying the sales, and the resorts to the brandy pubs"[54] compared the furore to the infernal regions. Much of the trade carried on at Montreal and its environs was illicit. Frontenac had received strict orders from the king to bring this unlawful bartering to an end. This he attempted to do as soon as he got to Montreal, but much to his surprise he found that the greatest offender of all was Governor Perrot, who on Ile Perrot was openly employing *coureurs de bois* who brought to him furs that were destined for Montreal, which were then sold on the foreign market at a good profit to the governor himself.

When Frontenac became aware of what was going on he ordered Perrot to proceed to Quebec (1673) to give an explanation of the transactions on Ile Perrot. Among the entourage accompanying Perrot was the Abbé Fénelon, who had gone to Quebec at Frontenac's request in order to impress upon the Governor of Montreal the enormity of the crime he had committed, and also to represent the seigneurial interests of the Sulpicians. Fénelon was no partisan of Perrot, but he conceived his own function as that of mediator between the two governors; when Frontenac decided, with very little regard for legal niceties, to demote and imprison Perrot and appoint a retired officer, La Nouguère, as Governor of Montreal, Fénelon demurred and vented his feelings in a blistering sermon condemning Frontenac's high-handed action.[55] The Sulpician superior, Dollier de Casson, repudiated the sermon, but this did not appease the infuriated Frontenac who summoned the offending preacher before the Sovereign Council. By this time the council was becoming restive and was refusing to be merely the mouthpiece of the governor. Frontenac, rather than put up with any procedural delay, shipped both Perrot and Fénelon back to France to stand trial for insubordination. It was perhaps a poor move as far as Frontenac was concerned, for Fénelon, it appears, convinced the authorities in Paris, including Colbert, of the correctness of his position. Colbert, however, did not think it would be in the interest of peace to send Fénelon back to Montreal, but for some reason he restored Perrot to his post and also appointed a new intendant, Jacques Duchesneau, with instructions to watch over and report carefully on the conduct of both the governor and the clergy.[56]

It seems fairly evident that in their first brush with Frontenac the Sulpicians were the victors, but it was a Pyrrhic victory, for Frontenac outwitted them by making an alliance with the reinstated Perrot, and began to emulate his example. On his first visit to Montreal, Frontenac had built a fort at the mouth of the Cataraqui on the north shore of Lake Ontario (where Kingston now stands) and named it after himself. The original intention in erecting the fort was to deflect the Indian trade from Albany; but after his failure to unseat Perrot the governor-general decided to carry on at Fort Frontenac a personal trade in furs similar to that conducted on Ile Perrot. Thus Montreal had two rivals instead of one.

These were evil days for Saint-Sulpice; with falling revenues it was necessary to cut down on ambitious missionary projects. Frontenac was encouraging the Recollets to go to his fort on Lake Ontario and to be prepared to fill in the vacuum left by the Sulpicians. But perhaps the most ominous portent of all was the eagerness with which the Jesuits were beginning to return to their old stamping grounds in the west.

MISSIONARIES AND EXPLORERS

After their expulsion from Huronia the Jesuits hoped to redeem their losses by converting the hostile Iroquois, or the Five Nations as they called themselves, to Christianity. It was an imaginative scheme of returning good for evil, but despite the daring and courage with which it was pursued under the leadership of Simon Le Moyne it was never possible to get all the Five Nations to agree on a peace treaty with France. Le Moyne had made a firm friend and a strong French partisan out of the Onandaga chief, Garakontie. But this "good friend of the French,"[57] as the Jesuits described him, could not keep the Mohawks and Oneidas from treacherously turning on the French when it suited their purposes; this treachery was only brought to an end when Governor Tracy established military posts along the Richelieu River and at Lake Champlain. The Jesuits had missions at all these posts, but the converts gained under military protection were somewhat sullen. As soon as it was possible for the Jesuits to return to their old haunts in the west, they were eager to resume the long journeys into the unknown country, first initiated by the Recollets.[58]

Justin Winsor in his admirable study of western discoveries thinks that Bancroft overstated the case when he said, "Not a cape was turned, not a river entered, but a Jesuit led the way." Winsor rightly points out that very often a "trader rather than a priest" led the way;[59] nevertheless, wherever a trader went a priest was not far behind. Two traders who trekked off into the west on their own for a time were the famous brothers-in-law from Trois-Rivières, Pierre Radisson and Médard des Groseilliers; in 1658-59 they wintered on the shores of Lake Superior. But by 1660 the aged Jesuit priest René Ménard was there working among the Ottawas, and when he perished in the wilderness on his way back to Quebec he was soon replaced by younger and more vigorous missionaries.[60]

The journeys of Radisson and des Grosseilliers around Lake Superior stimulated interest not only in what lay west and south but in the far north as well; it is supposed that these pioneers in their wanderings westward reached James Bay where they foresaw great possibilities for trade through the Hudson Bay, an idea which failed to impress the French; and so they turned to the English (1664) and to some extent changed the course of history in the New World.[61]

It is not quite true to say that the French were entirely indifferent to the north at this time. Jean Talon tried to establish a base in the vicinity of Hudson Bay and to this end sent Father Charles Albanel up the Saguenay to begin a mission among the Indians as near as possible to the bay. This mission, described in great detail by Father Dablon in his *Relation* of 1671-72,[62] was the object of considerable interest for a while but was soon lost to view in the stirring events associated with a mission at Sault Ste Marie, situated at the junction of three of the Great Lakes.

The Sault had become a gathering place for traders and priests whose primary interest was not trade nor missions but exploration. The intendant, Talon, shared in this interest but decided that, before these adventurers went forth in search of new rivers that might lead to China or India, it would be discreet to make a formal claim for France of all the new country that might be mapped on the way. To Nicolas Perrot, an adventurer well versed in the Indian way of life and familiar with many dialects, Talon assigned the task of lining up several Indian tribes for a ceremonial proclamation of France's claim to the as yet unmapped west. At the top of a hill at the Sault in 1671 an instrument was read before a gathering of soldiers, Indians and four Jesuits, proclaiming that the French king had assumed power over all territory from the north to the south sea and extending to the ocean on the west.[63] Such a proclamation was a challenge to all those present to start searching for the elusive river that would lead to either the southern or western seas. There were rumours that La Salle while travelling with the Sulpicians in 1670 had discovered the Mississippi,[64] but these were not well founded and there seems little doubt that the honour of being the first white men to reach the Mississippi must go to the Canadian-born Louis Jolliet and Father Jacques Marquette.

Jolliet had been educated by the Jesuits at Quebec for the church, but the call of exploration proved stronger than the priesthood. It was Talon who recognized Jolliet's talents as an explorer and suggested that he be put in charge of a company that was being organized to find the elusive Mississippi. When a choice had to be made for a priest to accompany this party the Jesuits had no hesitation in recommending Marquette whose facility with Indian languages and eagerness for exploration made him an ideal companion for Jolliet.

The story of the finding of the Mississippi is told, in what was once regarded as Marquette's journal, in great detail,[65] but unfortunately the authorship of this journal has been called in question; or at least it has been thought that it was recast by Father Claude Dablon with the aid of other sources. Whatever may be the truth of these accusations (they are very much controverted)[66] the journal must be considered a substantial account of Marquette's voyage with his friend Jolliet; it is indeed a fascinating saga of courage, improvisation and determination and ends upon a note of triumph when finally the two heroes floated down the mighty river almost to the Gulf of Mexico. They stopped short of the gulf because of fear of the Spaniards. The sequel, unfortunately, is not too happy a story: on his way back to Quebec Jolliet's canoe was swamped in the Lachine Rapids where two men were lost along with valuable maps and papers. Marquette had left the party before this doleful accident, but he lived only a short time to enjoy the prestige that had come to him as an explorer. He died in 1670 during a second voyage to the Illinois and was buried in the forest; later his remains were carried to the mission of Saint-Ignace which he himself had founded on the north shore of the straits of Michilimackinac.[67]

Frontenac after a long conversation with Jolliet at Montreal resolved to exploit to the full the possibilities for trade and commerce along the Mississippi; he chose for a partner in this project Sieur de La Salle. The latter had begun his career as an explorer in company, as we have seen,[68] with some Sulpician missionaries from Montreal. His association with the Sulpicians was due to the fact that his brother was a Sulpician priest in Montreal and had helped him to secure a grant of land from the Gentlemen of Saint-Sulpice which he turned into the Seigneurie of Lachine.

Earlier he had studied for the priesthood under the Jesuits at their college in Rouen,[69] but like Jolliet he decided to abandon theology for the life of exploration. In fact, he was so much the adventurer that he sold his seigneuric back to the Sulpicians in order to secure the money to finance explorations into the southwest. His real opportunity came when he met Frontenac who was so much taken with his enthusiasm that he made him the Seigneur of Fort Frontenac, where he joined forces with the Recollets for a new expedition to the Mississippi.[70] The most interesting and controversial of the Recollets at Fort Frontenac was Louis Hennepin whose account of La Salle's trip through the Mississippi Delta has long been regarded as partly fictitious.[71]

When La Salle and his faithful lieutenant, Henri de Tonti, started on their historic journey to the Gulf of Mexico in August, 1679, they were accompanied by Father Hennepin and three other Recollet fathers, all Flemings as was Hennepin. It is far beyond the compass of this study to detail the many false starts and setbacks, including the loss of the *Griffon*, the first sailboat on the Great Lakes, before the party finally reached the Gulf of Mexico on April 9, 1682. On this day La Salle claimed the valley of the Mississippi for the French crown and the country of *Louisiane* was born. It is reported that among the spectators of this historic event were some New England Indians—outcasts after King Philip's War—and that they regarded the ceremony as the birth of a new Acadia,[72] to serve as an asylum for both French and Indians so frequently dispossessed by aggressive English settlers on the Atlantic coast. Such prevision was fulfilled some seventy-five years later when the unfortunate Acadians, expelled from their homeland by a harsh English command, sought to find shelter in Louisiana, and their descendants to this day are known as *cadiens* or *cayens* (Cajuns).[73]

EXCOMMUNICATION AND THE LIQUOR PROBLEM

In the midst of the excitement of discovering new nations and new lands, in which "black Jesuits and grey Recollets" played a prominent role and mingled on fairly equal terms with the swarthy "*voyageurs* and painted savages", the evils of illicit trade and the perils of serving liquor to Indians were almost forgotten. One man, however, Bishop Laval, did not forget; in 1675 he had at long last been made Bishop of Quebec in his own right and had returned to his diocese accompanied by the new intendant, Duchesneau. Immediately there was tension in Quebec. Frontenac had decided it was impossible to prevent *coureurs de bois* from carrying liquor to the Indians in their cabins and, like his predecessors, decided to allow the Indians to buy alcoholic beverages within the French settlements.[74] The bishop still remained unimpressed by this arrangement and proceeded to excommunicate all who sold liquor to the aborigenes. Frontenac was furious at what he considered the church's intrusion into the affairs of state and encouraged the tavern keepers to defy the bishop's spiritual weapon. This time Laval had the support of Intendant Duchesneau, who reported to the king that Frontenac and his partner La Salle were conducting an illicit trade in both furs and brandy with the Indians. About this time the theologians of the Sorbonne upheld the bishop's right to excommunicate anyone who sold alcohol to the Indians for the purpose of producing intoxication.

The Sorbonne decision, coming on top of the intendant's report, forced the king to make some move to ameliorate the strained relations of church and state in New France. He felt that somehow the colonists themselves ought to be able to solve the problem, so he ordered the governor to call a meeting of the leading inhabitants of the colony and devise ways and means to bring to an end a trade that was manifestly debauching the aborigine population of New France. Frontenac complied with the king's order and called a meeting in 1678 but, as most of those invited were directly or indirectly involved in the trade, they soon agreed that it was impossible to bring the traffic to an end and that the sale of liquor within the settlements did help to curb illicit sales in the forests. This decision was a stunning blow to Laval who now resolved to return to France and make a personal plea to the king himself. An audience was secured through the good offices of the king's confessor, but all he got from Louis was an ordinance which forbade the "carrying of liquor to the cabins of the Indians outside the French habitations,"[75] an ordinance which hardly differed from those of the Sovereign Council.

Disorders however, continued to increase: despite the king's latest ordinance, young men still scampered through the woods selling brandy to the Indians. At the same time government-distributed seed was being left to rot on the ground. So great was the confusion which was reported to the king that he recalled Frontenac in 1682 and replaced him with a *noblesse de robe*, Le Febvre de La Barre, a man of weak character and quite unable to control the lawless elements in New France, particularly when he himself indulged in illegal traffic with the English at Albany. His greatest disservice to New France was to make what was generally regarded as a shameful treaty with the Iroquois;[76] and this along with his well-known dishonesty compelled the king to recall him in 1684, the same year that Laval resigned his episcopate.

LAVAL RETIRES

It does not appear to have been a very happy time in the affairs of Canada when Laval handed over his responsibilities to a young man in the person of Jean Baptiste de Saint-Vallier. The tumultuous society of 1684 stood in sharp contrast to the godly community that had been the boast of the Jesuits in the eras of Champlain and d'Argenson. Yet, despite the turmoil, Laval could still look back upon his career as a comparatively successful one. The church under his leadership had grown greatly in size and grandeur; its physical equipment was enormous and its authority was something that no governor, not even Frontenac, could ignore with impunity.[77] Much credit for its continuing powerful influence in an era more concerned with wealth than piety must go to Laval. Even in the confusion of settling the officers and soldiers of the Carignan Regiment, many of whom came from the most unruly elements in France, into a much extended seigneurial system, Laval upheld with vigour the rigid standards of conduct that had prevailed in Champlain's pious family around Fort Saint-Louis.

His task of organizing a parochial system had been greatly hampered by the civil authorities who wanted to impose an Old World church polity with independent curacies upon a sparsely settled frontier community. Such primitive settlements were never able to provide stipends out of their own resources for independent parish priests.[78] Nevertheless, an edict from the king in 1678 insisted that permanent curacies must be set up in Canada. Laval, against his better judgment, made some attempt to carry out this order: in 1681 he and Intendant Duchesneau drew up boundaries of parishes in which fifteen were served by curés with permanent appointments. During his episcopate he established some twenty-five parishes and missions, which he visited regularly.

It was during his most extensive parish visitation, from Cap Saint-Ignace to Lachine, that he recognized that his health was beginning to fail: heart tremours and dizzy spells assailed him. He finally decided that his huge diocese extending from Acadia to Lake Michigan must be handed over to a more youthful and vigorous man. After performing what he considered the crowning act of his episcopate, the creation of a cathedral chapter at Quebec,[79] he formally presented his resignation; but this by no means meant a complete withdrawal from the affairs of New France. He continued to live on at Quebec and some of the most controversial episodes of his long life still lay before him.

NOTES TO CHAPTER NINE

1. Vide Marcel de Grandpré, "Traditions of the Catholic Church in French Canada" in J. W. Grant, ed., The Churches and the Canadian Experience (Toronto: Ryerson, 1963), pp. 1-13, for an interesting comment on the colonists' shifting for themselves.

2. Vide John W. Berry, "The Peopling of Canada: A Statistical Analysis of Population Growth in Canada" (McGill University Thesis; Montreal, 1933), p. 44. The earliest dated census for Canada, 1665-66, gives a total population for Canada, excluding aborigines, 3,215 in 1665.

3. According to G. Lanctot, A History of Canada, Vol. I: From its Origins to the Royal Regime, 1663 (trans. J. Hambleton; Toronto & Vancouver: Clarke, Irwin, 1963), p. 339, "The year 1663 closes the heroic period in Canadian history."

4. Vide M. Roy, The Parish and Democracy in French Canada (Toronto: University of Toronto Press, 1950), p. 15, for a discussion of "a type of religious grouping to be found nowhere else perhaps but French Canada."

5. A.-H. Gosselin, Le Vénérable François de Montmorency-Laval (Quebec: Dessault et Proulx, 1901), p. 14.

6. Ibid., p. 56.

7. Vide R. G. Thwaites, ed., The Jesuit Relations and Allied Documents (Cleveland: Burrows, 1896-1901), Vol. XLV, p. 12 et seq. for a detailed description of the battle of the symbols.

8. The decree is included in Mandements, Lettres pastorales et Circulaires des Evêques de Québec, ed. H. Têtu and C.-O. Gagnon (Quebec: Coté, 1887), Vol. I, pp. 14-15.

9. Quoted by F.-X. de Charlevoix, History and General Description of New France (trans. and ed. J. G. Shea; New York: F. P. Harper, 1900), Vol. III, p. 53.

10. Abbé Richaudeau, ed., Lettres de la Révérende Mère Marie de l'Incarnation (Tournai: Casterman, 1876), Vol. II, p. 222.

11. Vide P. J. O. Chauveau's Introduction to Jugements et Délibérations du Conseil Souverain de la Nouvelle-France (Quebec: Coté, 1885), Vol. I, pp. 14-61, for a concise description of the origin and activities of the Sovereign Council.

12. E.-M. Faillon, Histoire de la Colonie française en Canada (Villemarie: Bibliothèque Paroissiale, 1865-66), Vol. III, p. 67.

13. Jugements etc., op. cit., Vol. I, p. 26.

14. Vide E.-M. Faillon, op. cit., p. 97 et seq.

15. Vide Father Jérôme Lalemant's interpretation of the significance of the earthquake in Thwaites, ed., op. cit., Vol. XLVIII, pp. 41-57.

16. Ibid., Vol. XLIX, p. 159.

17. *Jugements etc., op. cit.,* Vol. I, p. 344.

18. Quoted by W. B. Munro, *The Seignorial System in Canada* (New York: Harvard Historical Studies, 1907), p. 21.

19. *Ibid.,* p. 183; quoted from H. R. Casgrain *Une Paroisse Canadienne au XVIIe siècle,* pp. 40-1.

20. *Vide* M. Roy, *op. cit.,* p. 17; also *Mandements, op. cit.,* Vol. I, pp. 28-30, for ordinances relating to the election of church wardens.

21. *Vide* A.-H. Gosselin, *op. cit.,* p. 178 *et seq.*

22. *Vide* A.-E. Gosselin, *L'Instruction au Canada sous le Régime français 1635-1760* (Quebec: Laflamme et Proulx, 1911), p. 388 *et seq.*

23. *Vide* A.-H. Gosselin, *Laval, op. cit.,* p. 183.

24. *Vide* W. B. Munro, *op-cit.,* p. 183; also *Jugements, op-cit.,* Vol. I, p. 18.

25. *Vide infra,* pp. 161-2.

26. *Vide* A.-H. Gosselin, *Laval, op. cit.,* p. 187; also A.-E. Gosselin, *L'Instruction au Canada, op. cit.,* p. 346 *et seq.*

27. A.-H. Gosselin, *Laval, op-cit.,* p. 219.

28. This bull of Pope Alexander VII is included in the *Mandements, op. cit.,* Vol. I, pp. 54-6.

29. Richaudeau, *op cit.,* Vol. II, p. 310.

30. For a laudatory report on Colbert *vide* P. Magne's "Rapport à l'Empereur" in P. Clement, ed., *Lettres, Instructions et Mémoires de Colbert* (Paris: pub. d'après les ordres de l'empereur, 1861), Vol. I, pp. i-iii.

31. One of Colbert's first moves in relation to New France was to make a careful collection of the grants of territories made by the English kings in North America; these are still preserved in *Mélanges de Colbert,* 53, fol. 383 (Bibliothèque Nationale, Paris).

32. Thwaites, ed. *op. cit.,* Vol. XLIX, p. 213.

33. *Vide* Colbert's *Instruction au Sieur Talon,* P. Clement, ed., *op. cit.,* Vol. III², p. 389 *et seq.*

34. *Vide* F.-X. de Charlevoix *op. cit.,* Vol. III, pp. 84-85.

35. *Vide* Thomas Chapais, *The Great Intendant* (Toronto: University of Toronto Press, 1914), p. 19 *et seq.*

36. *Vide* P. Clement, ed., Vol. III², p. 395 *et seq.*

37. *Vide* W. B. Munro, *op. cit.,* pp. 71-72; also T. *Chapais, op. cit.,* pp. 54-6.

38. *Ibid.,* pp. 57-61.

39. *Vide* P. Clement, ed., Vol. III², pp. 390-391.

40. *Vide* Richaudeau, ed., Vol. II, p. 401 *et seq.* Even Laval in a letter written from Quebec, Oct. 15, 1667, pays his respects to the intendant for his success in building up the commercial life of the country. *Mélanges de Colbert 176, Correspondence de 1667 à 1670* (fol. ii) (Bibliothèque Nationale, Paris).

41. *Vide* C. de Rochemonteix, *Les Jésuites et la Nouvelle-France au XVIIe Siècle* (Paris: Letouzey et Ané, editeurs, 1895-96), Vol. III, p. 88 *et seq.,* for Jesuit reaction to the return of the Recollets.

42. *Ibid.,* Vol. III, p. 91.

43. *Vide* E.-M. Faillon, *op. cit.,* Vol. III, p. 108 *et seq.*

44. *Ibid., op. cit.,* Vol. III, p. 110.

45. For an interesting study of Perrot, *vide* E. S. Wardleworth, "François-Marie Perrot" (M.A. Thesis, McGill, 1931), *passim.*

46. *Vide* Dollier de Casson, *History of Montreal* (trans. R. Flenley; London and Toronto: Dent, 1928), pp. 327-9.

47. Laval's *Instructions* are included in the French edition of Casson's *Histoire* (Montreal: Société Historique, 1868), pp. 260-3.

48. *Vide* de Casson (English trans.), p. 333.

49. *Vide* L. Fallue, *Histoire Politique et Religieuse de l'Eglise Métropolitaine et du Diocèse de Rouen* (Rouen: Le Brument, 1850-51), Vol. IV, p. 176 *et seq.;*

Fallue points out that François de Harlay once ruled the great monastery of Jumièges and took the American church in his stride and had no intention of diminishing the power and prestige of his immense diocese. Among *Mélanges de Colbert, op. cit.,* is a rather pathetic letter from Laval to Colbert pleading for the minister's assistance to get the necessary bulls to make him Bishop of Quebec: "François, évêque de Petrée," 164, fol. 77.

50. *Vide* W. J. Eccles, *Frontenac the Courtier Governor* (Toronto: McClelland and Stewart, 1959), pp. 18-30 for the background of Frontenac.

51. F. Parkman, *Count Frontenac and New France under Louis XIV* (4th ed.; Boston: Little, Brown, 1877), p. 15.

52. *Ibid.,* p. 22; *vide* also W. J. Eccles, *op. cit.,* p. 59.

53. *Ibid.,* p. 43.

54. Dollier de Casson, *op. cit.,* p. 18.

55. *Vide* W. J. Eccles, *op. cit.,* pp. 39-50.

56. *Vide* P. Clement, ed., *op. cit.,* Vol. III², pp. 549-600 for "Instructions à Duchesneau."

57. Thwaites, ed., *op. cit.,* Vol. XLIX, p. 103.

58. *Vide supra,* p. 73.

59. Justin Winsor, *Cartier to Frontenac* (Boston and New York: Houghton, Mifflin, 1894), p. 177.

60. *Ibid.,* p. 187 *et seq.*

61. *Vide* J. Holland Rose, "The Struggle for Supremacy in America" in *The Cambridge History of the British Empire* (Cambridge: Cambridge University Press, 1929-36), Vol. VI, p. 78 *et seq.*

62. Thwaites, ed., *op. cit.,* Vol. LVI, p. 149 *et seq.*

63. *Ibid.,* Vol. LV, p. 105 *et seq.*

64. *Vide* F. Parkman, *La Salle and the Discovery of the Great West* (Boston: Little, Brown, 1927), p. 19 *et seq.*

65. For Journal *vide* Thwaites, ed., *op. cit.,* LIX, p. 88 *et seq.*

66. *Vide* J. Monet, "Marquette, Jacques, Jesuit, Missionary" in *Dictionary of Canadian Biography* (Toronto: University of Toronto Press, 1966), Vol. I, pp. 491-2 for a discussion of the Steck accusations.

67. Thwaites, *op. cit.,* LXI, p. 201 *et seq.*

68. *Vide supra,* p. 143.

69. The *Collège* still stands, but is now known as the *Lycée Corneille de Rouen* and La Salle has his place in the *Galerie des Illustres; vide Lycée Corneille de Rouen* (Rouen: Imprimerie Lecerf, n.d.), p. 43.

70. F. Parkman, *Frontenac, op. cit.,* p. 27 *et seq.*

71. F. G. Thwaites, in his introduction to *A New Discovery of Vast Country in America by Father Louis Hennepin* (Chicago: McClurg, 1903), Vol. I, p. xxix, says "Some of the father's statements, especially as given in the book here reprinted are quite impossible of credence. . . ." For a careful study of the value of Hennepin's writings *vide* Jean Delangley, *Hennepin's Description of Louisiana: A Critical Essay* (Chicago: Institute of Jesuit History, 1941), *passim.*

72. *Vide* J. Winsor, *op. cit.,* p. 295.

73. *Vide* E. Lauvrière, *La Tragédie d'un Peuple* (Paris: Librairie Henry Goulet, 1924), Vol. II, p. 189 *et seq.*

74. *Vide* W. J. Eccles, *op. cit.,* p. 65 *et seq.*

75. A. H. Gosselin, *Laval, op. cit.,* p. 317 *et seq.*

76. F.-X. de Charlevoix, *op. cit.,* p. 253, describes the treaty as a peace made on dishonourable conditions; W. J. Eccles, *Canada Under Louis XIV, 1663-1701* (Toronto: McClelland & Stewart, 1964), pp. 135-7, thinks La Barre incompetent, but indicates that there was no alternative but to sign a peace treaty.

77. For an interesting comment on the resignation of Laval *vide* Rochemonteix, *op. cit.,* Vol. III, p. 306 *et seq.*

78. *Vide* A.-H. Gosselin, *Laval, op. cit.,* p. 322 *et seq.*

79. *Ibid.,* p. 342.

TEN

The Era of Saint-Vallier

A revival of religious fanaticism in the closing decades of the seventeenth century cast a deep shadow over the episcopate of Jean Baptiste de La Croix de Chevrières de Saint-Vallier. In France the Edict of Nantes, which had guaranteed for over eighty years comparative security for the Huguenots, was revoked in 1685; once again these industrious subjects of the French king were being exiled or tortured to death; while across the channel loyal Roman Catholic subjects of the English king were being executed on the perjured evidence of Titus Oates and other unscrupulous witnesses.[1]

The bitterness engendered by this revival of religious bigotry was soon carried across the Atlantic to New France and New England and produced an era of frightfulness that led to unpitying massacres of men, women and children on the frontier settlements of America.

A PERIOD OF TREACHERY

One of the chief proponents of a policy of frightfulness was Comte de Frontenac[2] who returned as governor of Canada in 1689; but the seeds of such a policy had already been sown by his predecessor in office, Jacques-René de Brisay, Marquis de Denonville, whom the king had chosen as governor after the failure of Le Febvre de La Barre to secure peace with the Iroquois. Shortly after his arrival in Canada Denonville was convinced that the English were abetting the Iroquois in raids upon the Canadian settlements and he came to the conclusion that the only permanent security for New France would be the removal of the English from the continent of North America; and so he embarked upon a continental struggle reaching from Hudson Bay and Illinois to New England and New York; a struggle in which both French and English missionaries would play a very ambiguous role.[3]

The opening phase of this contest for a continent was marred by an act of treachery for which New France would pay dearly: Louis XIV had been asking for Iroquois prisoners to serve as slaves in his galleys; Denonville, without much forethought, acquiesced in what at the time was not an unusual request. The first boat load of these slaves was secured by the intendant, Jean Bochart, Chevalier de Champigny, who seized by stealth some friendly Iroquois among whom the Recollets had been carrying on a mission. Before sending these surprised Indians to France, de Champigny had humiliated them by chaining them to wooden stakes which had wrung from them a defiant death chant. Denonville, instead of repudiating his colleague's treachery, also sent his own quota of prisoners to France from among the Iroquois that he had captured during a foray into the Seneca country.[4]

Since the French had now embarked upon a policy of bad faith towards the Iroquois, one of their allied Huron chieftains, Kondiaronk, commonly called the Rat, decided to outdo both the French and the Iroquois in the art of deception; after murdering some Iroquois chieftains on their way to a peace conference with Denonville, he spread abroad the rumour that the governor himself had ordered the slaughter and thus made impossible any peace negotiations between the Iroquois and the French.[5]

Again the French settlers were constantly under attack by a stealthy enemy who would suddenly emerge from the most unexpected hiding places; the cruelest of these attacks was the fearful massacre at Lachine on August 5, 1689, when helpless women under the terrified gaze of Montrealers on the opposite bank of the river, were compelled "to turn the spit in which their children were roasted to death."[6] Shortly before this terrifying event the king had recalled Denonville and replaced him with Comte de Frontenac. After the Lachine massacre it was agreed by friend and foe alike that the only Frenchman capable of winning the confidence of the Iroquois enough to get them to a conference table, and thus save New France from extinction, was Frontenac.

ATROCITIES ON THE FRONTIER

On his arrival in Canada Frontenac found that he had been preceded by his former critic Mgr Laval; the two old antagonists, however, were now united in saving Canada from the allied attacks of the English and the Iroquois. During his stay at the Foreign Missions in Paris, while awaiting for the consecration of his successor, Laval had become alarmingly aware of the worsening situation in Canada —he had even heard that France was contemplating abandoning the colony[7]—and he longed to be back among his *canadois*, whom he had consoled and encouraged through so many similar crises. No sooner was his successor consecrated[8] than Laval was on his way to New France and reached there in time to welcome both the new bishop and the reinstated governor, and also to play his part as spiritual adviser in the new kind of warfare that Frontenac initiated during his second term as governor.

Laval may not have entirely agreed with the ferocity with which Frontenac conducted his campaign against the English settlements, but he did not publicly rebuke it; he probably thought it was partially justified after the Lachine massacre, which was regarded as having been instigated by the English of New York. Be that as it may, the church under the joint leadership of Laval and Saint-Vallier became closely identified, particularly through its Indian missions,[9] with a most violent struggle for a continent. During this long protracted war the fires of religious fanaticism were fanned to such heat that the reconciliation of Protestants and Catholics after the British conquest has remained a hope long deferred.

What is still today Canada's major problem began on the colonial frontiers of France and England where both sides were committed to a policy of frightfulness and terror. Sudden night attacks and indiscriminate slaughter of half-awake victims were common occurrences; in 1690 the little villages of Schenectady in the province of New York, Salmon Falls (now Portsmouth, New Hampshire), and Fort Loyal (now Portland, Maine) suffered almost as cruelly as did Lachine. As G. M. Wrong puts it, "When policy seemed to require it Frontenac knew no restraint in savagery"; the same writer adds that Fitz-John Winthrop, who led an English attack against LaPrairie, "in spirit if not in effectiveness rivaled the barbarity of Frontenac."[10]

It would indeed be difficult to apportion blame for the atrocities on the frontiers during the eighty years of conflict, with a few peaceful interludes, that followed upon the outbreak of war between France and England in 1699; each side could call the roll against the other with an ever growing list of massacres and martyrdoms. New Englanders were convinced that the Jesuit missionary to the Abenaki, Sébastien Râlé, was the instigator of a massacre at Deerfield, Massachusetts, in 1704; twenty years later Massachusetts sent an expedition against Râlé's mission at Norridgewock, in what is now the state of Maine and "took nearly thirty scalps among them that of Râlé." Thus New England got its revenge for the slaughter at Deerfield as well as for the murder of its own congregational minister Joseph Willard of Rutland, whose scalp had shortly before been sent as a trophy to Quebec.[11]

One of the major triumphs of New France during the so-called King William's war was the repulse of a New England fleet besieging Quebec; this crusading armada, led by Admiral William Phips who left Boston in 1690 with the fervent blessing of Cotton Mather, a fiery preacher dedicated to the destruction of New France. During the bombardment of Quebec the clergy took a prominent part in the defence of the city; Bishop Saint-Vallier called upon his flock to fight "the enemies not only of the French people, but of our faith and our religion;"[12] Mgr Laval arranged to have a flag with the Holy Family emblazoned on it, flown from the *clocher* of the cathedral as a supernatural protective shield for the defenders of Quebec; and there it fluttered safely all through the bombardment. When Admiral Phips finally admitted defeat and returned to a much downcast Boston, there was great rejoicing in Quebec; all were agreed that the clergy had played a courageous role in sustaining the soldiers during the downpour of shots and shells, and in keeping the people from panic. With the disappearance of Phips' fleet, church and state joined in a procession with the captured flag of the enemy; then followed a service of thanksgiving conducted in the Lower Town Church which was renamed Notre-Dame-de-la Victoire.[13]

Despite the severe famine that followed upon the siege and the continuing Iroquois raids, there was a great upsurge of pride and confidence among the *canadois*. Out of this period come some of the most inspiring tales of heroism in the annals of New France; the most remarkable is the story of how Madeleine de Verchères, a girl of fourteen, with the help of her two younger brothers foiled an Iroquois attack on her father's seigneurie.[14]

No one was more moved by these tales of heroism than citizen-priest Mgr Laval; they gave him a renewed pride in the emerging nation that he had adopted as his own; yet there was always an element of sadness in this identification with a young country not yet firmly established. Laval was too far-seeing not to know that New England, with a much larger population than New France, was now sufficiently aroused to put forth every effort to expel the French from North America. Although the Treaty of Ryswick (September 20, 1697) which brought King William's war to an end restored to France Admiral Phips' conquests in Acadia, yet Laval would probably have agreed with Cotton Mather that Phips' ill-fated attack upon Quebec had at least shown "that to go by sea to Quebec was the true path of the conquest of New France."[15]

OBSERVATIONS OF A VICAR GENERAL

There were other and more immediate matters to sadden Laval in his partial retirement in Canada, not the least being what he considered the strange ways of his youthful successor to the See of Quebec.[16] Why he should have chosen a high-spirited aristocrat from Grenôble to become a bishop of an admittedly difficult missionary diocese is a bit of a mystery. Mature missionaries in Canada, familiar with the historic tensions that had developed among the various religious orders of New France, would no doubt have avoided many of the errors made by the brash young man from the court of Louis XIV. But Laval was of noble lineage and he probably chose Saint-Vallier because of the latter's patriarchal background and the influence he wielded as a royal chaplain. As it was going to be some time before any bulls of consecration could be secured from Rome, because of the strained relations between the courts of Versailles and Rome following upon the famous declaration of the French clergy in 1682, Laval made Saint-Vallier his vicar general in Canada. Immediately the youthful cleric was away on a tour of his prospective diocese. During the years 1685 and 1686 he visited nearly every institution, parish and mission of New France from Montreal to Port-Royal, Acadia; and on his return to France in 1686 he wrote a *Relation* on the state of the church in Canada as he had found it.[17]

This *Relation* is one of the most important documents extant for the history of the church at the time of the transition from the era of Laval to that of Saint-Vallier. It reflects real enthusiasm on the part of the new bishop-elect for the work of Laval and all the pioneer missionaries of New France. He speaks very highly of the Quebec Seminary which he made his home while in Quebec and to which he made a gift of his library and a sum of money he had received at the termination of his chaplaincy at Versailles. All the orders and institutions at Quebec received like praise, as did the very pious governor, Denonville. Similarly in Montreal he had nothing but praise for the courteous way he was received by Governor de Callières and the Gentlemen of Saint-Sulpice.

The *Relation* reveals that many changes had taken place in Montreal's religious houses since Governor Maisonneuve had led his little band of pioneers to this island of visions: the house of the Sulpicians was still on its original foundation, but the fathers were about to build a large stone church on Notre Dame Street; the Hôtel-Dieu and the Congregation of Notre-Dame had grown enormously in personnel and in clients, but both were struggling with heavy financial burdens; Jeanne Mance who had been adept at finding money had been several years dead, but Marguerite Bourgeoys "still presided with vigor over the destinies of her *famille religeuse*."[18] A new venture in social welfare was being initiated by François Charron, who was attempting to combine in a general hospital the care of the old, indigent and orphans; the latter were to receive an elementary education.[19] This pioneer attempt to combine nursing and teaching was probably the stimulus behind Saint-Vallier's own attempt to found a General Hospital at Quebec.

If the vicar general was enthusiastic about what he observed in Montreal and Quebec, the same could not be said of what he found in France's oldest American colony on the Atlantic seaboard. Although Acadia had been restored to French rule by the Treaty of Breda in 1667, no attempt had been made to integrate this province of New France into the diocese of Quebec until nine years later when Abbé Petit arrived at Port-Royal as the grand vicar of Bishop Laval; he had been preceded, however, by Abbé Thury who went to Miramachi in 1674; this to some extent was an experimental adventure by the Seminary of Quebec in missionary activity.[20] Petit also had been trained at the seminary and both priests proved that the seminary could graduate excellent missionaries. But however dedicated they might be it was not possible for them to look after adequately the spiritual needs of the eight hundred or more French-speaking inhabitants scattered sparsely over the vast territory of Acadia, to say nothing of the once flourishing Indian missions; consequently Acadia immediately became one of Saint-Vallier's continuous concerns. After his return to France, he tried through his *Relation* to impress as strongly as possible upon the French public the Church's neglect of Acadia in the hope of securing volunteers for the missions of the New World.

In the meantime he left behind him in Acadia the two Sulpician priests who had accompanied him on his journey: Abbé Trouvé who took up residence at Beaubassin and Abbé Geoffrey who became an assistant priest to Abbé Petit at Port-Royal. The latter, with the aid of a sister whom Saint-Vallier sent from the Congregation of Notre-Dame, Montreal, opened a school for girls and it looked for a short time as if Port-Royal was about to resume the cultural development begun under d'Aulnay but so rudely brought to an end by Major Sedgwick's fleet in 1654. This new hopeful start in bringing some

literacy to Acadia was again brought to an end by another fleet from
Boston under the command of Admiral Phips, who in 1690 plundered
the colony just as ruthlessly as all his English-speaking predecessors
had done. Father Petit was taken a prisoner to Boston, but Abbé
Geoffrey escaped to France by way of Canada and it was some years
before he returned to win great fame in the Parish of Champlain.[21]

Before these unhappy events occurred, Saint-Vallier had made a
second visit to Acadia in 1688 following upon a tour of Newfoundland and the islands of Saint-Pierre and Miquelon, where he found
the few French settlers in a more deplorable condition spiritually
than in Acadia. Unfortunately the bishop did not keep a journal on
this trip for he was at the time engaged in a controversy with the
Quebec Seminary and in no mood to make notes, as he had previously done, on the state of the church in New France. This omis-
sion is to be regretted since so little is known about conditions in
Newfoundland towards the end of the seventeenth century. We do
know, however, that the bishop appointed a Recollet priest, Sixte
Latac, curé of Plaissance with the title of vicar general, and that
he left behind two secular priests to minister to the spiritual needs
of settlers on the islands of Saint-Pierre and Miquelon.[22]

QUEBEC SEMINARY DENOUNCED

Shortly after his return to Quebec as bishop in 1689 Saint-Vallier
began to have second thoughts about the seminary where he was
making his headquarters. He only stayed three months, and then
moved on to a house he had bought on one of the most scenic prom-
ontories in the Upper Town and where he ultimately built a most
imposing bishop's palace. Apparently he had come to the conclusion
while staying at the seminary that he was not really a full-fledged
bishop if he followed Laval's practice of sharing the administration
of the diocese with the directors of the seminary, who were also his
hosts; evidently they had made it clear to him that they expected
to be consulted on all policy decisions.[23]

Saint-Vallier was probably not aware, when he began his attack
upon the seminary, that he was taking on an opponent that had in
a very brief time become thoroughly integrated into the ecclesiastical
and social life of New France. The original purpose of the seminary
over and above Laval's desire to make it a home for both active and
retired curés, was to train young ordinands in administering the
sacraments, catechising and preaching; in other words, to fulfil the
functions of the priesthood. Training in intellectual subjects was to

be given by the *collège* of the Jesuits, but it did not seem to work out as Laval had planned; perhaps the curriculum at the Jesuit college was too exclusively classical for the pioneer community it was trying to serve, consequently, the more practical courses at the seminary grew in favour while those at the Jesuit college declined. Even the Petit Séminaire which was originally intended as a boarding house became a popular preparatory school for the Grand Séminaire; their graduates permeated French-Canadian society and their loyalty for their alma mater became so infectious that it made the Quebec Seminary, which later evolved into Laval University, one of the most venerated institutions in French Canada.[24] It is possible that this latent *esprit de corps* from which Saint-Vallier felt exluded caused the second Bishop of Quebec to turn so bitterly upon his predecessor's most valued contribution to the social development of New France.

The opening round of this contest was a rather petty affair. After leaving the seminary and establishing a separate residence the bishop wanted back his library of books and the money he had deposited with the directors during his first visit to Quebec; the directors took the position that a gift is irreversible and refused to accede to the bishop's request.[25] This rebuff led Saint-Vallier to impose some harsh regulations upon the seminary: the union of the seminary with the cures was to come to an end; the distribution of diocesan revenue was from now on to be the sole responsibility of the bishop; most shattering of all the regulations was the order that priests returning from their cures must not, without the bishop's consent, visit the seminary which they had so long regarded as their true home. By these regulations the bishop was reducing the seminary to one function alone, to be a training school for theological students; at the same time, however, he was planning to erect on his own property a rival institution.

The dispute was carried into other areas when the bishop suspended Henri de Bernières, the superior of the seminary, along with two colleagues, M. de Maizerets and M. de Glandelet, from their functions, because they had protested against the installation of M. de Colombière, a former Sulpician and a close friend of the bishop, to the cathedral chapter. The aggrieved ecclesiastics appealed to the Sovereign Council, and asked it to compel the bishop to restore them to their offices. Such an appeal to a civil authority over the spiritual authority of the church infuriated the bishop who retorted by interdicting the three priests from preaching and hearing confessions.

This unusually harsh discipline brought to the defence of the three ecclesiastics all the leading citizens of Quebec, including the governor and Mgr Laval. To see three highly regarded priests deprived of the most elementary functions of the priesthood was a very shocking sight indeed for the citizens of Quebec, who began to agitate for the recall of their diocesan.[26]

Regardless of his growing unpopularity, Saint-Vallier proceeded to stir up even greater opposition in his attempt to found a General Hospital to take care of the aged and indigent. In order to secure a revenue for such an establishment he decided to use the funds administered by the Bureau of the Poor, which he felt would be displaced by his new foundation. Another institution that would no longer be necessary was a House of Providence which had only been established two years earlier by the Sisters of the Congregation of Notre-Dame. The latter under the guidance of the venerable Marguerite Bourgeoys, who at the request of her bishop made a perilous journey on foot from Montreal to Quebec, co-operated in the new venture;[27] the officers of the bureau, however, protested vigorously against what they considered a high-handed alienation of funds that had been entrusted to them. With so much opposition frustrating him at every turn, the bishop decided to return to France to secure additional authority to carry out his plans.

His visit to Versailles in 1691 could not have been made under more favourable circumstances, for he brought with him the good news of the defeat of the English before Quebec. As a reward for such pleasing information the court was ready to grant all his requests; thus he was able to return to Canada in 1692 with his own regulations for the reform of the seminary confirmed by the court, and with a royal permit to found a General Hospital.[28]

AN IMPERIOUS BISHOP

All now seemed to be clear for the bishop to introduce the reforms he had in mind for the better administration of his diocese and for the advancement of his most cherished projects. But Saint-Vallier had a genius for stirring up opposition and creating enemies. For eight years the history of the church in New France is a chronicle of *affaires* from which the bishop was seldom absent.[29] Except for his absolute dedication to the priestly office and his genuine sympathy for the poor and unfortunate he might well be written off as a ridiculously proud cleric who merited nothing but contempt. In his later years he was to redeem much of his youthful arrogance by a more humble and self-abasing ministry, but never to his dying day did he shirk controversial issues.

It is beyond the scope of this study to chronicle all the affairs that kept buzzing through the conversation at social gatherings in Montreal, Quebec and Trois-Rivières. The *prie-dieu affaire* was perhaps the most embarrassing for the bishop since it involved him in a most prolonged duel with the Recollets of Montreal, whom he had established there over much opposition. While attending a service at the Recollet Church in Montreal the bishop decided that the governor's *prie-dieu* was in too prominent a position and ordered it removed; when the Recollets, menaced by the governor, felt they were powerless to carry out the bishop's command he placed their church under an interdict. Such an extreme measure seemed to spark a series of reckless accusations on the part of the bishop against former friends. He denounced the Recollets for allowing ladies to enter their refectory gardens as if there were something scandalous in this form of diversion; he gave credence to a rumour that one of these ladies, the sister of the superior, was the mistress of de Callières. Then followed similar accusations of adultery against several officers of the army, who were deprived of the sacraments. Such disciplinary measures annoyed Governor Frontenac who, surprisingly enough, got along very well with the bishop until the latter began to excommunicate army friends.

The breaking point with Frontenac came, however, when the governor proposed to put on Molière's satirical play *Tartuffe,* a play which Saint-Vallier knew had been condemned by the Archbishop of Paris. The Bishop of Quebec had published a *mandemant* condemning blasphemous plays; he was convinced *Tartuffe* came under this condemnation and he took it as a personal insult that the governor should contemplate sponsoring it at the château. He was still further infuriated when he learned that Sieur de Mareuil, a rather unsavoury character, was to play the leading role. In order to avoid what he considered would be a most scandalous performance he went to the governor and offered to pay him a hundred *pistoles* if the play were cancelled. Frontenac, who was amused by the offer, accepted the money, which he proposed to distribute among the poor, and promised that *Tartuffe* would not be produced. All might have been forgotten if the bishop had not then proceeded to bring to the Sovereign Council charges of impiety and blasphemy against the would-be leading actor at the château, de Mareuil. When the council detained de Mareuil for examination, Frontenac's patience gave out and he ordered the prisoner released.[30] Such a state of tension now existed in Quebec that some of de Mareuil's friends released their exasperation by smashing windows at the bishop's residence. All these tumultuous events were reported to Louis XIV, and so the bishop decided that he must again return to France to give to the king his own version of the stories that were told about him.

With practically the whole colony against him, Quebec took it for granted that it had seen the last of Mgr Saint-Vallier. Pontchartrain, the minister who examined the bishop's dossier,[31] was also of the opinion that Saint-Vallier's usefulness in Canada had come to an end, and he advised the king to demand that the bishop resign his see. The king accepted the advice. But when the minister conveyed the king's will to Saint-Vallier he received a surprising answer: the bishop admitted that he could not return to his diocese without the king's consent, "but to give my resignation," he said, "that depends upon me and never will I give it; I will govern my diocese from here."[32] For three years he held firmly to his resolution and the king finally decided he could no longer leave Canada without a bishop. After warning Saint-Vallier that he must establish peace in his diocese or he would be recalled, never to return, he allowed him to sail for Canada.

On his return the bishop sincerely tried to heed the king's warning: he became reconciled with the Recollets, the seminary and even with the governor. But he did not have much time to cultivate his renewed friendship at the château, for Frontenac died in 1698, shortly after the bishop's return. Saint-Vallier conducted the funeral, but he graciously allowed the superior of the Recollets to give the eulogy.[33]

When the Governor of Montreal, Chevalier de Callières, arrived in Quebec to succeed Frontenac it was feared that the peace between church and state would be rudely shattered. But nothing of the kind happened and the new governor was able to write to Versailles, "that since the bishop returned we have lived in a manner as if nothing had occurred between us; and I hope it will continue."[34]

All might have gone well if the bishop had not become so engrossed in the development of the General Hospital. He drew so heavily from the sisters of the Hôtel-Dieu to get personnel for the new foundation that the mother superior began to protest, and when the intendent, Champigny, came to her support, Saint-Vallier decided that it would perhaps be better to have two separate orders of sisters; and so he made the General Hospital a separate house, independent of the Hôtel-Dieu. But he reckoned without the court of Versailles which was in no mood to multiply orders. It was not long before word came from France that the patent for the General Hospital was cancelled and that the sisters already there were to return to the Hôtel-Dieu.[35]

Consternation now reigned in Quebec, for even the opponents of Saint-Vallier in his dispute with the mother superior did not wish to destroy the General Hospital. Although the bishop realized that he might never be allowed to return to his diocese if he went back to France to plead the cause of the General Hospital, yet he felt he must.[36] In so doing he saved his hospital but he did not see his diocese again for thirteen years. Four of these were spent as a prisoner in England; the French ship on which he was returning to Canada was captured by the English (1704) and he was seized as a hostage.[37]

UNSHEPHERDED YEARS: THE RELIGIOUS ORDERS

During the long absence of Bishop Saint-Vallier from his diocese, the religious orders of New France naturally became self-reliant in the discharge of their duties, but at the same time less conventional in the observance of their rules. They were not completely without episcopal supervision for Mgr Laval came out of retirement to assume once more episcopal responsibilities. It was necessarily somewhat less vigilant rule than the former bishop had been inclined to impose in his younger days; he was now an octogenarian and his exercises of piety, as recorded by his attendant, Hubert Houssard (an almost incredible catalogue of discomfort), must have made it impossible for him to supervise very closely the far flung diocese of Quebec.[38] His long and fruitful life came to an end on the 6th of May, 1708, at the age of eighty-six. It was Mgr Laval's dying wish to be buried in the chapel of the seminary; but it had been destroyed by fire in 1701 and had not been rebuilt by 1708, and so the dead bishop was interred in the cathedral. One hundred and sixty years later the lead coffin containing the bishop's body was solemnly transferred from the cathedral to the chapel of the seminary where it reposes to this day.

For five years Canada was without a resident bishop; during these unshepherded years the religious orders of New France never lost sight of the original purpose of their presence in the New World— the conversion of the aborigines; this was as true of the Seminary of Quebec as of any of the regular orders. After its reconciliation with Saint-Vallier in 1698 it was given, in co-operation with the Foreign Missions at Paris (and much to the chagrin of the Jesuits), a mission to the Tamarois, who were of the Illinois in the Mississippi valley.[39]

Here the missionaries met La Salle's faithful lieutenant, Henri de Tonti, who was a useful source of information about the unknown country in which they were casting their lot. Sieur de La Salle was no longer there to advise, as he had been murdered by a band of greedy assassins from his own country. It was wild and dangerous territory into which the Seminary and Foreign Missions were adventuring and in a short time this junior missionary society had its own calendar of martyrs: Fathers Foucault and Saint-Cosme died at the hands of Indians, "victims of their apostolic zeal."[40]

The Jesuits who would have liked exclusive jurisdiction in Louisiana had little to complain about, for they still administered, under the overall direction of the superior-general at Quebec, a vast missionary empire in North America. Besides their sedentary missions reaching from Montreal to Acadia and down into New York State, they were again extending into the western plains. The superior-general of this area ordinarily resided at Michilimackinac (now Mackinac), an island at the top of Lake Michigan. Here he presided over a fairly populous community made up of three separate villages: French, Huron and Ottawa. There was in the area a French fort, the residence of the commander of the post.

This combination of mission and trading post had, whenever tried, produced serious friction between the religious and commercial interests represented; such friction was not absent from Michilimackinac. Covering a very large radius from this centre the missionaries found new tribes of Indians very receptive to their message of salvation, but Jesuit preaching and teaching were constantly frustrated by the coureurs de bois. These young men "lost to civilization"[41] and far from the moral restraints that Laval and Saint-Vallier had rather successfully imposed upon the settled portions of New France, lived a life of unrestrained licence among the natives whom they debauched with liquors which they exchanged for furs. A particularly acute situation developed for the missionaries after the appointment of Antoine Laumet de Lamothe de Cadillac in 1694. According to one commentator "evil was allowed full swing." Father Etienne de Carheil, who was the "soul of resistance"[42] to the ruthless exploitation of the Indians by the traders and adventurers, was also a thorn in the side of Cadillac who accused him of traitorous conduct towards France.[43] For a time de Carheil's protests had some effect, for in 1696 Louis XIV ordered all the western trading posts, with the exception of Fort Saint-Louis under the command of Tonti, closed. But whatever benefit might have been obtained for the Indians by this rescript was nullified when, at the urging of Pontchartrain, the king permitted Cadillac to establish a new trading post on the St. Clair River, between Lake Erie and Lake Huron; the new post was named Pontchartrain, but later was called Detroit.[44]

In 1701 Cadillac and Tonti, as second in command, left Montreal with their wives, accompanied by some fifty soldiers and colonists. They were not merely occupying a trading post, but founding a new city. In a brief time all the evils that prevailed at Michilimackinac were revived at Detroit. The new colony attracted Indians from as far away as Michilimackinac and even farther, despite all the efforts of the missionaries to prevent such migrations; consequently, the Jesuits had to follow their converts to Detroit where the mood was to give free play to the white man's greed for gain, unshackled by any humane considerations.[45] From Jesuit correspondence at that time one gets the impression that the founding of Detroit coincided with the unleashing of those destructive forces which undermined the Indians' capacity to adjust to Western civilization. From then on until their dissolution in 1763 the Jesuits were completely frustrated in their attempt, which began in Huronia in 1626, to build a novel Christian civilization on an aboriginal foundation in western Canada. At this time nothing seemed to irk them more than conditions in Louisiana where they were compelled to abandon their missions, giving place to the Capuchins and the Quebec Seminary. They were also much chagrined that the bishop refused to make their superior a grand vicar.[46]

If the Seminary at Quebec was coming into its own in the opening decades of the eighteenth century, so also was the Seminary at Montreal. Like the Quebec Seminary it exercised in a smaller way the supervision of curés on the Island of Montreal, and furnished directors for the Hôtel-Dieu and the Congregation of Notre-Dame; it also had its Indian missions, a particularly notable one for Iroquois at La Montagne, which was later moved to a more favourable site called Saint-Louis. Montreal, however, was no longer an exclusively Sulpician preserve: besides a Jesuit House there was also a Recollet House which had been established with the aid of Saint-Vallier, who had accorded to the Recollets military chaplaincies and also encouraged them to extend their work into the much neglected missions in Acadia and Newfoundland. This was a distinct improvement from their status under Bishop Laval, who had not favoured their return to Canada. With the support of Frontenac they were often able to defy the unfriendly bishop, and it was with the governor's support that they were able to establish an infirmary close to the Quebec Cathedral. In the frequent tensions between church and state they were usually on the side of the state; this defiance of ecclesiastical authority along with their works of mercy made the Recollets the most popular religious order in New France.[47]

ARCHITECTURE, ART AND MUSIC

Although religious orders occupy a large place in any history of the French-Canadian Church, yet the essence of the French-Canadian identity must be sought in parochial life, where the curé has long been the most influential person. It was the parochial system and not the religious orders that survived the shock of the British conquest unimpaired, and the French-Canadian parish has remained almost impregnable to the assimilating tendencies of American civilization. Out of a long struggle for revocable or irrevocable curés there slowly emerged a unique parochial life during the era of Saint-Vallier. The church building with its distinctive architectural form, around which so much of community life revolved, helped to shape the cultural heritage of New France.

During the heroic age (1608-1665)[48] these churches were not much to look at: they were little more than log cabins and there is no indication that they embodied any indigenous architectural design. These hastily constructed chapels shocked Laval when he first arrived in Canada and he refused to consecrate them. There was, however, one stone parish church built in 1647, before Laval's arrival, Quebec's Notre-Dame-de-la-Paix, which was to serve as a model for the stone churches that Laval insisted must replace the temporary wooden structures. It is this model that explains the consistent architectural tradition in French Canada: a Latin cross twice as long as it is wide, terminating in a rounded apse.[49]

Modifications of the original design were made by Claude Baillif, who arrived in Canada in 1675 to teach at Laval's school of arts and trades at Saint-Joachim and who became superintendent of church building.[50] He was working upon the cathedral when Saint-Vallier first visited Quebec. The bishop-elect who had been living among the magnificent structures of Versailles was not impressed with Baillif's attempt at monumental architecture, so he immediately arranged to bring out from France an architect by the name of Larivière along with six masons.[51] Baillif however, was not superseded, for he went on to build the church of Saint-Anne-de-Beaupré; it was to Baillif Saint-Vallier turned for the construction of the episcopal palace which became, under the bishop's direction, a typical seventeenth-century French château and one of the most elaborate buildings of New France.[52]

Buildings like Saint-Vallier's palace, the Jesuit church in Quebec, La Paroisse in Montreal, brought to Canada contemporary European architectural ideas, but they were considerably modified by the craft traditions on which Laval's few parish churches had been based. Nor were the modifications confined to church structures: from the seminary came a young man, M. Lebland, who showed great sculptural talent and who helped in the ornamentation of the interiors of the churches in a way that made them uniquely Canadian.[53] A little later (1720) Michel Levesseur and other Quebec smiths produced religious vessels and *objets d'art* "of startling beauty and originality." Under the leadership of the school at Saint-Joachim the French colonists began to work out a domestic architecture suitable to Canadian climatic conditions, particularly "those typical Canadian houses with their tall bellcast roof and overhanging eaves,"[54] which began to cluster around the parish church, thus forming the unique church-centered villages and towns of French Canada.

In the realm of music there does not seem to have been the same originality as in the other arts. As the Huguenots, who brought to Canada a psalmody drawn from the compilation of the French metrical psalter (completed in 1562)[55] and long adhered to in the New England colonies as the only appropriate music in church, so the French ecclesiastics in New France were inclined to stick rigidly to the Gregorian psalm-chant, varied sometimes with Palestrinian compositions. There were, however, some local compositions, such as Brébeuf's Christmas carol composed in the Huron dialect sometime between 1634 and 1648; some Ursulines at Quebec composed original melodies for the Indians, and Father René Ménard composed a few motets which were sung after the elevation of the host. All such productions can hardly be termed French-Canadian since their authors were recent arrivals from France. The honour of being the original French-Canadian composer goes to Charles-Amador Martin (1648-1711), a musician of quality who wrote "a piece of plain-chant of incontestable beauty."[56] To complete the record it should be noted that Louis Jolliet, the discoverer of the Mississippi and an organist at Quebec, was the first native Canadian to study music in France. On the whole New France was very conservative in the field of music, and traditional songs that have disappeared in old France are still to be heard in French Canada.[57]

It had been expected by the bishops that the seigneurs would grant land and build the stone churches that were insisted upon, but most of the seigneurs were far too poor to do so, and the first stone churches were largely subsidized by the religious orders. There came however to the parish of Champlain as curé in 1697 Abbé Louis Geoffrey, whom we have already met in Acadia, to show how stone churches might be constructed. Abbé Geoffrey was an architect as well as an educator, and it was partly beause of his architectural ability that Saint-Vallier persuaded him to return to Canada. Soon after his arrival in the parish of Champlain he began to design and build churches at Trois-Rivières, Sorel and Contrecoeur.[58] Tithes and gifts in kind began to come in to help the building program. As these churches were built in seigneurial domain, seating arrangements according to rank and office became an important part of the curé's parochial responsibility; disputes over such symbolic indications of one's status in life became almost as frequent in the parish of Champlain as in Quebec and Montreal. Many a dispute was carried beyond the parish to the Sovereign Council at Quebec.

There was, however, a far more cheerful aspect to parish life than litigation. According to J. Edmond Roy the French Canadians were an unusually gay people and on Sundays and fête days they visited one another to eat the fruits of the season, to play cards and to dance.[59] Their gaiety and fashionable clothes were a constant worry to the bishop, and supposedly to the curé as well, though he for the most part shared in the games and feasting. He also had to read frequently from the pulpit the bishop's pastorals condemning curled hair and the nudities of the neck and shoulders,[60] and many other warnings against the temptations of the flesh. These must have been fairly effective, for there never was in New France the same degree of licentious conduct as prevailed at the trading posts in the far west or at Versailles.

Perhaps the best defence against allurements of the world, the flesh and the devil was Saint-Vallier's catechism which he began to compose during his first retention in France.[61] The importance of this catechism in the shaping of French-Canadian life can hardly be overstressed. That Saint-Vallier placed great weight upon it as a method of combating sin is evident from the records of the four synods he called during his episcopate. At these synods he explained in detail how the catechism might be taught by the priests and how parents might be instructed to teach their children and domestics. For those about to be confirmed he had prepared a little catechism; for those preparing for communion there was an outline of Christian doctrine and holy history and for the more mature Christians he had prepared a catechism of the fêtes and a course in church history,[62] all of which made the Canadian a very literate Christian.

Bishop Laval had also used the catechetical method of reinforcing Christian doctrine and discipline and there is little doubt that the two bishops succeeded in impressing upon the pioneer families of Canada, who were not always drawn from the most stable elements in old France, a spirit of pious devotion and a religious outlook upon life that was not so generally evident in Europe in the eighteenth century. Travellers from Europe were frequently struck by this contrast between European and Canadian piety; but withal it was a light-hearted piety, very different from the rather gloomy piety of their Puritan neighbours to the South.[63]

PROBLEMS OF DISCIPLINE

That Canadians were on a path of their own soon became evident to Saint-Vallier after his return to his diocese in 1713. He came back, a much mellowed man, determined to live out his declining years as a humble ascetic. Instead of taking up residence at his magnificent palace which at the time was occupied by the intendant, Michel Begon, he went to live in a sparsely furnished room that had been prepared for him at the General Hospital.[64] All seemed very pleasant for a time: he had been welcomed back most cordially by the governor and the clergy.[65] But this cordiality quickly waned, when the bishop tried to put some restraint upon the unconventionality of the religious orders. He was greatly surprised to learn that Governor Vaudreuil casually entered convents to converse with the sisters and that he often took friends along with him. The bishop's rebukes apparently did not stop the practice which continued down to the time of Bishop Dosquet at least.[66]

Shocking also it was to find that some parishioners attended the church under the influence of liquors; also there was much quarreling and even swearing before the church doors, and some people left church before the service was finished. Such unseemly conduct had also been of great concern to Intendant Raudot, who had issued a severe ordinance against it. In order to get his ordinance more strictly enforced, the intendant tried to raise the prestige of the captains of militia and give them greater disciplinary power by allowing them to walk in procession after the church wardens and also to receive the blessed bread[67] before other members of the congregation. The bishop thoroughly approved of the intendant's ordinance against unseemly conduct but could not agree that captains of militia were entitled to the honours that had been conferred upon them. In this he again found himself opposed by the governor, who was supported by the king, much to the embarrassment of the bishop.[68]

Another disturbing scandal, still rife, was the sale of liquor to the Indians, a perennial problem that Saint-Vallier inherited from his predecessor. It was the suspicion of the Jesuits that the second Bishop of Quebec did not show the same rigour in opposing this evil trade as did the first. Father Chauchetière speaks of the reluctance of the bishop to open his mouth in protest. Abbé Gosselin thinks such criticisms unfair, for, as he points out, few of the bishop's pastorals failed to condemn the evils of the liquor trade and, moreover, in 1714 he made an unusually strong protest before the Superior Council on the evil consequences of debauching the Indians.[69]

Jesuit criticism of Saint-Vallier as failing to take a firm stand on a matter of conscience is somewhat ironic, for there seems little doubt that he was more rigid in condemning the sins of the flesh than were the Jesuits themselves: in point of fact it has been suspected that he was a Jansenist at heart or that at least he shared the Jansenists' suspicion that the Jesuits were lenient in the confessional. He would not allow Father Duparc to become spiritual director at the General Hospital because the Jesuits "taught and practised probabilism."[70] On the other hand Saint-Vallier was a strong papalist and after the pope condemned Jansenism in the bull, *Unigenitus*, he refused to allow any Jansenist books to circulate in his diocese. When it was discovered that François Poulet, a one-time recluse in the parish of Kamouraska, was a Jansenist he was immediately banished from the diocese of Quebec.[71]

Some of the "allied errors" of Jansenism, such as Quietism, may have been patronized by the bishop—that is if mystic visions can be equated with Quietism. Such visions had, long before Saint-Vallier's arrival, been part of the religious tradition of New France; Marie de l'Incarnation's mystic raptures were well known, as were those of some of the founders of Montreal, like Madame d'Ailleboust.[72] It is true that Saint-Vallier gave no credence to the "supernatural revelations" of Sister Tardif and rebuked two Sulpician priests who were inclined to accept them; but in the far more remarkable case of Mademoiselle LeBer he was quite lenient. This anchorite, who had taken a solemn vow of seclusion before Dollier de Casson, had unusual credentials: she was the daughter of one of the very pious settlers of Montreal, a goddaughter of Jeanne Mance and a pupil both of the Ursuline convent at Quebec and the Congregation of Notre-Dame at Montreal. In 1695 she secluded herself in a small cell close to the altar of the chapel of the Congregation of Notre-Dame and there she remained until her death. Saint-Vallier visited her in 1698 and was "highly gratified on beholding the edifying recluse of whom report said so much."[73] Miraculous assistance through the intercession of pious folk who died in the odour of sanctity was taken for granted by Saint-Vallier and most of his flock. The miracles that occurred at Sainte-Anne-de-Beaupré were common knowledge; the Intendant Campigny gave New France an additional national shrine by his devotion to the "pious Iroquois", Catherine Tekawitha, whose intercessions had restored his failing powers of speech; this daughter of an Algonkin squaw and a non-Christian Mohawk, was the first Indian to receive the appellation "venerable." Saint-Vallier himself testified to a remarkable cure at Trois-Rivières through the intercession of Frère Didace.[74]

DIOCESAN CONSOLIDATION

In his preoccupation with the supernatural the bishop never lost sight of the natural arrangements necessary for an episcopally governed diocese as he had known it in France. On July 30th, 1714, he was present at a meeting of the Superior Council when an anticipated royal letter putting an end to the cathedral chapter as it had been established by Mgr Laval, and replacing it by one worked out between Saint-Vallier and the Court,[75] was read to the assembled councillors. Members of the seminary were excluded from the chapter, which meant for the seminary a serious loss of revenue from the French abbeys they had been administering. In place of this revenue they were to receive an annual gift of three thousand livres from the king, but on condition that the state was to have a voice in the appointment of officials at the seminary; the state was also to have something to say in the appointment of the new cathedral chapter that Saint-Vallier was organizing.

As was to be expected, there was great discontent at the seminary over its exclusion from the chapter, but what must have grieved Saint-Vallier even more was the quarrelsomeness of the new canons at the cathedral who showed a reluctance to occupy their places in the choir during service.

One of Saint-Vallier's last important administrative acts was to make, in co-operation with the Intendant de Meulles, a new circumscription of his diocese: they redesigned the boundaries of eighty-two parochial districts destined to have settled curacies, thus bringing up to fifty the number of new parishes erected by the second

Bishop of Quebec.[76] No sooner was the circumscription completed than protests from all quarters assailed the ears of the bishop. The seminary protested not only the boundaries but warned of the impossibility of finding curés for so many new parishes.

As a matter of fact the seminary had never been enamoured of the ordinance of 1692 which called for the fixed tenure of parishes, and was still opposed to it, whereas Saint-Vallier was firmly convinced that a "resident priest is the soul of the parish,"[77] it was his opinion that the seminary did not make enough effort to train sufficient men for the priesthood. Indubitably there were not enough parochial priests to man all eighty-two parishes and without the help of religious orders many a parish would have been destitute of all spiritual care; even if there had been enough priests there would not have been sufficient revenue to pay them. Parishes were pitiably poor, the people were reluctant to pay tithes and the king's supplement was meagre.[78] All this tended to frustrate the new arrangement of 1721. Protests were registered not only from the Seminary of Quebec, but also from the Sulpicians of Montreal and from neglected parishes as well. Ten years later there were not more than twenty titled curés; the other parishes were served by simple missionaries. "Time and experience," says Abbé Gosselin, "had demonstrated the wisdom of the system established by Mgr Laval." The Abbé points out that "apart from Notre Dame at Quebec there never were in Canada irrevocable curés in the canonical sense of the word."[79] Although bishops nominated to parishes, yet they reserved to themselves, in their letters of nomination, the right of removing at will the priest whom they selected, and thereby circumvented the edict of 1692.

BURDEN OF OFFICE

The last few years of Saint-Vallier's episcopate remained troubled: the governor and intendant quarreled bitterly and their example was followed by the seminaries of Quebec and Montreal. The bishop was finding the burden of his office almost too heavy to bear; he wrote pathetically to the court asking for a priest of quality who might become dean and merit by his good qualities the right to fill his place.[80] Before returning to Canada in 1713 he had asked for a coadjutor to share his responsibilities and the king had nominated a member of a noble Breton family, Duplessis de Mornay, who was consecrated Bishop of Euménie in Phrygia. Saint-Vallier's immediate intention was to send his coadjutor to Louisiana, but Mornay, after he was given an allowance of three thousand *livres* a year, never left France;[81] consequently, the bishop still had to carry out all episcopal duties that could not be delegated to the lesser clergy. As late as 1725 he made a visitation of his diocese trying to appease parishoners who were still indignant over the parish boundaries set in 1721. He returned to Quebec greatly exhausted from what had proved to be his last visitation.

There was, however, a more cheerful side to the story of the last days of Saint-Vallier. After fatiguing visitations he could return to his beloved General Hospital which had become the most beautiful building in Canada, and to the tender care of its *bonnes religieuses* whose greatest pleasure was to look after every want of their most eminent boarder and founder.[82] Furthermore, Saint-Vallier had in 1726 ordained to the priesthood, a widower, M. de Lotbinière, a man well versed in the ways of the world, who in a brief time relieved the bishop of many troublesome chores. Saint-Vallier would have liked to make Lotbinière dean, but he was well aware that such appointment would have caused great indignation among the senior clergy, so he compromised by making him his grand vicar.[83] When the end was near it was to Lotbinière he turned for the last rites of the church. He passed away on Christmas Day, 1727, leaving behind him such a reputation for holiness and sanctity as to embarrass greatly the grand vicar in attempting to carry out the last wishes of the dead bishop—to be buried in the chapel of the General Hospital where he had spent so much time in prayer and meditation.

NOTES TO CHAPTER TEN

1. For an interesting comment on the revival of religious persecution *vide* Anne Whiteman, "Church and State" in *The New Cambridge Modern History* (Cambridge: Cambridge University Press, 1961), Vol. V, esp. pp. 138-48.

2. *Vide* E. B. O'Callaghan, ed., *The Documentary History of the State of New York* (Albany: Ward Parsons, 1849), Vol. I, pp. 297-302, for "An account of the most remarkable occurrences in Canada" by M. de Monseignat, Comptroller General of the Marine in Canada; he writes, "The orders received by M. le Comte (de Frontenac) to commence hostilities against New England and New York afforded him much pleasure and were necessary for the country." There follows a description of the use of Indian allies to surprise unsuspecting inhabitants with murderous slaughter; *vide* also G. Lanctot, ed., *New Documents by Lahontan* (Ottawa: The Oakes Collection, 1940), p. 31: Lahontan says the cruelties which took place at Schenectady "are scarcely believable."

3. *Vide* "Mémoire sur le Canada par Monsieur de Denonville à Quebec, le 12 Novembre 1688" in *Collection de Manuscrits . . . relatifs à la Nouvelle-France* (Québec: Coté, 1883-85), Vol. I, p. 348 *et seq.*; also *Lettre de M. de Denonville, Québec, 1688.* Vol. I, p. 442 *et seq.*

4. *Ibid.*, p. 418; "Mémoire du Roy à Mons. de Denonville": ". . . ces gens, qui sont vigoureux et accoutumez à la peine, peuvent servir utilement sur les galères de Sa Majesté"; also E. B. O'Callaghan, *op. cit.*, Vol. I, p. 233 *et seq.*, for a

memoir from the king to Denonville, 1687, in which the king "expects to learn at the close of this year the entire destruction of the greatest part of these savages . . . and as a number of prisoners may be made . . . His Majesty thinks he can make use of them in his galleys . . ."; also Thwaites, *op. cit.*, Vol. LXIV, p. 241, for a letter by Father Lamberville written in Paris in 1695 in which he recalls with bitterness Governor Denonville's decision "to ruin and annihilate, if he could, the Iroquois."

5. *Vide* F.-X. de Charlevoix, *History and Description of New France*, trans. J. B. Shea (New York: Harper, 1900), Vol. IV, pp. 12-4.

6. *Vide* G. M. Wrong, *The Rise and Fall of New France* (Toronto: Macmillan, 1928), Vol. II, p. 506.

7. *Vide* A.-H. Gosselin, *Le Vénérable François de Montmorency Laval* (Quebec: Dessault et Proulx, 1901), p. 352.

8. *Ibid.*, p. 355.

9. *Ibid.*, p. 374.

10. G. M. Wrong, *op. cit.*, Vol. II, p. 520; *vide* also E. B. Callaghan, *op. cit.*, Vol. I, pp. 302-4, for a list of the people killed at Schenectady on Feb. 9, 1690, preserved in Mortgage Book B. in County Clerk's office, Albany, N.Y.

11. On this incident Father de la Chasse wrote that the English "have succeeded in gratifying their passion of hatred and ridding themselves of an apostolic man"; Thwaites, *op. cit.*, Vol. LXVII, pp. 231-47. Contrasting accounts of these tragic events are to be found in F. Parkman, *A Half Century of Conflict* (Boston: Little, Brown, 1903), Vol. I, pp. 244-9, and W. I. Kipp, ed., *The Early Jesuit Missions in North America*, compiled and translated with notes from letters of French Jesuits (New York: Wiley and Putnam, 1846), pp. 69-78.

12. *Vide* H. Têtu et C.-O. Gagnon, *Mandements, Lettres Pastorales et Circulaires des Evêques de Québec* (Quebec: Coté, 1887-89), Vol. I, p. 265 *et seq.*: "Lettre Pastorale pour disposer les peuples de ce diocèse à se bien défendre contre les Anglais."

13. For a description of the conduct of the ecclesiastics during the siege by Michel Germain DeCouvert *vide* Thwaites, *op. cit.*, Vol. LXIV, pp. 41-53.

14. For a vivid account of the heroism of Madeleine de Verchères based on a *récit* made by order of M. de Beauharnois *vide* F. Parkman, *Count Frontenac and New France under Louis XIV* (4th ed.; Boston: Little, Brown, 1877), pp. 302-8.

15. G. M. Wrong, *op. cit.*, Vol. II, p. 529.

16. In a letter to the Archbishop of Paris Laval expressed the opinion that his successor felt that his episcopal character gave him guidance without any need for advice in the governance of his church. *Vide* C. de Rochemonteix, *Les Jésuites et la Nouvelle-France au XVIIe siècle* (Paris: Letouzey et Ané, 1896), Vol. III, p. 314.

17. The *Relation* is included in the *Mandements . . . des Evêques*, *op. cit.*, Vol. I, pp. 191-275.

18. Soeur Saint-Félix, *Monseigneur de Saint-Vallier et l'Hôpital Général de Québec* (Quebec: Darveau, 1882); p. 51.

19. An interesting account of the Congregation of Hospitallers of Montreal is given by Y. Poutet in an article entitled "Les Voeux des Frères Charon, Hospitaliers-Enseignants" in *Revue d'histoire de l'Eglise de France* (Paris 1964), Tome XLIV, No. 146, pp. 19-45.

20. *Vide* H.-R. Casgrain, *Les Sulpiciens et les Prêtres des Missions-Etrangères en Acadie* (Quebec: Pruneau et Kirouac, 1897), p. 18 *et seq.*

21. *Vide* Prosper Cloutier, *Histoire de la Paroisse de Champlain* (Trois-Rivières: Imprimerie "Le Bien Public", 1915), Vol. I, p. 191 *et seq.*

22. *Vide* A.-H. Gosselin, *L'Eglise de Canada depuis Monseigneur de Laval jusqu'à la Conquête* (Quebec: Laflamme et Proulx, 1911), Vol. I, pp. 63-4.

23. *Ibid.*, Vol. I, p. 53 *et seq.*

24. For an excellent summary of the educational institutions in Canada before the conquest *vide* J. Douglas, *Old France in the New World* (Cleveland: Douglas, 1905), p. 462 *et seq.*; for a more detailed account *vide* A.-E. Gosselin, *L'Instruction au Canada sous le Régime français* (Quebec: Laflamme et Proulx, 1911), p. 43 *et seq.*

25. *Vide* C. de Rochemonteix, *op. cit.*, Vol. III, 315.

26. *Ibid.*, Vol. III, p. 316 *et seq.*; also *vide* A.-H. Gosselin, *op. cit.*, Vol. I, p. 94.

27. *Ibid.*, p 62.

28. *Vide* Soeur Saint-Félix, *op. cit.*, p. 98

29. A.-H. Gosselin, *op. cit.*, Vol. I, pp. 116-27, a chapter devoted to the *affaires* of Mgr de Saint-Vallier; *vide* also C. de Rochemonteix, *op. cit.*, Vol III, p. 320 *et seq.*

30. For a gossipy letter by M. de Lamothe Cadillac (28 September, 1649), on the Mareuil *affaire vide Rapport de l'Archiviste de la Province de Québec pour 1923-24* (Quebec: Proulx, 1924), p. 80 *et seq.*

31. *Vide* "Lettre au Ministre de Pontchartrain sur l'Affaire du Sieur de Mareuil et Lettre sur l'Hôpital-Général de Québec, Le Conseil Souverain, La Justice, et cetera," in *Rapport de l'Archiviste de la Province de Québec pour 1922-23, op. cit.*, pp. 8-12.

32. A.-H. Gosselin, *op. cit.*, Vol. I, p. 132.

33. For a copy of the eulogy of Frontenac by Father Goyer *vide* F. Parkman, *Count Frontenac, op. cit.*, pp. 428-37.

34. A.-H. Gosselin, *op. cit.*, Vol. I, p. 160.

35. *Vide* Soeur Saint-Félix, *op. cit.*, p. 143 *et seq.*

36. H. Têtu, *Les Evêques de Québec* (Quebec: Hardy, 1889), p. 102 *et seq.*, tells in some detail the story of the founding of the General Hospital, for he says, "it shows Saint-Vallier for what he was."

37. *Vide* Soeur Saint-Félix, *op. cit.*, p. 180 *et seq.*

38. *Vide* A.-H. Gosselin, *Laval, op. cit.*, pp. 381-400.

39. *Vide* C. de Rochemonteix, *op. cit.*, Vol. III, p. 571 *et seq.*

40. A.-H. Gosselin, *Saint-Vallier, op. cit.*, Vol. I, p. 170.

41. *Vide* C. de Rochemonteix, *op. cit.*, Vol. III, p. 489.

42. *Ibid.*, Vol. III, p. 497.

43. For a letter from Father Etienne de Carheil to Governor Callières (1702) describing in minute detail the vicious lives of the traders and reflecting the despair of the missionaries for the future of the Indians *vide* Thwaites, *op. cit.*, Vol. LXV, pp. 189-253.

44. For an interesting account of the founding of Detroit *vide* F. Parkman, *A Half Century of Conflict, op. cit.*, Vol. I, pp. 17-33.

45. *Vide* "Mémoire au Ministre de Pontchartrain" on the problems of commerce at Detroit in *Rapport de l'Archiviste, op. cit.*, p. 51 *et seq.*

46. *Vide* C. de Rochemonteix, *op. cit.*, Vol. III, p. 583.

47. *Ibid.*, Vol. III, p. 361.

48. *Vide* Alan Gowans, *Church Architecture in New France* (Toronto: University of Toronto Press, 1955), p. 12.

49. *Ibid.*, pp. 41-2.

50. *Ibid.*, pp. 46-7.

51. *Ibid.*, pp. 50-1; *vide* also A. Roy, *Les Lettres, les Sciences et Les Arts du Canada* (Paris: Jouve, 1930), p. 153.

52. For pictorial representation of seventeenth-century art and architecture of New France *vide* Ramsay Traquair and G. A. Neilson, *The Architecture of the Hôpital Général de Québec* (Montreal: McGill University Publication series, 1931), 13, No. 31.

53. *Vide* A.-H. Gosselin, *op. cit.*, Vol. I, p. 174.

54. Jacques Monet, "The Foundations of French-Canadian Nationality," in *Culture* (Quebec, December 1965), Vol. XXVI, No. 4, p. 459.

55. *Vide* J. W. Smith and A. L. Jamison, eds., *Religious Perspectives in American Culture* (Princeton, N.J.: Princeton University Press, 1961), pp. 291-2.

56. Andrée Desautels, "Les trois Ages de la Musique au Canada," in *Grand Larousse Encyclopédie de la Musique* (Paris: Librairie Larousse, 1965), Vol. II, pp. 314-5.

57. *Vide Larousse de la Musique* (Paris: Librairie Larouse, 1957), Vol. I, p. 152.

58. *Vide* P. Cloutier, *op. cit.*, Vol. I, p. 193 *et seq.*

59. "Nos ancêtres avaient un fond d'inaltérable gaité qui tenait à leur sang français." Quoted by P. Cloutier, *op. cit.*, Vol. I, p. 200, from J. Edmond Roy's *Histoire de la Seigneurie de Lauzon*. *Vide* also Peter Kalm, *Travels into North America* (trans. J. R. Foster; London: Lowndes, 1770-1771), Vol. III, p. 81 *et seq.*

60. For a letter from Mgr Saint-Vallier to the governor and his wife urging them to set a good example to the people in the matter of dress, *vide Mandements, op. cit.*, Vol. I, pp. 169-74.

61. *Vide* A.-H. Gosselin, *op. cit.*, Vol. I, p. 132.

62. For an excellent study of Saint-Vallier's catechism and the catechetical method used in the diocese of Quebec, *vide* Fernand Porter, *L'Institution Catéchistique au Canada Français, 1633-1833* (Montreal: Les Editions Franciscaines, 1949), *passim*; also an article by Marcel de Grandpré, "Traditions of the Catholic Church in French Canada," in J. W. Grant, ed., *The Churches and the Canadian Experience* (Toronto: Ryerson, 1963), pp. 1-13.

63. *Vide* Max Savelle, *A History of Colonial America*, revised by R. M. Middlekauff (New York and Toronto: Holt, Rinehart and Winston, 1964), pp. 303-5, for comments on New England theology at this time.

64. *Vide* Soeur Saint-Félix, *op. cit.*, p. 227.

65. *Vide* A.-H. Gosselin, *op. cit.*, p. 254.

66. *Ibid.*, Vol. I, pp. 264-6.

67. "It was the custom," says M. J. Edmond Roy in his *Histoire de la Seigneurie de Lauzon*, "for the parishioners to offer by turn each Sunday a portion of bread to the church to be blessed and then to be shared among the faithful, which they ate with devotion." Quoted by P. Cloutier, *op. cit.*, p. 179.

68. *Vide* A.-H. Gosselin, *op. cit.*, Vol. I, p. 312.

69. *Ibid.*, Vol. I, p. 274.

70. *Ibid.*, Vol. I, p. 269.

71. *Ibid.*, Vol. I, pp. 325-31.

72. *Ibid.*, Vol. I, p. 425 *et seq.*; *vide* also Aegidius Fauteux, *La Famille d'Aillebout* (Montreal: Ducharme, 1917).

73. E.-M. Faillon, *L'Héroine Chrétiennne du Canada ou Vie de Mlle LeBer* (Villemarie: Chez les Soeurs de la Congrégation de Notre-Dame, 1860), p. 124 *et seq.*

74. *Vide* A.-H. Gosselin, *op. cit.*, Vol. I, p.p. 227 and 436.

75. *Ibid.*, Vol. I, p. 278.

76. *Ibid.*, Vol. I, pp. 349-55.

77. F. Porter, *op. cit.*, p. 56.

78. *Ibid.*, p. 57.

79. A.-H. Gosselin, *op. cit.*, Vol. I, p. 365.

80. *Ibid.*, Vol. I, p. 424.

81. *Vide* H. Têtu, *op. cit.*, pp. 157-69.

82. *Vide*, A.-H. Gosselin, *op. cit.*, Vol. I, p. 429; also Soeur Saint-Félix, *op. cit.*, pp. 279-80, for an account of the last days of Mgr Saint-Vallier.

83. *Vide* A.-H. Gosselin, *op. cit.*, Vol. I, p. 435.

ELEVEN

An Era of Dismay

The decline and fall of New France, which is the inevitable theme of this concluding chapter, has all the elements of a Greek tragedy with its moments of victory and deeper moments of tragic drama. The final phase of France's attempt to create a New World empire came at a very inopportune time in the civic and church life of New France; corruption in governmental circles particularly during the regime of the infamous intendant, Bigot, played an overwhelming part in the disaster that befell Quebec in 1759.[1] But the decline of the spiritual ardour of the church also made its contribution to the misery of the time.

Not the least important of the contributors to the final tragic act was William Pitt, Great Britain's ambitious prime minister, who represented domestic middle class virtues, so rare in the England of his day. These were enough to turn the scales in the struggle for a continent[2] especially when they were supplemented by a religious awakening in the English colonies that added a crusading fervour to New England's demand for the expulsion of the French from the North American scene.[3]

AN UNUSUAL BURIAL

That something ominous and portentous was happening to the religious life of New France was evident in the unusual proceedings that followed upon the death of Mgr Saint-Vallier. As miracles were anticipated at the tomb of the dead bishop the canons of the cathedral felt that they should take measures to avoid a stampede of the faithful to the General Hospital where the burial was to take place; consequently they quickly called a chapter meeting and appointed the curé of Quebec, Canon Etienne Boullard, capitular vicar of the diocese, and instructed him to make some unusual arrangements for the funeral. These included carrying the remains of the bishop from church to church in Quebec; at each of these churches the casket was to be ceremoniously received by the curé and his congregation and, when the procession was completed, the body was to be taken to the cathedral to lie in state for a while. After that Canon Boullard would conduct the funeral service and then proceed to the chapel of the General Hospital for the interment. In this way, the canons apparently thought they could forestall continual pilgrimages to Notre-Dame-des-Anges by people in search of miraculous cures. But their scheme was immediately challenged by Archdeacon Lotbinière, who pointed out that he was the acting administrator of the diocese until the arrival of the new bishop, Duplessis de Mornay, who as coadjutor had now automatically succeeded to the See of Quebec; he also refused to allow the removal of the body from the General Hospital.

The archdeacon's reaction to the suggestions of the canons was mild compared to that of Intendant Dupuy, who immediately suspected that the canons harboured some "dark design"[4] whereby they were going to bury the bishop at the cathedral. He then ordered the archdeacon to proceed with the funeral that very evening in Notre-Dame-des-Anges, the chapel of the General Hospital. In a very brief time the mortal remains of Mgr Saint-Vallier were deposited in the tomb he had chosen before his death.

No sooner was the service over than the canons, with the capitular vicar at their head, were knocking on the door of the locked chapel and demanding the body of the bishop; learning that the interment was a *fait accompli*, Canon Boullard placed both the mother superior of the hospital and the chapel of Notre-Dame-des-Anges under an interdict. The matter was carried to the Superior Council where Canon Boullard and Intendant Dupuy became engaged in a contest that was to embroil every religious and secular order in New France. Finally, Governor de Beauharnois resolved to intervene decisively to bring the controversy to an end: first he exiled two councillors to the country, in order to assure himself a majority in the council; he then forced through the council an ordinance which suppressed all controversy until the court had spoken.[5]

When news at last came from France it brought little comfort to anyone except perhaps to Lotbinière: Dupuy was called home, but Beauharnois was also rebuked for exceeding his powers, and the canons were censored for ignoring the prerogatives of Archdeacon

Lotbinière who was now confirmed by the bishop himself as the temporary administrator of the diocese. The bishop, however, took note of a long letter of complaint from the canons on the chaotic state of his diocese and promised that he would soon provide them with a coadjutor bishop with authority to act as if he himself were present.[6]

PROBLEMS OF A COADJUTOR

It was generally understood that Bishop de Mornay would not reside in his diocese because he was afraid to cross the ocean[7]— clear evidence of a sharp decline from the spiritual fervour of the church that had sent Laval and Saint-Vallier to the New World. That de Mornay should have continued to enjoy the revenue of the See of Quebec while sending another to do his work was also indicative of the general religious apathy that was sweeping eighteenth-century Christendom.

There was some delay before the bishop found a suitable coadjutor willing to make the perilous voyage across the ocean to Quebec. Fortunately, there was at Rome a former Sulpician, Pierre-Herman Dosquet, who had already been consecrated to the titular See of Samos for missionary service in the Orient.[8] He had spent two years in Montreal as director of the Sisters of the Congregation of Notre-Dame and he was quite willing to return to Canada in place of going to the Orient. So in 1729 he sailed for Quebec in company with M. Bertrand de La Tour who had just been appointed Dean of Quebec and Gilles Hocquart who was replacing the discredited Dupuy as intendant.

With these new appointments and some of the feudists removed from Quebec it was hoped by the court that peace would return to the church in New France. It was a vain hope, for the canons still continued to frustrate Archdeacon Lotbinière at every turn, even after he had been confirmed in his office by Bishop de Mornay. Somehow they managed to get the new Dean de La Tour off the ship carrying the coadjutor bishop to Quebec before it docked and the former read a speech of welcome for the new prelate, thus depriving Lotbinière of that honour.[9] By agreeing to this tactic of humiliating the archdeacon, neither the bishop nor the dean was contributing to the peace of the church.

It was indeed a time for firm measures and some sharp discipline, but unfortunately the new bishop did not have the stature or the courtly manners of his predecessors to command immediate respect.

One of his serious handicaps was that he was regarded by the French Canadians as a foreigner, since he had been born in the principality of Liège in 1691 and had to be naturalized before he could take his seat in the Superior Council.

Almost immediately problems of a rather trivial nature stirred up much ill will against Mgr Dosquet. Before he left France the court, concerned about the neglected Bishop's Palace, said he must reside there without delay. This brought him into conflict with the sisters of the General Hospital, who as legatees of the late Mgr Saint-Vallier were asked to repair the palace. This they refused to do and the matter was going into litigation when the court intervened and supplied the money for the repairs.[10] No sooner was the bishop settled in his palace than he found he could enjoy very little privacy for the grounds had become a strolling place for the populace of Quebec. When he resorted to putting up a gate to block the strollers it was torn down at once; after various attempts to secure some privacy in his own home, the bishop had to give up and allow the terrace to be accessible to all who wished to walk there.[11]

What was more serious than the ill will of the populace was the enmity of the Canadian priests. This he provoked by cancelling the appointments to curés made by the canons during the semi-vacancy of the See. When he asked one priest to go to Acadia, which was desperately in need of missionaries, he received an abrupt refusal, and when he sought the aid of the canons to help in administering some much-needed clerical discipline he received very little cooperation. "The canons," he wrote "acknowledge neither rules nor statutes nor superiors. They treat the dean as their inferior and the bishop as their equal. . . ."[12] Relations with the religious orders were not much better, particularly with the nursing orders. Their opinion of the coadjutor is well reflected in the remark of the superior of the Hôtel-Dieu at Quebec: "We have," she writes, "a new prelate who does nothing by himself. He has a grand vicar of twenty-eight to whom he has given over the details of the diocese"; she accused this young man of having so distorted things "that we know not where we are."[13]

Many of the bishop's problems were due to the long periods in the Canadian church when there had been no firm hand in control of the administration; but not all were caused by this. There was also an increasing nationalism developing among the Canadian clergy that resented the appointment of French ecclesiastics to all the influential offices in Canada. Despite the fact that nearly half the missions were still served by Sulpician, Jesuit and Recollet missionaries the native

Canadian curés were slowly and painfully trying to establish themselves as canonically parish priests in communities that were awk-
wardly strung out along a river or a road, known as the côte or rang,
"the elementary unit of social cohesion"[14] in early French Canada. It
was uphill work to create anything like an old-country parish in this
early form of settlement, but the Canadian curés were tireless in their
efforts to create solid parochial units and to become the most
important persons in the parishes they served.

To some extent Bishop Dosquet tried to put a damper on this
development. On the matter of fixed curés he took the position of
Laval: he regarded the parishes too large and too poor to be assigned
permanently to one priest; he also considered it too much of a risk to
give permanent tenure, as the canons had done, to young and immature graduates of the seminary.[15] But perhaps he provoked the
greatest resentment among the Canadian clergy when he tried to curb
their independence of action by placing priests from France in
parishes between two others served by Canadians—to act as a brake
upon over-exuberance. The new dean fresh from France did little to
help bring peace to the diocese; like the bishop himself he was
imperious and demanding; as clerk of the council he had been a very
contentious person and when at the end of two years in Canada he
returned to France, no one, not even the bishop, regretted his
departure.[16]

Overshadowing all other problems facing the bishop was the lack
of revenue; his income as coadjutor was so limited that he fell into
debt, a condition shared by most of the religious institutions in New
France at this time. In desperation he asked for a seigneurie in the
hope that he might receive from it some additional revenue. The
request was granted and he was given some land in the environs of
Trois-Rivières where he built a house and a church, around which
emerged a village known as the Villa de Samos. This example, says
Gosselin, started "a veritable epidemic of commercial and industrial
enterprises among the Canadian clergy. For a time the influence of
the curés must have declined drastically as many of them, like the
curé, Le Page, who had acquired the seigneurie of Terrebonne,
seemed more interested in their lands and mills than in their
congregations.[17]

It was not without murmurs of discontent that the people saw their
clergy becoming men of commerce. Both the governor and the intendant had been reluctant to allow men of the cloth to engage in
industry; they did, however, acquiesce in some cases in order that the
church might reduce its debts, but drew the line when Abbé Martin

asked to be allowed to establish a fish factory in Labrador.[18] Nevertheless, there was good reason for the coadjutor and clergy to look around for new ways to raise money for a church no longer receiving the generous support it once had from wealthy benefactors in France. Indeed the bishop residing in Paris was taking for his personal use revenue from abbeys that was intended to be expended in Canada while many of the religious institutions such as the seminary in Quebec and the Ursuline convent at Trois-Rivières were to all intents and purposes insolvent. Mgr Dosquet, commenting on the condition of the latter, writes, "There are in Trois-Rivières thirty Ursulines who have not together more than five hundred and sixty five *livres* of revenue. If the bishop does not do something to relieve their misery, he will seem unfeelingly hard."[19] Finally the coadjutor gave over to his grand vicars the administration of the church in Canada and returned to France in October, 1732, to inform the court personally that Bishop de Mornay was evading his responsibilities to New France.

The king's minister, de Maurepas, on being informed of how de Mornay was abusing his trust ordered the latter to proceed to Canada at once; the bishop, however, escaped this fate by placing his resignation, pure and simple, in the hands of the king, September 12th, 1733.[20]

Mgr Dosquet, much to his surprise, now found himself in full charge of the diocese of Quebec, but with much less revenue from the abbeys than he had expected; this stringency, however, does not seem to have inspired him to cut down on his own personal expenses. On the boat which brought him back to Quebec in 1734 he had with him a *maître d'hôtel*, a valet, a cook, a cook's assistant, a coachman, a footman and a Negro. "Alas!" writes Abbé Gosselin, "what has become of the times of Laval and Saint-Vallier, who were content with one or two servants!" Also on the same ship, the *Rubis*, were several priests "more or less badly chosen, some of whom were in great need of clerical instruction."[21] After a brief stay at his palace, which he found too uncomfortable, the bishop moved on to the more healthful environment of Villa de Samos.

He was not long back in Canada before he found himself engaged in a bitter controversy with the seminary at Quebec. At the time the seminary was severed from the cure of Quebec and allowed no association with the chapter it had lost its chief source of revenue and was now continually in debt; it was the bishop's suggestion that it might be amalgamated with the seminary at Montreal. Such a suggestion was greatly resented by the Canadian clergy, most of whom

were its graduates; neither Saint-Sulpice nor the Jesuits had produced a single Canadian priest.[22] To thus alienate the Canadian
clergy by threatening the extinction of their Alma Mater made it
practically impossible for the bishop to govern his diocese as a
father-in-God, particularly when the priests he had brought over with
him on the *Rubis* were complaining that they did not receive enough
to live on and were anxious to return to France. Although he tried
hard to make them remain at their posts he finally gave up the
struggle himself and returned to Paris in 1735, pleading ill-health as
his excuse.[23]

CANADIANIZATION: MONSEIGNEUR DE LAUBERIVIERE

For four years Canada was without a resident bishop, and during
this time native Canadians were more and more getting control of
their own church. Since France was failing to make adequate pro-
vision for the administration and upkeep of the church in Canada, it
was only natural that the Canadians should try to replace the incompetent clergy that were now coming out from France, particularly in
the higher echelons, with more competent native sons. In 1738
Lotbinière was made dean, the first native Canadian to hold this
office. There was a slight pause in this Canadianization when the
chapter was informed that the king had nominated, in 1739, Abbé du
Pourroy de Lauberivière to succeed the ailing Dosquet as Bishop of
Quebec. It was M. de l'Orme the very faithful representative of the
Canadian church at the court of Versailles who informed the chapter
in Canada what their new bishop was like. He observed that he was
a very pious young man of good looks and polished manners. "All I
fear," he wrote, "is that he has sucked too much of the milk of Saint-
Sulpice."[24]

Unfortunately, the consecration of this young man was to give New
France only a brief respite from its shepherdless condition. He was
consecrated on July 16, 1739, in the Seminary of Saint-Sulpice in
Paris by the former Bishop of Quebec, Mgr de Mornay, with another
former bishop Mgr Dosquet taking a part in the consecration.[25] In
1740 he sailed on a plague-stricken ship for Quebec and for a brief
time he charmed all with his gracious manners and gentle spirit. Then
he fell ill with the plague on August 13, and was dead by August 20
and buried the same day "without pomp because of the nature of his
illness."[26] As a tribute to his saintliness he was buried in the cathedral alongside the tomb of Mgr Laval: in the words of his biographer:
"two saints sleep now, one beside the other, very different in age, but
equally dear to God and man."[27]

Once again the Canadian church had to rely on its own resources. On the same day that Mgr de Lauberivière died the chapter met and made some appointments hurriedly: it nominated M. de Miniac, a Sulpician who had succeeded Lotbinière as archdeacon, vicar general for the whole diocese; and M. Courtois, of Saint-Sulpice, grand vicar and superior of the regions and communities in the city and government of Montreal. This latter nomination was a distinct slight to M. Normant du Faradon, the superior of Saint-Sulpice, who had been unjustly accused of engaging in a dishonest business transaction. By passing over the superior and nominating M. Courtois grand vicar the chapter was indirectly supporting the accusation of dishonesty.[28] Under the circumstances M. Courtois refused to accept the proffered title, and the chapter was compelled to make another nomination. This time it went outside the seminary, an unusual step, and nominated Etienne Marchand, curé of Boucherville, the first Canadian to hold the office of grand vicar. This was done, apparently, under the pressure of the Canadians in Montreal where local pride in native sons was as evident as at Quebec.

The same kind of pressure was making things very difficult for M. de Miniac in Quebec; suddenly he slipped away incognito to France without informing either the chapter or the dean that he was leaving Canada.[29] The chapter met once again and, as was the case at Montreal, it elected a Canadian, M. Thierry Hazeur, capitular vicar. Unhappily for the Canadian cause he was not a fortunate choice, as he had no talent for administration, and there can be little doubt that he was glad to be relieved of his administrative duties with the arrival in Canada on October 12, 1741, of Mgr Henri Dubreuil de Pontbriand, as the sixth Bishop of Quebec.[30]

THE ENLIGHTENMENT

At the time that de Pontbriand left France new and enlightened ideas represented by Voltaire and the Encyclopedists under the patronage of Mme de Pompadour were beginning to circulate freely in a France that would one day proclaim to a startled world a gospel of liberty, equality and fraternity.[31] These ideas based upon methods of thought drawn from Newtonian science were not confined to France alone, but had also reached the New World, particularly New England.[32] It would seem highly probable that the bishop, who had studied at the Jesuit Collège in La Flèche before proceeding to the house of the Sulpicians in Paris for his philosophy and had ultimately become a doctor of the Sorbonne, was aware of the "winds of change" blowing through his native land. That he was not always sheltered in orthodoxy is evident in that he embraced for a time, as Gosselin expresses it, *"les erreurs jansénistes"* but these we are told he retracted in a manner solemn and touching.[33] Nevertheless he must have been of an inquiring mind.

One can only speculate as to how well he would be aware of the new ideas that were circulating within the English colonies to the south and were giving a renewed impetus to the expansionist spirit of New England. Whether he knew about it or not in the year that he landed at Quebec, a great religious awakening "which aroused all New England"[34] was sweeping through most of the English colonies and was to have a profound effect on the future of the North American continent. It had been preceded by an acquaintance on the part of many New Englanders with Newton's *Principia Mathematica* which proclaimed an orderly world with natural laws and did much to undermine Puritan orthodoxy as formulated in Cotton Mather's *Magnolia Christi Americana* (1702) and Samuel Willard's *The Compleat Body of Divinity* (1726), in which unswerving natural laws are not very prominent. Isaac Newton did not achieve his victory for natural laws unaided; he was ably assisted by John Locke (1632-1704) who translated the "new scientific notions into the language of philosophy, psychology, morals, religion and government."[35] It is this devotion on the part of the philosophers, and sometimes theologians, to the canons of rationalism and "reasonableness" that put an end to the Salem witch-hunts and brought the English colonies into the full sweep of the enlightenment. The religious thinker who did most to unite New England theology with the enlightenment was Jonathan Edwards. At the age of fourteen, while at Yale, he came upon John Locke's *Essay on Human Understanding* and from it drew the inspiration for "his argumentative treatises on the Religious Affections, Freedom of the Will and Original Sin."[36] He thus established the empirical tradition that has given the United States its experimental and dynamic civilization and which even today remains a threat to any doctrinally based culture such as New France tried to achieve.

The more profound aspects of the religious awakening, combined with the enlightenment in eighteenth-century New England, could hardly have been evident to contemporary New France; what was patently evident was the deeper antagonism of this revived religion towards the Church of Rome. When, for example, Captain William Pepperell of Kittery, Massachusetts, decided to lead a force of New Englanders to attack the French outpost at Louisbourg, George Whitefield, the great English revivalist who had been preaching at

Kittery, gave the expedition its motto: *nil desperando Christo duce,* thus sanctifying the enterprise as a crusade against medieval darkness. The senior chaplain of the expedition took along an axe "to hew down the altars of anti-Christ and demolish his idols."[37] It was in such defiant terms as these that New France learned about the great religious awakening in the English colonies—hardly in a form to invite emulation.

There is evidence, however, that New France was not completely cut off from the intellectual ferment of the eighteenth century, even during the troublesome episcopate of Bishop Dosquet. In one of his rare *mandements,* published in 1735, the bishop indicates great concern for educational opportunities in Canada, and notes with satisfaction that there are Latin schools in Montreal and also a new college in Quebec, but these he felt were not enough and he urged the curés in the country districts to instruct children in their presbyteries. This kind of instruction had been initiated by Laval and continued by Saint-Vallier, but Bishop Dosquet can be credited with having increased the number of presbyterial schools. In an organized parish (unfortunately these were very few), the *fabrique* or parochial corporate body occasionally built a school and assumed the responsibility for primary education: towards the end of the seventeenth century there were about twenty-four of these under the direction of Les Dames de la Congrégation or the curé. Sometimes a lay teacher was hired by the *fabrique.* In the presbyterial schools the curés prepared children for the seminary, but included in the curriculum was instruction in music, chanting and training for participation in the liturgical offices.[38]

Right from the beginning of his episcopate Mgr de Pontbriand showed deep concern over the illiteracy that he discovered in French Canada, since he felt it was largely responsible for the disorder and impiety of the times.[39] To combat these disturbing manifestations he fell back upon the catechetical methods of Laval and Saint-Vallier. According to Father Porter the work of de Pontbriand in furthering the catechetical method of his predecessors "was truly admirable,"[40] perhaps the most noteworthy achievement of his episcopate. Although it may seem like a very low-key response to the challenging ideas that were whirling around in New England, nevertheless, the catechetical system of New France must not be underestimated. Perhaps no other method, under the circumstances of the time, could have saved French-Canadian culture, particularly after the conquest, from absorption into the dynamic culture of the Thirteen Colonies. As Father Grandpré has pointed out, "the catechism was the tool by which the Canadian Catholic was shaped."[41] It was by no means a mere "rote" education, since the vocabulary of the catechism and the methods of reasoning were drawn from scholastic philosophy; even the French-Canadian peasant had through his catechetical training become intellectually alert and could hold his own in dealing with abstract problems.

MONSEIGNEUR DE PONTBRIAND

New France was indeed fortunate to receive in the middle of the eighteenth century, when the church was being inundated with time-serving prelates, such a dedicated bishop as Mgr de Pontbriand. Though not of the same strength of character as Laval or Saint-Vallier, he had good organizing ability and there is no question but that he gave himself unstintingly to the welfare of the church. His first move in this direction was to strengthen the chapter by making some worthwhile appointments to fill up the vacancies that had occurred during the interregnum. These for the most part turned out to be very judicious appointments; like the bishop himself the new men were of Breton stock and firm upholders of seventeenth-century Catholic culture. One of them, Abbé Gosselin, was a celebrated botanist; another, Henri Briand, would one day become bishop and successfully guide the church through the trying years of adjustment after the British conquest;[42] a third, M. de la Ville-Angevin, he chose for his vicar general rather than Thierry Hazeur, who as capitular vicar had quarreled constantly with many diocesan officials. In Mont-real he left M. Marchand to one side and appointed M. Normant du Faradon his grand vicar, thus "repairing the unmerited injury that the chapter of Quebec had done to Saint-Sulpice;"[43] but at the same time reversing the trend towards an indigenous church.

The bishop's next most serious problem was to bring the religious orders, which had got seriously out of hand during the vacancies, back to their former disciplined life. Obstinacy was particularly rampant at the Ursuline convent, and the General Hospital had never really regained peace after the unusual burial of Saint-Vallier. With the careful selection of confessors for these institutions, a better spirit soon prevailed and, rather surprisingly, the bishop was able to bring to an end the casual entrance of visitors into the cloisters—something that not even Saint-Vallier had been able to achieve.

A parochial visitation in 1743 revealed that many quarrels were marring the religious life of New France; a good part of the bishop's tour was taken up trying to appease offended curés and parishioners.

He had some difficulty disciplining one or two priests who indulged in excessive drinking but he came to the conclusion, from first hand knowledge, "that the Canadian clergy in general were exemplary in conduct."[44] Since he could get very few priests to come out from France to fill up the vacant parishes, he relied chiefly upon native Canadian ordinands to keep the parishes in good running order. He ordained ninety-seven of them during his episcopate. He also inaugurated a series of retreats for the clergy and organized conferences for the purpose of instruction on the catechism. He himself spent considerable time teaching seminarists and thus he secured devout and well trained Canadian priests most of whom were to render invaluable service in maintaining the continuity of the Catholic Church in remote parishes after the conquest.[45]

Mgr de Pontbriand played an active role in the Superior Council, but it is the opinion of his most laudatory biographers that he was not firm enough in standing up for the rights of the church against secular officials. He did not challenge the exclusive right of the court to erect parishes and he never attempted to create a new parish without first referring the matter to the king's representative.[46] His one strong protest to the government against the large number of Protestants entering Canada was countered by some statistics to the effect that three quarters of the commerce of the colony was now carried on by Protestants and to expel them would do great financial harm to Canada's material welfare.[47] Mgr de Pontbriand was enough of an eighteenth-century utilitarian to find this plea convincing; but one can imagine what Laval's reply would have been to such an argument.

By the autumn of 1744 the bishop had completed his personal survey of the diocese and was about to work out a general policy for improved administration and expansion of parochial services when the outbreak of war between England and France brought an abrupt end to such peace-time planning.

WARTIME AND MISSIONS

In wartime it was always the more remote missions that absorbed the bishop's attention; after the outbreak of the war of the Austrian Succession in 1744 de Pontbriand had to make some hard decisions in relation to Acadia and the far west.

During the uneasy years of peace following upon the treaty of Utrecht (1713) the English and French were continually coming into contact with one another along an ever lengthening border. The English, as Parkman put it, flowed westward "in obedience to natural laws."[48] France regarded most of North America as belonging to her by right of discovery and hoped to dam up the English overflow by building forts at strategic centres. From Fort Rouge on the Red River in what is now Manitoba there was a long string of forts and trading posts, reaching down deep into what is now the United States, such as Fort Crêvecoeur, south of Lake Michigan, Fort Ponchartrain (Detroit), Fort Duquesne (Pittsburgh) and Fort Sainte-Anne to guard against New Yorkers and New Englanders, and so on to Louisbourg on Cape Breton Island. These forts constituted a challenge to nearly all of the English colonies and drove them together into a loose confederation.

As these French forts increased in number and attracted a considerable population around them, so did the jurisdiction and responsibilities of the bishop extend and increase. One of the most vexatious of all these forts was Louisbourg,[49] on Ile Royale off Cape Breton, which the French had built shortly after signing the Treaty of Utrecht to compensate for the loss of the Acadian Peninsula, or Nova Scotia, to the English. The majority of the population at Louisbourg came from Placentia, which the French had to evacuate after ceding Newfoundland to the English in the Treaty of Utrecht. For those Acadians who did not wish to live under British rule Ile Royale was an ever present alternative; with its strong fortifications it was in some sense a pledge that Acadia would one day be brought back into the French family of colonies. Some of the missionaries encouraged this hope,[50] even though the bishops had forcibly urged upon them the necessity of prudence in their relations with the occupying power.[51]

At the time of its foundation the spiritual life at Louisbourg was entrusted to the Recollets; there was also another order, known as the Religieux de la Charité, in charge of a hospital. A house of instruction for young girls had been placed under the direction of the Congrégation de Notre-Dame de Montreal. There were the usual religious dissensions that seem to afflict all pioneer colonial projects; the Recollets, who were inclined to act as if they alone were in complete charge of the post, did not take kindly to the bishop's grand vicar and were not always prudent in their relations with the officials of British-controlled Acadia; but far greater imprudence was shown by the secular authorities, particularly the *commissaire-ordonnateur* and Governor Du Quesnel. The moment these two heard that war had broken out between France and Great Britain in 1744, they immediately embroiled Louisbourg in an ill-fated attempt to restore all of Acadia to France by attacking Canso and Annapolis, and so aroused the New Englanders that they began their crusade against Ile Royale under the leadership of William Pepperell. In a short time Louisbourg was in British hands and the senior chaplain of the fleet was able to use his axe on Roman altars.[52]

The fall of Louisbourg was a serious set-back to missionary activity in Acadia; besides the loss of Louisbourg itself as a sanctuary for disaffected Acadians, the ill will stirred up by the military operations made it doubly difficult for those Catholic missionaries in Nova Scotia who had been following the rule of prudence and assuring the British authorities that they were not engaged in subversive activities.[53] Even against these dedicated missionaries the British were beginning to harden their hearts.

Nor were the Jesuit missionaries to the Abenaki any less embarrassed. They also had been attempting to follow a policy of prudence towards the British, but their mission bordered on French territory as well as British and the court had been using the missionaries to enroll the Abenaki on the side of the French during the war of the Austrian succession; they had even subsidized the mission to the extent of four thousand *livres*.[54] More and more the missionaries were becoming involved, whether they wanted to or not, in the military strategy of France, which in the long run would prove very detrimental to the primary task of evangelizing the Indians.

In western Canada it was the same story: the Recollets at Frontenac and Niagara became involved in France's commercial fortunes, as were the Jesuits at Detroit and Michilimackinac, and were being accused of putting commerce above the gospel; they were also being seriously thwarted in their missions to the south by the enmity of the Indians themselves. In 1727 Fathers Guignas and de Gonner had established a mission among the Miamis; suddenly, they found themselves menaced by two allied Indian bands, the Foxes and Sakis, who had built a fort on the Des Moines River. The attack upon the French by the Foxes and Sakis, who "rivalled the Iroquois in astuteness and courage"[55] was probably urged on by the British in the hope of diverting commerce away from the French to the English colonies.

Nothing daunted, however, the Jesuits still sought other fields to conquer by following French explorers and fur traders into the far West. When Pierre de La Vérendrye decided in 1731 to renew La Salle's project of finding a pathway to the western sea, the Jesuits were on hand to accompany him. On the first expedition Father Messaiger accompanied the famous explorer as far as the Assiniboine River, and preached to all the Indians they met on the way.

On a second attempt to reach the Pacific, in 1735, he had as a companion a young Jesuit, Charles Aulneau, fresh out from France; but he like many of his predecessors met a martyr's death at the beginning of his career. While camping on an island in the Lake of the Woods with a party of men he was killed and scalped by a band of Sioux, along with the whole company, including a son of La Vérendrye.[56] Because of the lack of support by the French court, due in part to jealousy among rival fur traders, La Vérendrye never reached the Pacific. He did however get to the foothills of the Rockies, accompanied by Father Coquart.

CHURCH BUILDING AND FESTIVALS

It was also partly because of the war with England that New France failed to reach the West Coast at this time. The war, however, came to an end in 1748 with the signing of the Treaty of Aix-la-Chapelle which restored Ile Royale, including Louisbourg, to the French much to the consternation of the New Englanders. The bishop, who had been encouraging his flock during the war with stirring patriotic *mandements*,[57] was now able to turn to more peaceful projects. A matter that had been very much on his mind at the outbreak of war was a proposal to repair his palace and rebuild the cathedral, which had become too small for the growing congregation at Quebec; another problem was that of reducing the excessive number of fête days in Canada.

It was the bishop's expectation that he would receive aid from France to help rebuild the cathedral; but when this was refused he turned to the Canadians themselves and put on a most vigorous fund-raising campaign throughout the diocese. Curés were asked to appeal directly to their congregations; by also establishing founders' masses he raised almost enough money to complete the cathedral before the outbreak of the Seven Years War.

It is Gosselin's opinion that Mgr de Pontbriand's rebuilt cathedral, without being a masterpiece, was beautiful "at least for the epoch."[58] The design was worked out by Chaussegros de Léry, the best known of New France's eighteenth-century architects.[59] He endeavoured to add a twin-tower façade to the original design but most of his work was concerned with the interior, which was widened by the construction of side aisles. These were completed by de Léry, but funds ran out before he could complete the towers; or at least they remained very similar to the towers of *La Paroisse* in Montreal, which probably served as his model: one tower was completed, the other reached only to the first storey. Twin towers had apparently been first conceived by the Sulpicians at Montreal, but the adoption of this façade for the cathedral started a trend in de Pontbriand's time and "twin towers appeared in parish church architecture as the mature Quebec tradition developed."[60] Many elaborate parish churches were built in the short span of peace that followed upon the Treaty of Aix-la-Chapelle; the development was brought to an end with the outbreak of the Seven Years War and would not be renewed until many years after the conquest.

Apparently the Canadians enthusiastically supported the bishop in his building projects, but they were not so enthusiastic when he tried to reduce the number of festivals of obligation that brought the people to church during the week and also provided them with holidays. At the beginning of de Pontbriand's episcopate there were about thirty-three festivals of obligation observed by the Canadians; sometimes there would, by a conjunction of festivals, be a stoppage of work for three continuous days. The court had been suggesting to both the civil and religious authorities that this very uneconomic practice should be brought to an end by a suppression of several of these festivals or by transferring them to a Sunday observance. Mgr de Pontbriand, who was inclined to be deferential to state officials, agreed to suppress some, but he also translated several to Sunday, leaving still about fourteen days of obligatory festivals.[61] Canadians, however, were greatly attached to their holy days, particularly those observed in honour of their own special saints or the patron saints of their town or village. The bishop did little to enhance his popularity by yielding to the importunities of the governing authorities in this matter.

THE GREY NUNS

Such co-operation with state officials was to result in many humiliations for the well-intentioned bishop; never more so than when it brought him into conflict with one of the most outstanding personalities of the eighteenth-century church of New France, Mme d'Youville, the foundress of the Grey Nuns. Mme d'Youville, baptized Marie-Marguerite Du Frost de Lajammerais,[62] born at Varennes, Quebec, in 1701, was a truly Canadian girl. At an early age she married François d'Youville and went to live in the Market Place of Montreal. With the death of her husband, in 1730, she was compelled to make her own way in the world; even before her husband's death she had opened a store on the first floor of their house and her business continued to flourish so that she was able to educate two sons for the priesthood.

In the market place Mme d'Youville saw much crime and suffering and she resolved to do something about it. Her first opportunity came through her election as Superior of the Confraternity of the Holy Family in 1735. Among members of the confraternity she found some women who, like herself, wished to consecrate themselves to the service of the poor, wayward and unfortunate; soon they were going about together in the market place doing deeds of mercy and helping the poor, sometimes with gifts of money. Among the gossips the question was raised whether the liquor traffic in which Mme d'Youville's husband had been engaged before his death had provided the money these women were distributing among the poor. Drunken Indians used to stagger into Mme d'Youville's store and this gave the gossips additional reason to shout at the little group of women as they went about the market place: *Voilà les sœurs grises* –There go the tipsy sisters. Since *grise* can be translated into either tipsy or grey, the sisters good-naturedly accepted the scornful sobriquet and ultimately became an order known as the Grey Nuns.[63]

It was Father Normant du Faradon, the superior of Saint-Sulpice, who recognized the organizing ability and unusual business acumen of Madame d'Youville and suggested that she and her little band of women should take over and manage the General Hospital. At the time the hospital was under the feeble control of the Charon Brothers. It was originally intended to be both a hostel for old folk and a school for orphans, but this turned out to be an impossible combination[64] and the hospital had been gradually deteriorating in service and accumulating debts so that by 1747 it owed to creditors the sum of thirty-eight thousand *livres*.

In point of fact the sisters had been asked to take over a ruin, but it was the kind of challenge they had been looking for; in no time at all they had the place cleaned up and also got two farms connected with the hospital, one at Chambly and the other at Pointe-Charles, in good running order. Several wealthy ladies, impressed by the cleanliness of the hospital at Pointe-à-Callières, asked if they could live there as boarders. They were accepted gladly to help defray costs; the old men whom the sisters had inherited from the Charon Brothers, along with two old members of the community, were comfortably lodged in a section set aside for men; one floor was fitted up to receive prostitutes who had abandoned their profession. Women of Jericho, as the prostitutes were called, were a problem to house in the same building as the wealthy paying boarders, but somehow Mme d'Youville managed it.

All seemed to be going well until the arrival of François Bigot in Canada, in 1748, to replace Hocquart as intendant. Bigot was aware that the court wished, in the interest of economy, to reduce the number of religious houses in Canada; he decided he would begin by closing the General Hospital in Montreal and absorbing its patients and furnishings into the General Hospital at Quebec.[65] He was able to persuade both the governor, La Jonquière, and the bishop to agree to this drastic move. It was a considerable shock to the people of Montreal, who heard the ordinance closing the hospital read to them to the accompaniment of drums in the Market Place, to find that the bishop's signature led all the rest. They had by this time changed their opinion about Mme d'Youville and her tipsy sisters and were determined that she should be allowed to run the hospital in peace.[66] In this determination they had the whole-hearted support of the superior of Saint-Sulpice.

By transferring as quickly as possible all the movable assets of the hospital to Quebec, Bigot was trying to make sure there would be no reversal of the ordinance; Abbé Normant, on the other hand, was determined to accomplish just that. He finally convinced the governor that a serious injustice had been done to the poor of Montreal and also to the Grey Nuns. Together they got in touch with the superior of the Sulpician Seminary in Paris and asked him to present their case to the court. The superior accepted the assignment and succeeded remarkably well in convincing Louis XV's advisers that Mme d'Youville was performing a great service for the court by assuming all the debts of the hospital which otherwise would have to be assumed by the king's treasury. This was an argument that proved decisive at Versailles and soon word arrived in Canada that the General Hospital was to continue in Montreal with Mme d'Youville in charge. The exultant mood of the hospital itself is reflected in the following from Sister Fitts' story of the Grey Nuns: "At last, three years after the thunder of drums in the Market Place had announced the storm of opposition which would beat upon the General Hospital, the skies cleared and the sun shone in full glory."[67]

Shortly after the reversal of attitude by the court, letters patent designating a new religious order of Grey Nuns was signed by Louis XV (January 3, 1753), and the most prosperous religious order ever founded in Canada was started on its adventurous career. It was indeed remarkable that it should have originated in the tumultuous Market Place of Montreal in a century apathetic to religious orders;

also a matter of wonder was that it should have come to birth despite the opposition of the bishop, who had the humiliation of confirming the rules necessary for the spiritual discipline of the sisters.[68]

DISQUIETING TIMES: EXPULSION OF THE ACADIANS

The *affaire* of the General Hospital appeared in retrospect to be a rather minor irritant after the outbreak of the Seven Years War in 1756. Once again it was the outlying portions of the diocese that caused the bishop most distress. Even before the outbreak of war Louisiana was becoming a very troublesome problem: the Capuchins were threatening to leave the country if their superior was not given a title equal to the Jesuit superior. Both superiors resided at New Orleans, where about a dozen Ursulines ran a hospital, rather badly, according to the testimony of the *commissaire* and the Capuchins. The latter became so insistent on their right to govern the church in Louisiana as they saw fit that the bishop felt compelled to put two of them under an interdict; they then made a direct appeal to Rome against the bishop's interdiction, but the proceedings were long-drawn-out and nothing was decided up to the time of the conquest. In the meantime the superior of the Jesuits remained the only grand vicar in Louisiana until the suppression of the Society of Jesus in 1763.[69]

Their missions in this area were not a great success. The Indians proved almost impervious to the gospel message,[70] and after the Jesuits withdrew from Louisiana they, with the exception of the Tamarois and some Kaskaskias bands, returned to paganism. Even the Tamarois mission was to a large extent deserted by the seminaries of Quebec and the Foreign Missions at Paris. At the time of the Conquest there was only one missionary at Tamarois and he, in despair, sold the property of the seminaries for a trifling sum and allowed the mission to disappear.[71]

At Michilimackinac it was somewhat the same story: the Jesuit mission there was continually being depleted by the migration of the Indians to the Detroit area; most of the missionaries moved on to Detroit where they laboured valiantly to keep the surviving Hurons loyal to the church, but against desperate odds. Father de La Richardie wished to remove them to a more sheltered home near Montreal, but this suggestion was frowned upon both by his society and the governing authorities at Quebec. He was replaced by Father Potier, who created a new Huronian parish some distance from the French settlement at Detroit. He was followed by Father Pluie, who took over the work in 1751 and remained for thirty years, conducting a model Huronian parish until his death in 1781; but this was about the only cheerful aspect in the western missions where so much blood and tears had been expended in the seventeenth century; they were now decaying through lack of recruits and despair for the future of French Canada.[72]

All this was very disquieting to Bishop de Pontbriand, but his greatest anxiety lay in Acadia. The founding of Halifax as a strongly fortified town by the British in March, 1749, as a compensation to New England for the return of Louisbourg to the French, was an ominous sign to the Acadians that the English were in Nova Scotia to stay. Governor Cornwallis, firmly established in the new capital, warned the Acadians, that if they were to remain in possession of their lands and to practise their religion freely they must take an oath of allegiance to the King of England. As this oath implied bearing arms in defence of the English cause, they refused to do so; for a time the English authorities left the matter in abeyance, but the Acadians now knew they were in serious peril. Many of the French clergy, like Abbé Daudin at Annapolis Royal and Abbé Maillard at Louisbourg, urged upon their flocks great prudence in their relations with the English authorities, but their prudence was nullified by the fiery Abbé Le Loutre at Beauséjour, who with his Indian following carried on a guerilla warfare against the hated English.[73] These tactics so provoked the New Englanders that they raised an army of about two thousand soldiers, sailed up the Bay of Fundy in 1755 and captured Beauséjour. Abbé Le Loutre escaped from the fort and reached Quebec, where he was severely reprimanded by the bishop for his imprudence in bringing the wrath of the New Englanders down upon the Acadians; but he received great praise from the court. During his attempt to return to France he was captured by the British and held a prisoner until the end of the Seven Years war.

Although a state of war had not yet been declared between England and France at the time of the capture of Beauséjour, a cruel fate lay in store for the Acadians; after the fall of Beauséjour most of their missionaries were rounded up and taken to Halifax and then despatched to Portsmouth, whence they finally got back to France. It was Colonel Lawrence who as acting governor finally made the cruel decision to solve the Acadian problem by deporting all the Acadians from Nova Scotia.[74] Many of them escaped to the woods, two thousand reached Canada, but some seven thousand of them between 1755 and 1757, sometimes separated from their closest relatives, were scattered throughout the English colonies—a heart-rending action which brought no word of indignation from France, since such expulsions were part of the code of international morality. The harsh process of deportation in which 11,000 out of 15,000 were uprooted from their homes continued until 1762, and won for Colonel Lawrence the promotion to the governorship of Nova Scotia, indicating England's approval of his cruel deed.

DEFEAT AND SURRENDER

The expulsion of the Acadians was accepted by the Canadians as a warning of what to expect if they did not put up a strong resistance to English aggression. When war was belatedly declared the bishop in a *mandement* used Acadia as a spur to his flock to fight bravely: "That which happened to the Acadians", he wrote, "renders suspect all these their (the English) promises, and you would soon be saddened by seeing the detestable errors of Luther and Calvin introduced into this diocese where the Faith has always been so pure."[75]

To Abbé Maillard for whom the English had considerable respect, the bishop assigned the difficult task of caring for the spiritual needs of the Acadians who survived the expulsion. For a time Maillard resided at Louisbourg, where he was shocked by the licentiousness of its inhabitants; nevertheless, this den of iniquity as Maillard called it displayed great courage under bombardment, but finally had to surrender to the British in July 1758; and in the summer of 1759 the victorious fleet now under the command of James Wolfe was on its way to Quebec. Abbé Maillard did not, however, desert his Acadians but moved on to Halifax where he sought out his scattered and disheartened flock and also welcomed back those Acadians who were allowed to return to Nova Scotia after 1763; he also rendered great service to the English by persuading the Micmacs not to terrorize their new masters.[76]

As the British fleet moved up the St. Lawrence in the last days of June Bishop de Pontbriand was the spectator of greater excesses in Quebec than those witnessed by Abbé Maillard at Louisbourg. The chief offender was the profiteer, Intendant Bigot, whose ostentatious banquets in the midst of famine scandalized the bishop, as did also Bigot's mistress Mme Péan, who has been described as the Mme de Pompadour of New France.[77]

During the final epoch of New France there were some cheerful interludes at Quebec. The bishop records in a *mandement* the joy of the Canadians at the appointment of Marquis de Vaudreuil, a native of Canada, as the new governor; but the joy was short-lived as the new governor did little to curb the profiteering of Bigot and his *grande société*. Strangely enough, the bishop remained the partisan of the Canadian governor to the end and refused to agree, when the evidence appeared overwhelming, that his friend was responsible for allowing General Wolfe to reach the Plains of Abraham.[78]

With the arrival of General Montcalm in Canada the bishop was subject to a new anxiety, for the general and many of his officers were imbued with the ideas of Voltaire and were assiduous readers of the *Encyclopédie*. Montcalm himself does not seem to have been favourably impressed with the bishop, whom he describes as "a holy man indeed, of good morals," but who "has all the prejudices of a Canadian although born in France."[79] The bishop's fears for the "errors" that Montcalm's men might leave behind in their passage through Canada, were soon forgotten in his joy over the victories won by the intrepid general. Each victory is recorded in a *mandement*; after the capture of a group of forts at the head of Oswego River in 1756 he wrote: "What dear brothers are your sentiments on this action, so humiliating for the English, so glorious for our army, so useful to our commerce, so advantageous to the colony and I dare say so favourable to our religion."[80] His *mandement* was generally hailed with enthusiasm by those who read it, except for one discordant note from Montcalm who wrote to Maréchal de Lévis: "Your friend the Bishop has just issued the most ridiculous *mandement* in the world, but take good care not to say it, for it is the admiration of Canada."[81] A *mandement* proclaiming the capture of Fort George was properly subdued because of the slaughter of the English captives by the Indian allies of the French.[82]

From now on the bishop's *mandements* take on a very sombre tone, for the troops from France had brought with them some contagious diseases: four hundred victims died of the plague at the General Hospital in 1757 and an additional three hundred in 1758.[83] Already famine was stalking the land to be followed shortly by Wolfe's cruel devastation of the countryside and his persistent bombardment of the citadel of Quebec.

The bishop was now convinced that New France was in danger because of its sins: "It is not the number of our enemies we have to fear," he wrote, "but rather the deplorable thieving and injustices," an obvious reference to Bigot and his *grande société*. Not yet, however, did he despair; there was still one last recourse: "Our faith teaches us that a sincere conversion will stop the arm of vengeance of the divine justice."[84] But by this time de Pontbriand's health was perceptibly failing; he left Quebec for Charlesbourg, accompanied by the directors of the seminary, whence he proceeded to Montreal to take up residence at the Seminary of Saint-Sulpice. Before he left Quebec he had made Henri Briand his representative to negotiate for the freedom of the church, if Quebec should be occupied by the enemy. After the fall of Quebec he sent from Montreal wise words of advice: priests and nuns were warned not to speak of religion to the English and Briand was advised to be prudent to the officials of the new foreign government, thus putting the future Bishop of Quebec on the road of prudence which served the church so well after the British conquest. Mgr de Pontbriand lived only a year longer after his withdrawal to Montreal; he died on June 8, 1760, at the age of fifty-one in a little room set apart for him in the Sulpician Seminary, knowing[85] that three British armies were closing in on Montreal.

A BLEAK OUTLOOK

It was a black moment in the life of the church: it now found itself under foreign rule without a bishop; nevertheless, the sacraments were still administered, bringing balm to many a troubled soul, and that "pure religion and undefiled"[86] which dedicates itself to the afflicted was never more in evidence than when Canada fell under British rule. Although the physical plant of the church had been terribly battered, particularly in Quebec and also in many parts of the war-torn countryside, there were still one hundred and eighty-one priests in Canada at the time of the conquest and these were to play a vital role in the rehabilitation of French Canada under foreign rule.[87] Most conspicuous of all was the contribution of the hospital sisters during the difficult years of transition; these made a very favourable impression upon the occupying armies.

The General Hospital, situated at Point-à-Callières outside Montreal, was in the path of General Amherst's army. In this hospital British fugitives had frequently been hidden by Mme d'Youville and afterwards allowed to escape; one of these, a young man from Williamstown, Massachusetts, was near General Amherst when he was about to bomb the hospital, fearing that it might be a disguised fortress. The young man pleaded with the general to make an investigation before shelling it; the latter sent some officers forward to reconnoitre and when they ventured into the hospital they found wounded British soldiers being well cared for; they were then invited into the refectory where biscuits and wine had been laid out for them by Mme d'Youville.[88]

Very similar deeds of mercy could be recounted of all the nursing orders of Canada. So impressed were the British authorities with the nuns at Quebec and Montreal that there was never any question but that they should "be preserved in their constitutions and privileges." This was stated in the articles of capitulation; but not so for "the communities of Jesuits and Recollets and the priests of Saint-Sulpice at Montreal," who were refused any recognition until "the King's pleasure be known."[89] Thus was brought to an end, for the time being, a century and a half of missionary endeavour among the aborigines of North America, the original motive for the presence of these communities in Canada. It had been a noble endeavour to save a primitive people from being exploited by greedy Europeans.

To be compelled to abandon these aborigines at a time when Europe was in its most expansive mood and was manifesting a great indifference to the welfare of primitive people who might get in the way of so-called progress was indeed a great frustration for those religious communities. They had come to America in the seventeenth century to win souls for Christ; right up to the day of capitulation they had endeavoured to save their primitive flocks from the ruthless exploitation of the French fur traders. They had learned through personal experience how reckless and inhumane cupidity can be, and how much worse it might be when freed from all religious restraints, or if it should become allied with a philosophy of manifest destiny. That had seemed to be the case in New England which had come close to committing the crime of genocide.

If these religious communities had been able to peer into the future (and no doubt they tried), they might have found some consolation in knowing that during their stay in America each community had, in its own way, contributed to the promotion of a French-Canadian society based upon a scale of values that belong to a humanistic tradition that goes back through St. Thomas Aquinas to Aristotle and to which French Canada has been unusually loyal. This loyalty, "favoured and safeguarded by their church" has given the French Canadian a "sense of security and conviction"[90] which has enabled him to maintain a way of life distinct from the rest of North America in spite of his almost daily contact with one of the most assimilative cultures in modern history. But this is an epic theme to be dealt with in later volumes of the story of Christianity in Canada.

NOTES TO CHAPTER ELEVEN

1. *Vide* Guy Frégault, *François Bigot, Administrateur Français* (Ottawa: The Author, 1948), *passim*.

2. For an account of "Pitt's Great Administration" *vide* Shortt and Doughty, *Canada and Its Provinces* (Toronto: Brook, 1914-17), Vol. I, p. 260 *et seq.*

3. For source material on religious awakenings in New England *vide* D. C. Douglas, ed., *English Historical Documents*, Vol. IX: *American Colonial Documents to 1776* (London: Eyre and Spottiswoode, 1955-59), pp. 534-51.

4. A.-H. Gosselin, *L'Eglise du Canada depuis Monseigneur de Laval jusqu'à la Conquête* (Quebec: Laflamme et Proulx, 1911), Vol. I, p. 456; *vide* also *Rapport de l'Archiviste de la Province de Québec pour 1920-21*, pp. 78-105, for "Mémoire de M. Dupuy . . . sur les troubles arrives à Québec en 1727 et 1728 après la mort de Mgr de Saint-Vallier, évêque de Québec."

5. *Vide* Soeur Saint-Félix, *Monseigneur de Saint-Vallier et l'Hôpital Général de Québec* (Quebec: Darveau, 1882), pp. 275-80, for a very frank account of an embarrassing interlude in the history of the General Hospital.

6. *Vide* H. Têtu, *Les Evêques de Québec* (Quebec: Hardy, 1889), p. 166, for a copy of the letter to the chapter.

7. *Vide* H. Têtu et C.-O. Gagnon, eds., *Mandements . . . des Evêques de Québec* (Quebec: Coté, 1887), Vol. I, p. 526, for comments on the bishop's reluctance to leave France.

8. *Vide* H. Têtu, *op. cit.*, p. 117 *et seq*, for biographical details on Bishop Dosquet.

9. *Vide* A.-H. Gosselin, *op. cit.*, Vol. II, p. 46.

10. *Vide Report concerning Canadian Archives for year 1904* (Ottawa: The King's Printer, 1905), appendix K, p. 290, for memorandum from the king to de Beauharnois concerning the episcopal palace.

11. *Vide* A.-H. Gosselin, *op. cit.*, Vol. II, p. 72.

12. *Ibid.*, Vol. II, p. 79.

13. Quoted by A.-H. Gosselin, *op. cit.*, Vol. II, p. 90.

14. *Vide* Jean-Charles Falardeau, "The Seventeenth Century Parish" in M. Rioux and Yves Martin, eds., *French Canadian Society* (Toronto: McClelland and Stewart, 1964), Vol. I, pp. 19-32.

15. *Vide Mandements, op. cit.*, Vol. I, p. 547 for a copy of the revocation of the curacies granted by the chapter.

16. *Vide* A.-H. Gosselin, *op. cit.*, Vol. II, p. 100.

17. *Ibid.*, Vol. II, pp. 199-201.

18. *Ibid.*, Vol. II, p. 202.

19. *Ibid.*, Vol. II, p. 207; *vide* also *Ursuline des Trois-Rivières depuis Leur Etablissement jusqu'à Nos Jours* (Trois-Rivières: Ayotte, 1888), Vol. I, p. 227.

20. *Vide Mandements, op. cit.*, Vol. I, p. 526.

21. A.-H. Gosselin, *op. cit.*, Vol. II, pp. 266-7.

22. *Ibid.*, Vol. II, p. 284.

23. *Vide* H. Têtu, *op. cit.*, p. 193.

24. Quoted by A.-H. Gosselin, *op. cit.*, Vol. II, p. 358.

25. *Vide Mandements, op. cit.*, Vol. I, p. 553.

26. A.-H. Gosselin, *op. cit.*, Vol. II, p. 390.

27. H. Têtu, *op. cit.*, p. 212.

28. *Vide* A.-H. Gosselin, *op. cit.*, Vol. II, p. 411 *et seq.*

29. *Vide Report concerning Canadian Archives for the year 1905* (Ottawa: The King's Printer, 1906), part v, p. 286, for a despatch from the king, March 27, 1741: Abbé Miniac says he had no other reason in coming to France than to prevent the results which his quarrel with the chapter respecting the curé of Château Richer might have had.

30. *Vide Mandements, op. cit.,* Vol. I, p. 560, for only recorded *mandement* of Hazeur.

31. *Vide* Louis Ducros, *French Society in the Eighteenth Century,* trans. W. de Geijer (London: Bell, 1926), pp. 226-41; also A. Dansette, *Religious History of Modern France* (trans. J. Dingle; London and Edinburgh: Nelson, 1961), Vol. I, p. 3, *et seq.*

32. *Vide* A. Cobban, *A History of Modern France, Old Regime and Revolution, 1715-1799.* (A Pelican Book, 1957), Vol. I, pp. 83-101, for an interesting discussion of the origins of the Revolution.

33. A.-H. Gosselin, *op. cit.,* Vol. III, p. 22; *vide* also H. Têtu *op. cit.,* pp. 220 *et seq.*

34. C. C. Goen, *Revivalism and Separatism in New England* (New Haven: Yale University Press, 1962), p. 8; *vide* also E. S. Gaustad, *The Great Awakening in New England* (New York: Harper, 1957), especially Chap. IV, pp. 42-60: "The Flood, 1741-1742."

35. *Vide* J. W. Smith and A. L. Jamison, eds., *Religion in American Life* (Princeton: Princeton University Press, 1901), Vol. I, pp. 240 54, for a discussion of Jonathan Edwards and the New Divinity.

36. *Ibid.,* Vol. I, p. 248.

37. F. Parkman, *A Half Century of Conflict* (Boston: Little, Brown, 1903), Vol. II, p. 80.

38. *Mandements, op. cit.,* Vol. I, pp. 543-5; *vide* also Rioux and Martin, eds., *op. cit.,* Vol. I, pp. 29-31.

39. F. Porter, *L'Institution Catéchistique au Canada* (Montreal: Les Editions Franciscaines, 1949), p. 65.

40. *Ibid.,* p. 68.

41. J. W. Grant, ed., *The Churches and the Canadian Experience* (Toronto: Rycrson, 1963), p. 4.

42. *Vide* H. Têtu, *op. cit.,* p. 193 *et seq.*

43. A.-H. Gosselin, *op. cit.,* Vol. III, p. 25.

44. *Ibid.,* Vol. III, p. 75.

45. *Vide* F. Porter, *op. cit.,* Chapter III, especially pp. 65-8: "La Garde du Dépôt."

46. *Vide* A.-H. Gosselin, *op. cit.,* Vol. III, p. 228.

47. *Ibid.,* Vol. III, p. 236.

48. F. Parkman, *op. cit.,* Vol. II, p. 45.

49. *Vide* T. B. Akins, ed., *Selections from Public Documents of the Province of Nova Scotia* (Halifax: Annand, 1869), pp. 49-52.

50. *Vide* H.-R. Casgrain, *Les Sulpiciens et les Prêtres des Missions-Etrangères en Acadie* (Quebec: Pruneau et Kirouac, 1897), pp. 367-8; also Du Boscq de Beaumont, *Les Derniers Jours de l'Acadie* (Paris: Lechevallier, 1899), pp. 15-6.

51. *Vide* A.-H. Gosselin, *op. cit.,* Vol III, p. 532.

52. *Vide supra,* p. 189.

53. *Vide* H.-R. Casgrain, *op. cit.,* p. 358 *et seq.*

54. *Vide* A.-H. Gosselin, *op. cit.,* Vol. II, p. 238.

55. *Ibid.,* p. 240.

56. *Vide* R. G. Thwaites, ed., *The Jesuit Relations and Allied Documents* (Cleveland. Burrows, 1900 1901), Vol. LXIX, pp. 36 65 for two letters from Father Luc François Vau to Mme Aulnau, the mother of Father Charles Aulnau.

57. *Vide Mandements, op. cit.,* Vol. II, p. 51.

58. A.-H. Gosselin, *op. cit.,* Vol. III, p. 106.

59. *Vide* A. Gowans, *Church Architecture in New France* (Toronto: University of Toronto Press, 1955), p. 49.

60. *Ibid.,* p. 80.

61. *Vide Mandements, op. cit.*, Vol. II, p. 40 for *Mandement pour transférer la solennité de quelques fêtes au dimanche.*

62. *Vide* Abbé Faillon, *Vie de Mme d'Youville* (Villemarie: Soeurs de la Charité, 1852), for a well documented life of Madame d'Youville, listing MSS available; Sister Mary Pauline Fitts' *Hands to the Needy* (New York: Doubleday, 1950), is an interesting monograph in English.

63. *Ibid.*, pp. 92-6.

64. *Vide* Y. Poutet, "Les Voeux des Frères Charon Hospitaliers-Enseignants" in *Revue d'histoire de l'Eglise de France* (Paris, 1964), XLIX, No. 146, pp. 19-45 for an interesting article on the work of the Charon Brothers and their failure in combining nursing and teaching.

65. *Vide* G. Frégault, *op. cit.*, Vol. II, p. 12.

66. *Vide* M. P. Fitts, *op. cit.*, p. 110 *et seq.*

67. *Ibid.*, p. 176.

68. *Vide* Abbé Faillon, *op. cit.*, Vol. LXX, p. 108 *et seq.*

69. *Vide* Thwaites, *op. cit.*, Vol. LXX, pp. 213-301 for the story of the Jesuits in Louisiana by Philburt Watrin.

70. *Ibid.*, p. 245.

71. *Vide* A.-H. Gosselin, Vol. III, p. 323.

72. *Vide* Thwaites, *op. cit.*, Vol. LXIX, pp. 241-77, for an account of the practical side of the mission to the Hurons at Detroit.

73. *Vide Collection de Manuscrits . . . relatifs à la Nouvelle-France* (Quebec: Coté, 1884), Vol. III, pp. 437-39 and 456-61 for letters written by Abbé Le Loutre from Louisbourgh, July 29, 1749, and from Beaubassin, Oct. 4, 1749.

74. *Vide* J. B. Brebner, *op. cit.*, Chapter VII, "Caught between the Duellists."

75. *Mandements, op. cit.*, Vol. II, pp. 105-14.

76. *Vide* H.-R. Casgrain, *op. cit.*, pp. 435-44.

77. *Vide* G. M. Wrong, *op. cit.*, Vol. II, p. 832.

78. *Vide* J.-B. Ferland, *Cours d'Histoire du Canada* (Quebec: Coté, 1865), Vol. II, p. 584.

79. A.-H. Gosselin, *op. cit.*, Vol. III, p. 446.

80. *Mandements, op. cit.*, pp. 122-24.

81. Quoted by A.-H. Gosselin, *op. cit.*, Vol. III, p. 461. Montcalm's letters frequently reflect his annoyance with the bishop's *mandements*. *Vide* H.-R. Casgrain, ed., *Lettres de M. de Bourlamque au Chevalier de Lévis* (Quebec: Demers, 1865), Vol. II, p. 584.

82. *Mandements, op. cit.*, p. 110.

83. Soeur Saint-Félix, *op. cit.*, p. 331.

84. *Mandements, op. cit.*, Vol. II, pp. 134-37.

85. *Vide* A.-H. Gosselin, *op. cit.*, Vol. III, p. 551.

86. Jas. 1: 27.

87. *Vide* A.-H. Gosselin, *op. cit.*, Vol. III, p. 556.

88. M. P. Fitts, *op. cit.*, p. 220.

89. Articles of Capitulation of Montreal are to be found in Shortt and Doughty, *Documents relating to the Constitutional History of Canada* (Ottawa: Taché, 1907), Vol. I, pp. 21-29.

90. *Vide* Edmond Gaudron, "French Canadian Philosophers" in *The Culture of Contemporary Canada*, ed. Julian Park (Toronto: Ryerson, 1957), pp. 274-291, especially p. 280.

Bibliography

BOOKS

Akins, T. B. (ed). *Selections from Public Documents of the Province of Nova Scotia.* Halifax: Annand, 1869.

Anghiera, Pietro Martiro d'. *Do Orbo Novo.* Translated by Paul Gaffarel. Paris: Leroux, 1907.

Aubert, R. *Historical Problems of Church Renewal.* Vol. VII of *Concilium; Theology in the Age of Renewal.* Glen Rock, N.J.: Paulist Press, 1965.

Ballard, Edward, *Memorial Volume of the Popham Celebration.* Portland, Maine: Bailey and Noyes, 1863.

Barth, Karl. *The Church and the Political Problem of Our Day.* London: Hodder, 1939.

Beard, Charles and Beard, Mary. *The Rise of American Civilization.* New York: Macmillan, 1933.

Benoit, Pierre. *Maisonneuve.* Tours: Mame, 1960.

Bernard, A. *Le Drame Acadien depuis 1604.* Montreal: Les Clercs de Saint-Viateur, 1936.

Berry, John W. *The Peopling of Canada: a Statistical Analysis of Population Growth in Canada.* McGill University Thesis. Montreal, 1933.

Bertrand, C. *Monsieur de La Dauversière.* Montreal: Les Frères des Ecoles Chrétiennes, 1947.

Biggar, H. P. *The Early Trading Companies of New France.* Toronto: Toronto University Press, 1901.

Bishop, M. *Champlain.* New York: Knopf, 1948.

Bishop, M. *White Men Came to the St. Lawrence.* Montreal: McGill University Press, 1961.

Bornkamm, H. *Luther's World of Thought.* Translated by M. H. Bertram. St. Louis: Concordia, 1958.

Bossuet, J. B. *The History of the Variations of the Protestant Church.* 2 vols. New York: Sadlier, 1845.

Bradford, William. *Of Plymouth Plantation, 1620-47.* New edition with introduction by S. E. Morison. New York: Knopf, 1963.

Bremond, H. *Histoire Littéraire du Sentiment Religieux en France.* 11 vols. Paris: Bloud et Guy, 1924-33.

Brennan, Louis A. *No Stone Unturned: an Almanac of North American Prehistory.* New York: Random House, 1959.

Bultmann, Rudolf Karl. *History and Eschatology.* Edinburgh: Edinburgh University Press, 1957.

Butterfield, H. *The Origins of Modern Science.* London: Bell, 1949.

Calvin, Jean. *Tracts and Treatises in Defence of the Reformed Faith*. Translated by Henry Beveridge. 3 vols. Edinburgh and London: Oliver, 1958.

Canadian Indian. Ottawa: Dept. of Citizenship and Immigration, 1932.

Carrington, Phillip. *A Church History for Canadians to 1900 A.D.* Toronto: General Board of Religious Education, 1946.

Casgrain, H.-R. *Histoire de la Mère Marie de l'Incarnation*. Quebec: Desbarats, 1864.

Casgrain, H.-R. (ed.). *Lettres de M. de Bourlamque au Chevalier de Lévis*. Quebec: Demers, 1865.

Casgrain, H.-R. *Les Sulpiciens et les Prêtres des Missions-Etrangères en Acadie*. Quebec: Pruneau et Kirouac, 1897.

Catholic Encyclopedia. 16 vols. New York: Encyclopedia Press, 1913-14.

Champlain, Samuel de. *Works*. Translated and edited under general editorship of H. P. Biggar. 6 vols. Toronto: Champlain Society, 1922-1936.

Chapais, Thomas. *The Great Intendant*. Toronto: University of Toronto Press, 1914.

Charlevoix, F.-X. de. *History and General Description of New France*. Translated and edited by J. G. Shea. 6 vols. New York: Harper, 1866-72.

Clark, S. D. *Church and Sect in Canada*. Toronto: University of Toronto Press, 1948.

Cloutier, Prosper. *Histoire de la Paroisse de Champlain*. Trois-Rivières: Imprimerie "Le Bien Public", 1915.

Cobban, A. *A History of Modern France, Old Regime and Revolution, 1715-1799*. Gloucester, Mass.: Peter Smith, 1957.

Coffin, R. P. T. *Kennebec, Cradle of the Americas*. New York: Farrar and Rinehart, 1937.

Collection de Manuscrits Contenant Lettres, Mémoires, et autres Documents Historiques relatifs à la Nouvelle France. 4 vols. Quebec: Coté, 1883-85.

Collier, J. *Indians of the Americas*. New York: Norton, 1947.

Collier, J. *Indians of the Americas*. Abridged edition. New York: New American Library, 1953.

Collingwood, R. G. *The Idea of History*. Oxford: Clarendon Press, 1946.

Cosmas Indicopleustes. "Topographia Christiana." Text found in Migne, J. P., *Patrologia Graeca*, Vol. LXXXVIII. Paris: Migne, 1909.

Couillard Després, A. *Charles de Saint-Etienne de La Tour et son Temps, 1593-1666*. Arthabaska: Imprimerie d'Arthabaska, 1930.

Cronin, Vincent. *A Pearl to India: the Life of Roberto de Nobili*. London: Dutton, 1959.

Dansette, A. *Religious History of Modern France*. Translated by J. Dingle. 2 vols. London: Nelson, 1961.

Dawson, C. *The Dynamics of World History*. Edited by J. J. Malloy. New York: Sheed and Ward, 1957.

Dawson, C. *Group Settlement: Ethnic Communities in Western Canada*. Toronto: Macmillan, 1936.

Dawson, C. *The Movement of World Revolution*. New York: Sheed and Ward, 1959.

Delangley, Jean. *Hennepin's Description of Louisiana: a Critical Essay*. Chicago: Institute of Jesuit History, 1941.

Denys, Nicolas. *The Description and Natural History of the Coasts of North America.* Translated and edited by W. F. Ganong. Toronto: Champlain Society, 1908.

Dollier de Casson, F. *A History of Montreal.* Translated and edited by R. Flenley. London: Dent, 1928.

Douglas, D. C. (ed.). *English Historical Documents.* 9 vols. London: Eyre and Spottiswoode, 1955-59.

Douglas, D. C. (ed.). *English Historical Documents. Vol. IX: American Colonial Documents to 1776.* London: Eyre and Spottiswoode, 1959.

Douglas, J. *Old France in the New World.* Cleveland: Douglas, 1905.

Doyle, J. A. *The English in America.* 2 vols. London: Longmans, Green, 1882.

Du Boscq de Beaumont, Gaston. *Les Derniers Jours de l'Acadia.* Paris: Lechevallier, 1899.

Ducros, Louis. *French Society in the Eighteenth Century.* Translated by W. de Geijer. London: Bell, 1926.

Durant, Will. *The Story of Civilization. Vol. VI: The Reformation.* New York: Simon and Schuster, 1957.

Eastman, M. *Church and State in Early Canada.* Edinburgh: Constable, 1915.

Eccles, W. J. *Canada under Louis XIV, 1663-1701.* Toronto: McClelland and Stewart, 1964.

Eccles, W. J. *Frontenac, the Courtier Governor.* Toronto: McClelland and Stewart, 1959.

Eden, R. *The Decades of the Newe Worlde.* Edited by Edward Arber. Birmingham: Turnbull, Spears, 1885.

Encyclopedia Canadiana. 10 vols. Ottawa: The Canadian Company (Grolier), 1957-58.

Eusebius Pamphili, Bp. of Caesarea. *The Ecclesiastical History and the Martyrs of Palestine.* Translated with an introduction and notes by H. J. Lawlor and J. E. L. Oulton. 2 vols. London: Society for Promoting Christian Knowledge, 1927.

Faillon, E.-M. *L'Héroine Chrétienne du Canada ou Vie de Mlle LeBer.* Villemarie: Ches les Soeurs de la Congrégation de Notre Dame, 1860.

Faillon, E.-M. *Histoire de la Colonie française en Canada.* 3 vols. Villemarie: Bibliothèque Paroissiale, 1865-66.

Faillon, E.-M. *Vie de Mme d'Youville.* Villemarie: Soeurs de la Charité, 1852.

Faillon, E.-M. *Vie de M. Olier.* 4th ed. 3 vols. Paris: Vattelier, 1873.

Fallue, L. *Histoire Politique et Religieuse de l'Eglise Métropolitaine et du Diocèse de Rouen.* Rouen: Le Brument, 1850-51.

Fauteux, Aegidius. *La Famille d'Aillebout.* Montreal: Ducharme, 1917.

Fédération des Collèges Classiques. *Brief Submitted to the Commission of Inquiry in Education.* Quebec: the Queen's Printer, 1963.

Fénelon, Abbé de. *See* Salignac.

Ferland, J.-B.-A. *Cours d'Histoire du Canada.* 2 vols. Quebec: Coté, 1865.

Fisher, G. P. *The Reformation.* New York: Scribner, 1916.

Fiske, John. *The Discovery of America.* 2 vols. Boston and New York: Houghton, Mifflin, 1892.

Fitts, Mary Pauline. *Hands to the Needy.* New York: Doubleday, 1950.

Fliche, Augustin et Martin, Victor. *Histoire de l'Eglise depuis les Origines jusqu'à Nos Jours.* Vol. XVIII: Willaert, Leopold. *Après le Concile de Trente; la Restauration catholique, 1563-1648.* Paris: Bloud et Guy, 1945.

Fliche, Augustin et Martin, Victor. *Histoire de l'Eglise depuis les Origines jusqu'à Nos Jours.* Vol. XIX: Preclin, E. *Les Luttes Politiques et Doctrinales aux XVIIe et XVIIIe siècles.* Paris: Bloud et Guy, 1956.

Floquet, A. *Anecdotes Normandes.* Rouen: Cagniard, 1883.

Foran, J. K. *Jeanne Mance or the Angel of the Colony.* Montreal: Herald Press, 1931.

Franciscans. *Les Frères Mineurs.* Montreal: Revue du Tiers-Ordre et de la Terre-Sainte, 1915.

Frank, Waldo. *The Rediscovery of Man.* New York: Braziller, 1958.

Frégault, Guy. *François Bigot, Administrateur Français.* Ottawa: The Author, 1948.

Garneau, F.-X. *History of Canada.* Translated by A. Bell. 3rd revised ed. 2 vols. Toronto: Belford, 1876.

Gaustad, E. S. *The Great Awakening in New England.* New York: Harper, 1957.

Gibbon, J. M. and Mathewson, Mary S. *Three Centuries of Canadian Nursing.* Toronto: Macmillan, 1947.

Goen, C. C. *Revivalism and Separatism in New England.* New Haven: Yale University Press, 1962.

Gosselin, A.-E. *L'Instruction au Canada sous le Régime français, 1635-1760.* Quebec: Laflamme et Proulx, 1911.

Gosselin, A.-H. *L'Eglise du Canada depuis Monseigneur de Laval jusqu'à la Conquête.* 3 vols. Quebec: Laflamme et Proulx, 1911.

Gosselin, A.-H. *La Mission du Canada.* Evreux: Imprimerie de l'Eure, 1909.

Gosselin, A.-H. *Le Vénérable François de Montmorency Laval.* Quebec: Dessault et Proulx, 1901.

Gowans, A. *Church Architecture in New France.* Toronto: University of Toronto Press, 1955.

Goyau, G. *Une Epopée Mystique: les Origines Religieuses du Canada.* Paris: Grasset, 1924.

Grant, J. W. (ed.). *The Churches and the Canadian Experience.* Toronto: Ryerson, 1963.

Guizot, F. P. G. and Guizot, DeWitt. *France.* Translated by R. Black. 8 vols. New York: Collier, 1898.

Hakluyt, R. *The Principal Navigations, Voyages and Discoveries of the English Nation.* London: Everyman's Library (Dutton), 1907.

Harvey, D. C. *The French Regime in Prince Edward Island.* New Haven: Yale University Press, 1926.

Hawkes, J. and Wooley, L. *History of Mankind; Cultural and Scientific Development.* Vol. I. *Prehistory and the Beginning of Civilization.* New York: Harper, 1959.

Hennepin, Louis. *A New Discovery of a Vast Country in America.* 2 vols. Chicago: McClurg, 1903.

Herring, H. *A History of Latin America.* 2nd revised ed. New York: Knopf, 1961.

Hosmer, J. K. *Winthrop's Journal.* 2 vols. New York: Scribner, 1908.

Hughes, E. C. *French Canada in Transition.* London: Routledge and Kegan Paul, 1946.

Huizinga, J. The Waning of the Middle Ages. London: Arnold, 1924.

Hutton, W. H. The English Church from the Accession of Charles I to the Death of Queen Anne. London: Macmillan, 1913.

Innis, H. A. The Cod Fisheries: the History of an International Economy. New Haven: Yale University Press, 1940.

Ives, E. J. The Message of Thomas à Kempis. London: Student Christian Movement, 1922.

Jamet, A. Marguerite Bourgeoys. 2 vols. Montreal: La Presse Catholique Pan-Américaine, 1942.

Janelle, Pierre. The Catholic Reformation. Milwaukee: Bruce, 1948.

Jaspers, K. The Origin and Goal of History. London: Routledge and Kegan Paul, 1953.

Jedin, H. A History of the Council of Trent. Translated by E. Graf. 2 vols. Edinburgh: Nelson, 1957-61.

Jenks, David. Six Great Missionaries. Oxford: Oxford University Press, 1930.

Jenness, D. Indians of Canada. (Bulletin No. 65) Ottawa: Dept. of Mines, 1932.

Johnson, F. Man in Northeastern North America. Andover, Mass.: Phillips Academy, 1946.

Johnston, A. A. A History of the Catholic Church in Eastern Nova Scotia. Antigonish: St. Francis Xavier University, 1960.

Jones, Gwyn. The Norse Atlantic Saga. New York and Toronto: Oxford University Press, 1964.

Jugements et Délibérations du Conseil Souverain de la Nouvelle-France. Quebec: Coté, 1885.

Jury, Wilfrid and Jury, Elsie McLeod. Sainte-Marie among the Hurons. Toronto: Oxford University Press, 1954.

Kalm, Peter. Travels into North America. Translated by J. R. Foster. 3 vols. London: Lowdnes, 1770-71.

Kennedy, J. H. Jesuit and Savage in New France. New Haven: Yale University Press, 1950.

Kenton, Edna. Black Gown and Redskins. London: Longmans, Green, 1956.

Kidd, D. J. The Counter Reformation, 1550-1600. London: S.P.C.K., 1933

Kidd, B. J. (ed.). Documents Illustrative of the Continental Reformation. Oxford: Clarendon Press, 1911.

Kipp, W. I. (ed.). The Early Jesuit Missions in North America. New York: Wiley and Putnam, 1846.

Knox, R. A. Enthusiasm. New York: Oxford University Press, 1950.

Kraemer, Hendrik. World Cultures and World Religions. London: Lutterworth, 1960.

Lanctot, G. A History of Canada. Vol. I: From Its Origins to the Royal Regime, 1663. Translated by J. Hambleton. Toronto: Clarke, Irwin, 1963.

Lanctot, G. (ed.). New Documents by Lahontan. Ottawa: The Oakes Collection, 1940.

Langtry, J. History of the Church in Eastern Canada and Newfoundland. London: Society for Promoting Christian Knowledge, 1892.

Latourelle, René. Etude sur les Ecrits de Saint Jean de Brébeuf. 2 vols. Montreal: L'Immaculée Conception, 1952.

Latourette, K. S. *A History of the Expansion of Christianity*. 7 vols. 2nd ed. New York: Harper, 1941.

Lauvrière, E. *La Tragedie d'un Peuple*. 2 vols. Paris: Librairie Henry Goulet, 1924.

LaViolette, F. E. *The Struggle for Survival*. Toronto: University of Toronto Press, 1961.

Lavisse, E. *Histoire de France*. 4 vols. Paris: Colin, 1905.

Leblond de Brumath, A. *Bishop Laval*. Toronto: Morang, 1910.

Le Clercq, Chrestien. *First Establishment of the Faith in New France*. Translated by J. G. Shea. 2 vols. New York: Shea, 1881.

Lescarbot, Marc. *Nova Francia; a Description of Acadia, 1606*. Translated by P. Erondelle in 1609. 3 vols. Reprinted, London: Routledge, 1928.

Le Sueur, W. D. *Count Frontenac*. Toronto: Morang, 1910.

The Life of the Venerable Mother Mary of the Incarnation by a Religious of the Ursuline Community. Dublin and London: Duffy, 1880.

Lycée Corneille de Rouen. Rouen: Imprimerie Lecerf, n.d.

McCann, F. T. *English Discovery of America to 1585*. New York: Kings Crown Press, 1952.

McIntyre, J. *The Christian Doctrine of History*. Edinburgh & London: Oliver and Boyd, 1957.

MacNutt, F. A. *Bartholomew de las Casas*. New York and London: Putnam, 1909.

Maritain, Jacques. *On the Philosophy of History*. New York: Scribner, 1957.

Martin, Claude. *Marie de l'Incarnation: Ecrits Spirituels et Historiques*. 4 vols. Paris, Desclée de Brouwer, 1929.

Maycock, A. L. *Nicholas Ferrar of Little Gidding*. London: S.P.C.K., 1938.

Miller, P. *The New England Mind from Colony to Province*. Cambridge: Harvard University Press, 1953.

Miller P. and Johnson, J. H. *The Puritans*. New York: American Book, 1938.

Molinos, Miguel de. *The Spiritual Guide*. London: Hodder, 1928.

Mooney, J. *The Aboriginal Population of America North of Mexico*. Washington: The Smithsonian Institution, 1928.

More, Sir Thomas. *Utopia*. New York: Dutton, 1951.

Morison, S. E. *Admiral of the Ocean Sea*. Boston: Little, Brown, 1942.

Munro, W. B. *The Seignorial System in Canada*. New York: Harvard Historical Studies, 1907.

Nant, Candide de. *Pages Glorieuses de l'Epopée Canadienne*. Montreal: Le Devoir, 1927.

Neale, J. M. *A History of the So-Called Jansenist Church of Holland*. Oxford: Parker, 1858.

Neumann, Erich. *The Great Mother; an Analysis of the Archetype*. Translated by Ralph Manheim. London: Routledge and Kegan Paul, 1955.

Newton, A. P. *The Colonizing Activities of the English Puritans*. New Haven: Yale University Press, 1914.

Newton, A. P. *The Great Age of Discovery*. London: University of London Press, 1932.

Nichols, J. H. *History of Christianity, 1650-1950*. New York: Ronald Press, 1956.

O'Callaghan, E. B. (ed.). *The Documentary History of the State of New York*. 4 vols. Albany: Ward Parsons, 1849.

Palfrey, J. G. *A Compendious History of New England.* 4 vols. Boston and New York: Houghton, Miflin, 1883.

Parkman, F. *Count Frontenac and New France under Louis XIV.* 4th ed. Boston: Little, Brown, 1877.

Parkman, F. *A Half Century of Conflict.* Boston: Little, Brown, 1903.

Parkman, F. *The Jesuits in North America.* 11th ed. Boston: Little, Brown, 1878.

Parkman, F. *La Salle and the Discovery of the Great West.* Boston: Little, Brown, 1927.

Parkman, F. *Pioneers of France in the New World.* 5th ed. Boston: Little, Brown, 1867.

Pascal, Blaise. *Les Provinciales.* Paris: Flammarion, n.d.

Peers, E. A. *Studies of the Spanish Mystics.* 3 vols. London: S.P.C.K., 1927-30.

Pelikan, J. and Lehmann, H. T. (eds.). *Luther's Works.* Vol. XL: *Church and Ministry.* Saint Louis: Concordia, 1958.

Pohl, F. J. *The Lost Discovery: Uncovering the Track of the Vikings in America.* New York: Norton, 1952.

Porter, Fernand. *L'Institution Catéchistique au Canada Français, 1633-1833.* Montreal: Les Editions Franciscaines, 1949.

Prescott, W. H. *History of the Conquest of Mexico.* 3 vols. New York: Harper, 1843.

Prescott, W. H. *History of the Conquest of Peru.* 2 vols. New York: Harper, 1848.

Prowse, D. W. *History of Newfoundland.* London: Macmillan, 1895.

Ranke, L. von. *A History of the Papacy, Political and Ecclesiastical, in the Sixteenth and Seventeenth Centuries.* Translated by J. E. M. D'Aubigné. 2 vols. Glasgow: Blackie, 1855.

Rapport de l'Archiviste de la Province de Québec pour 1923-24. Québec: Proulx, 1924.

Report Concerning Canadian Archives for year 1904. Ottawa: The King's Printer, 1905.

Repplier, Agnes. *Mère Marie of the Ursulines.* New York: Sheed and Ward, 1931.

Richaudeau, Abbé. *Lettres de la Révérende Mère Marie de l'Incarnation.* 2 vols. Tournai: Casterman, 1876.

Rochemonteix, C. de. *Les Jésuites et la Nouvelle-France au XVIIe siècle.* 3 vols. Paris: Letouzey et Ané, 1896.

Rogers, Charles. *Memorials of the Earl of Stirling and the House of Alexander.* 2 vols. Edinburgh: Patterson, 1877.

Rousseau, Jean Jacques. *Du Contrat Social.* Paris: Gallimard, 1964.

Rousseau, P. *Histoire de la Vie de M. Paul de Chomedey, Sieur de Maisonneuve.* Montreal: Cadieux et Derome, 1886.

Rowse, A. L. *The Elizabethans and America.* London: Macmillan, 1959.

Roy, A. *Les Lettres, les Sciènces et les Arts du Canada.* Paris: Jouve, 1930.

Roy, M. *The Parish and Democracy in French Canada.* Toronto: University of Toronto Press, 1950.

Roy, Pierre-Georges. *A Travers l'Histoire de l'Hôtel-Dieu de Québec.* Lewis: Augustines Hospitalières, 1939.

Ruz, Alberto. *Uxmal; Official Guide.* Mexico: Institute Nacional de Antropologia e Historia, 1963.

Sagard-Théodat, G. *Histoire du Canada.* 4 vols. Paris: Librairie Tross, 1866.

Sagard-Théodat, G. *The Long Journey to the Country of the Hurons.* Translated by H. H. Langton. Toronto: Champlain Society, 1939.

Saint-Félix, Soeur. *Monseigneur de Saint-Vallier et l'Hôpital Général de Québec.* Quebec: Darveau, 1882.

Salignac de La Mothe-Fénelon, François de. *Pious Reflections.* London: Houlston, 1839.

Savelle, Max. *A History of Colonial America.* New York and Toronto: Holt, Rinehart and Winston, 1964.

Scott, H. A. *Bishop Laval.* London and Toronto: Oxford University Press, 1926.

Shortt, A. and Doughty, A. G. *Canada and Its Provinces.* 23 vols. Toronto: Brook, 1914-17.

Shortt, A. and Doughty, A. G. *Documents Relating to the Constitutional History of Canada.* Ottawa: Taché, 1907.

Smith, A. J. M. (ed.). *The Oxford Book of Canadian Verse.* Toronto: Oxford University Press, 1960.

Smith, J. W. and Jamison, A. L. (eds.). *Religion in American Life.* 4 vols. Princeton: Princeton University Press, 1961.

Smith, J. W. and Jamison, A. L. (eds.). *Religious Perspectives in American Culture.* Princeton: Princeton University Press, 1961.

Stanard, M. N. *The Story of Virginia's First Century.* Philadelphia and London: Lippincott, 1928.

Stephen, Sir J. *Essays in Ecclesiastical Biography.* 2 vols. London: Longmans, 1907.

Sweet, W. W. *Religion in Colonial America.* New York: Scribner, 1951.

Talbot, F. X. *Saint among the Hurons.* New York: Doubleday, 1949.

Têtu, H. *Les Evêques de Québec.* Quebec: Hardy, 1889.

Têtu, H. and Gagnon, C. O. (eds.). *Mandements, Lettres Pastorales et Circulaires des Evêques de Québec.* 4 vols. Québec: Coté, 1887-89.

Thomas à Kempis. *Of the Imitation of Christ.* (The World's Classics, Vol. XLIX). Oxford: Oxford University Press, 1920.

Thompson, J. E. S. *The Civilization of the Mayas.* 6th ed. Chicago: National History Museum, 1958.

Thompson, J. E. S. *Mexico before Cortez.* New York: Scribner, 1933.

Thwaites, R. G. *The Colonies, 1492-1750.* New York: Longmans, Green, 1920.

Thwaites, R. G. (ed.). *The Jesuit Relations and Allied Documents.* 75 vols. Cleveland: Burrows, 1896-1901.

Traquair, Ramsay and Neilson, G. A. *The Architecture of the Hôpital Général de Québec.* Montreal: McGill University, 1931.

Turner, F. J. *Rise of the New West.* New York: Harper, 1906.

Tyler, L. G. *Narratives of Early Virginia.* New York: Barnes and Noble, 1930.

Les Ursulines des Trois-Rivières depuis Leur Etablissement jusqu'à Nos Jours. Trois-Rivières: Ayotte, 1888.

The Voyages and Colonizing Enterprises of Sir Humphrey Gilbert. London: Hakluyt Society, 1940.

Wardleworth, E. S. *François-Marie Perrot.* McGill University Thesis, 1931.

Webb, W. P. *The Great Frontier.* Boston: Houghton, Mifflin, 1932.

Wertenbaker, T. J. *The Puritan Oligarchy: the Founding of American Civilization.* New York and London: Scribner, 1947.

Winsor, Justin. *Cartier to Frontenac*. Boston and New York: Houghton, Mifflin, 1894.

Wright, Louis B. *The American Frontier: Colonial American Civilization*. New York: Knopf, 1951.

Wrong, G. M. *The Rise and Fall of New France*. 2 vols. Toronto: Macmillan, 1928.

Zwemer, S. M. *Raymond Lull, First Missionary to the Moslems*. New York and London: Funk and Wagnalls, 1902.

ARTICLES

Campeau, Lucien. "La Grande Crise de 1612 à Port-Royal," in *Lettres du Bas-Canada*, XV, No. 1 (March, 1961), p. 8.

Colebrander, H. T. "The Dutch Element in American History" in the *Annual Report of the American Historical Association for the Year 1909*. (Washington, 1911), pp. 193-201.

Desautels, Andrée. "Les Trois Ages de la Musique au Canada" in *Grand Larousse Encyclopédie de la Musique*. (Paris: Librairie Larousse) Vol. II, pp. 314-315.

Deschamps, Leon. "Isaac de Razilly, Biographie-Mémoire Inédite," in *Revue de Géographie* (October, 1886), p. 282 et seq.

D'Olwer, Nicolau. "Comments on Evangelization of the New World", in *History of Religion in the New World*. (Washington, D.C.: Conference on the History of Religion in the New World during Colonial Times, 1958), pp. 63-74.

Falardeau, Jean-Charles. "The Seventeenth Century Parish" in *French Canadian Society*. Edited by M. Rioux and Yves Martin. (Toronto: McClelland and Stewart, 1964.) Vol. I, pp. 19-32.

Garigue, Philippe. "Change and Continuity in Rural French Canada", *Culture*, XVIII (December, 1957), pp. 379-92.

Gaudron, Edmond. "French Canadian Philosophers" in *Culture of Contemporary Canada*. Edited by Julian Park. (Toronto Ryerson, 1957), pp. 274-292.

Grandpré, Marcel de. "Traditions of the Catholic Church in French Canada" in Grant, J. W. (ed.), *The Churches and the Canadian Experience*. (Toronto: Ryerson, 1963), pp. 1-13.

Guindon, Hubert. "The Social Evolution of Quebec Reconsidered", *Canadian Journal of Economics and Political Science*, XXVI (November, 1960), pp. 533-51.

Handy, R. T. "Survey of Recent Literature: American Church History", *Church History*, XXVII (June, 1958), pp. 161-167.

Harbison, E. H. "The Meaning of History and the Writing of History", *Church History*, XXI (June, 1952), pp. 97-106.

Hay, David W. "The Christian Tradition and the Church Historian", *Canadian Journal of Theology*, XII, No. 1 (January, 1966), pp. 26-34.

Human Relations. Vol. V, No. 10. Toronto: Human Rights Commission, 1964.

Lanctot, G. "The Elective Council of Quebec, 1957", *Canadian Historical Review* (June, 1934), pp. 123-132.

Latourette, K. S. "Contribution of the Religion of the Colonial Period to the Ideals and Life of the United States", in *History of Religion in the New World.* (Washington, D.C.: Conference on the History of Religion in the New World during Colonial Times, 1958), pp. 4-19.

Magne, P. "Rapport a l'Empereur" in P. Clement (ed.), *Lettres, Instructions et Mémoirs de Colbert* (Paris, pub. d'après les ordres de l'empéreur, 1861), I, pp. i-iii.

Mead, S. E. "From Coercion to Persuasion," *Church History,* XXV (December, 1956), pp. 317-337.

Mead, S. E. "Professor Sweet's Religion and Culture in America," *Church History,* XXII (March, 1953), pp. 33-49.

Monet, J. "Marquette, Jacques, Jesuit, Missionary" in *Dictionary of Canadian Biography* (Toronto: University of Toronto Press, 1966), Vol. I, pp. 491-2.

Monet, Jacques. "The Foundations of French-Canadian Nationality", *Culture,* XXVI (December, 1965), p. 459 *et seq.*

Moreno, W. J. "The Indians of America and Christianity" in *History of Religion in the New World.* (Washington: Conference on the History of Religion in the New World during Colonial Times, 1959), pp. 75-95.

Newton, A. P. "The Great Immigration 1618-1648" in *The Cambridge History of the British Empire* (8 vols.; Cambridge: Cambridge University Press, 1929-36), Vol. I, pp. 136-181.

Poutet, Y. "Les Voeux des Frères Charon, Hospitaliers-Enseignants," *Revue d'Histoire de l'Eglise de France,* XLIV (1964), pp. 19-45.

Putnam, Ruth. "The Dutch Element in the United States" in the *Annual Report of the American Historical Association for the Year 1909* (Washington, 1911), p. 206.

Rose, J. Holland. "The Struggle for Supremacy in America" in *The Cambridge History of the British Empire* (8 vols; Cambridge: Cambridge University Press, 1929-36), Vol. VI, pp. 78-90.

Tilley, A. A. "French Humanism and Montaigne" in *Cambridge Modern History* (14 vols.; Cambridge: Cambridge University Press, 1907-12), Vol. III, pp. 53-72.

Trinterud, L. J. "The Task of the American Church Historian", *Church History,* XXV (March, 1956), pp. 3-15.

Wade, Mason. "The Culture of French Canada" in *Culture of Contemporary Canada,* edited by Julian Park (Toronto and New York: Ryerson, 1957), pp. 367-395.

Whiteman, Anne. "Church and State" in *The New Cambridge Modern History* (12 vols; Cambridge: Cambridge University Press, 1961), Vol. V, pp. 122-48.

Index